Slanted and Enchanted

Slanted and Enchanted

The Evolution of Indie Culture

Kaya Oakes

A Holt Paperback

Henry Holt and Company * New York

Holt Paperbacks
Henry Holt and Company, LLC
Publishers since 1866
175 Fifth Avenue
New York, New York 10010
www.henryholt.com

Library of Congress Cataloging-in-Publication Data

Oakes, Kaya.
  Slanted and enchanted : the evolution of indie culture / Kaya
Oakes.—1st Holt Paperbacks ed.
    p. cm.
  Includes bibliographical references and index.
  ISBN-13: 978-0-8050-8852-6 (pbk.)
  ISBN-10: 0-8050-8852-0 (pbk.)
  1. Indie culture—United States—History. 2. Arts and society—
United States. 3. Arts—United States—History. I. Title.
  E169.12.O18 2009
  700'.103—dc22   2008045286

Henry Holt books are available for special promotions and premiums.
For details contact: Director, Special Markets.

First Holt Paperbacks Edition 2009

Designed by Meryl Sussman Levavi

Printed in the United States of America

10 9 8 7 6 5 4 3 2 1

America after all it is you and I who are perfect
   not the next world.
Your machinery is too much for me.
You made me want to be a saint.

—Allen Ginsberg, "America"

Create the Condition You Describe

—San Francisco Diggers Motto

Contents

Preface

In many ways, the genesis of this book goes back to a specific decade in a specific place: the San Francisco Bay Area, and particularly the cities of Oakland and Berkeley, in the late eighties. As a teenager growing up there, I was introduced to the creative subculture of independent artists, writers, cartoonists, musicians, and thinkers. My first exposure to punk happened at Berkeley's collectively run performance space 924 Gilman Street. I attended my first small press poetry readings at Cody's Books on Telegraph Avenue. I created my first zine with a group of friends in high school, and did my first interviews with local bands to fill its pages, which I ran off at Krishna Copy on Telegraph, where many other zinesters and indie publishers were copying their own zines. I stayed up late listening to KALX, the venerable college radio station of UC Berkeley, and after college (a year of which I spent at Evergreen State in Olympia, Washington, where riot grrrl, grunge, and twee pop were beginning to foment), I worked in a bookstore where the owners were passionate about alternative comics. I ventured over to North Beach and the saloons where the independent artists of the fifties and sixties beat and hippie generations planted the roots of the subculture that eventually became known as indie. In 2005, I began teaching a writing course at the University of California, Berkeley, about the history and the future of independent, underground music—the same music that has been the soundtrack to my life. My roots as a writer and thinker are very much tied to the version of independent culture that was locally displayed in the eighties and early nineties: eclectic, open-minded, a little nerdy, and intellectually challenging. The Bay Area was a fantastic place to discover camaraderie among like-minded artists, and that same independent spirit fueled similar local scenes all over the country. Today, however, the meaning of indie as a subculture has changed.

Every semester that I teach my underground music course, I ask my students what they think the word "indie" means, and somebody inevitably gives the same answer: skinny pants. I want to come clean here and tell everyone that I have never worn skinny pants; they look awful on me. But the answer is telling. The idea of skinny pants as a signifier may be what leather jackets were in the eighties or tattoos in the early nineties. These trappings had previously been a signal from one member of the indie subculture to another that we were alike, that we'd have something to talk about, and, most important, that we might be able to help one another out with a place to play a gig, crash, or make art. Once these kinds of signifiers cross over into the mainstream, that context is lost, and my students, being as media savvy as they are, know that skinny pants are not a signal of being tuned in but of being sold to. They've been sold indie not as a philosophy but as a genre, and thus they are logically cynical about it. It's an interesting moment. Indie *is* a backlash, and when there's a backlash against indie there has to be some sort of reinvention.

Since I began researching and writing this book, people have frequently asked me what I think indie means. That's the question I've tried to answer in these pages. I've interviewed scores of people, read tons of books and articles, visited many locations, and from that research I've tried to deduce an answer. Indie has historically been a subculture that operates outside of the mainstream, but technology and changing times have made the line of demarcation between mainstream and indie almost unrecognizable. However, indie culture is very much alive and well today, and I predict it will continue to be well into the future. No matter how it's repackaged and reimagined for a mass-consuming audience, indie is remarkably resilient and always manages to reinvent itself. The Internet has enabled musicians in particular to take charge of distributing, recording, and engineering their own music in a manner they've never been able to before. Writers are also seizing technology as an advantageous tool that's totally adaptable to DIY; we blog, we publish online journals, and we pass work back and forth with ease, all without any kind of outside support or interference. Crafting balances the dichotomy between handmade objects and online communities so dexterously that it's growing faster than any other art form I wrote about. In spite of some signals that indie's been exploited to death, it's actually alive and kicking. But it also looks different every day.

Astute readers will note that I did not manage to interview a number of people who they may have liked to hear from, but because indie is so sprawling, decentralized, and self-defining it would be impossible to get more than a glimpse of each of the decades I write about or more than a couple of interviews per chapter unless I were assembling an encyclopedia. However, one lesson learned from everyone I talked with and read about is that indie is not just about DIY, though DIY remains its central tenet. It's about serving your community, self-actualization via creativity, and it's about empowerment, all of which occur as a result of DIY. None of this book would be possible without the examples put forth by the people who passed that idea down to my generation, nor would I be able to write without the examples of the people who are reinventing indie today. My own version of indie may have begun in the Bay Area back in 1986, but today it encompasses a more global kind of definition. This book is just the beginning of trying to understand how independence changes art and forges communities. What's missing are simply the other parts of a story that I hope will never end.

Slanted and Enchanted

Introduction: Scenes from an Independent America, 2007

After a hot and stuffy Fourth of July, hungover and weary revelers woke on the fifth to find the San Francisco Bay Area covered in a more typical summer blanket of fog. As Friday the sixth rolled around, the organizers of Oakland's Art Murmur, a monthly gallery walk that had recently grown into a full-blown hipster street fair, expected that the crappy weather and lingering sour stomachs from barbecue and beer would probably keep people at home. It was a prospect welcomed by some of the store owners on the route in question. Art Murmur has become something of a conflict between scale and idealism. Launched a year earlier by three scrappy, funky galleries within a block's proximity of one another whose owners hoped to attract a bigger clientele, it rapidly attracted a cadre of young and middle-aged indie artists, musicians, crafters, and hangers-on who, enticed by the prospect of an artists' community, began to crowd downtown and West

Oakland in search of cheaper rent and the camaraderie of other artists. Lower Telegraph Avenue, where the Murmur occurs, had in the 1980s and '90s become home to several sketchy bars and boarded-up businesses, as well as a brisk trade in male prostitution. Visitors drawn to the area by its newer populace of artists are likely to spot paint-spattered eccentrics in skinny jeans among the neighborhood's majority population of immigrant store owners, street hustlers, and newly arrived loft dwellers, and all those skinny-jeans-wearing artists love congregating on First Fridays. More than once, the cops were called by unfriendly neighbors intolerant of the influx of noise and crowds that broke into the usual run-down but quiet monotony of the street. A recent crackdown on drinking on the block due to crowd control issues followed, and signs posted on street corners notify patrons of the ban. The festivities had even taken a violent turn at the May Art Murmur, when someone took a pipe to the head in a fight.

Jen Loy, one of the owners of Mama Buzz Café and Gallery, which has, in its three years of business, become a combination playhouse, gallery, and performance venue for the local indie set that frequents the Murmur, leans over the counter and confides that "hopefully with this weather everyone'll stay home." Jen is tiny—just under five feet tall—but her size belies a tough personality and limited tolerance for bullshit. Over the past few months, her job on First Fridays has become half police work, half counseling service, and she's getting tired of scolding her ostensible peers. Jen wipes down the café counter as she speaks, clearly alert to the particular annoyances the day will bring. A customer tries to transfer her pint of beer to a take-out coffee cup, earning an admonition from Jen and a shake of the head. Jen and her business partner Nicole Neditch bought Mama Buzz from its previous owner when the revival of Oakland's art scene was in its nascent stages; only one other gallery, Ego Park, was in the neighborhood at that point, and it was more of a home and studio space to its owner, Kevin Slagle, than a full-time gallery. But Mama Buzz tapped into a need in the neighborhood—a need for a gathering space, a need for the sympathetic ear of the two young, creative women who owned it, and a need for affordable coffee and food in a neighborhood with few restaurants and grocery stores nearby. Within a year of the café's opening, business had grown and, with it, the neighborhood began to change. But Mama Buzz was just part of the changing face of the neighborhood where the Murmur takes place, which went from being an affordable area for artists to being home to a Starbucks, a Whole Foods, and multiple loft buildings within a couple of years. Similar transformations in formerly undesirable neighborhoods were taking root around the country: Brooklyn, a mostly sleepy and seedy place in the sixties and seventies, was discovered by artists in the eighties and is now swarming with hipsters and baby strollers as rents increase and condo developments pop up along with the arrival of chain retail and grocery stores like Trader Joe's, American Apparel, and Urban Outfitters; the west side of Portland, Oregon, a haven for small art galleries for years in the eighties, is now home to designer lofts, a massive Whole Foods emporium, and a Restoration Hardware store that threaten the artists who preceded them, and similar shifts are occurring in Chicago's Wicker Park, Providence's west side, and even in farther-flung outposts of independent art like Omaha and Missoula.

In Oakland, the evolution went like this: more collective and shambolic galleries moved into lower Telegraph in the wake of Mama Buzz and Ego Park, including 21 Grand, a mixed performance space and gallery. They were followed by Rock Paper Scissors Collective, a DIY dream space of zines, hand-sewn objects, printmaking classes, and knitting nights, and, most recently, two slick and Manhattanesque art spaces that stick out among the tattered buildings housing neighboring galleries like upscale loft developments stick out among nearby derelict flats and liquor stores. Esteban Sabar Gallery opened in early 2006, its owner having in turn been priced out of San Francisco's Castro neighborhood, which had become home to tony boutiques and pricey restaurants. Sabar's gallery reflects the upscaling that is beginning to bleed into lower Telegraph; on that foggy July evening, as patrons squeezed into his gallery's multiple rooms and gawked at tasteful black-and-white photos, he waved a Chinese paper fan in front of his face and, in response to a question about the swelling size of Murmur crowds, sardonically replied, "That's a bad thing?" Sabar has never been secretive about his ambitions for his gallery, whereas his neighbors at Mama Buzz and Rock Paper Scissors are beginning to feel overwhelmed and resentful of the crowds. Around the corner from his space, the recently opened, slickly designed Johansson Projects hosts a show called "Wunderkammer," a mixed-media set of sculpture mimicking the seventeenth century's "cabinets of curiosity" and their collections of mammalian and aquatic skeletons and remains. A large-scale painting of a blowfish done on a mirror is selling there for fourteen thousand dollars; around the corner at Rock Paper Scissors (aka RPS), you can purchase, for five bucks, a knit cozy made to house a mix tape.

The crowd is equally high and low, rich and poor, young and old. Younger people still outnumber the more monied San Franciscans and the hill-dwelling, Prius-driving types Sabar admits he's trying to attract. Still, there are a number of graying heads in the crowd, mixing with the kids in jeans, ponchos, elaborate facial hair, and eyeglasses of every conceivable shape and size. The street outside RPS is closed off to traffic, and tables are set up where artists hawk T-shirts, buttons, burned CDs, and other homemade crafts. At one table, a shopping cart stuffed full of thrift-store clothing is labeled with a handmade sign reading "Pick a garment, pick a screen." The available assortment of print images displayed on the table features mostly stylized appliances like toasters and eggbeaters. Patrons also have the option to pay five dollars and have a custom-made item cranked out right then by the bearded proprietor, an affable guy in his late twenties who's sporting a battered railroad cap along with a shirt identical to the ones on the table. At another table, two dreadlocked African American teenage boys in basketball jerseys try to hype the crowd and sell a mix CD they've made of "authentic Oakland hip-hop." At another, two women in their thirties wearing shirts screenprinted with political slogans pass out flyers for Team Abolition, a prisoners' literacy project, and talk seriously and quietly with people about their activism. The zine rack inside RPS displays titles ranging from *Biofuel and Genocide* and *Former Fetus: An Abortion Journal* to *Junk Pirate* and *Broccoli Cheese and Crackers*. As a middle-aged couple in fleeces and Birkenstocks poke their way among the racks of revamped thrift-store dresses and colorfully painted light-switch covers, the woman leans over to her husband and confides, "I didn't know there was art in Oakland."

By 8:30 in the evening, as the light begins to dim, Mama Buzz is packed wall to wall, the air above the outside patio blurring with the fog of cigarette smoke and an occasional cloud of pot. People are crammed into Johansson Projects, banging against the sculpture of branches and headless birds that protrudes over the space of one wall. In Ego Park, the massive zoetrope built by Christopher Loomis—which requires patrons to walk up, spin it, and peer in to see images of the zoetrope itself being built—has a line of people waiting to do just that. Crowds jostle one another on the sidewalk, and a young guy in a knit cap shouts to his friends, "Whatever gallery you see my bike at, I'll be there!" Toddlers ramble around, their tattooed moms chasing them. Red dots appear on half the art for sale, and the trays full of carrot sticks dwindle to tiny piles. Though Murmur organizers had hoped to shut things down by 9 p.m., it seems unlikely anyone will take off by the appointed hour as the crowds continue to swell and swell.

Three thousand miles away, on a humid summer day, Park Slope, Brooklyn, looks like something out of a Woody Allen film from the seventies, embodying the idealized New York in which people will shell out a lot of money to live well. The air shimmers with a golden hue, trees are lush and thick with greenery, and the people walking the streets, released from the bondage of winter wear, are letting their skin breathe in shorts and strapless dresses. Music and barbecue smoke from the Park Slope Fifth Avenue Fair drift down Bergen Street, and it's a perfect day for being outdoors. In the midst of this clamorous idyll, independent literary culture is quietly trying to stake a claim in the neighborhood. Unnameable Books is tucked away on one of these picturesque side streets, just down from the Bergen Street 2 and 3 stop. From the outside the store looks modest: a jumble of books on a cart parked on the sidewalk, a tiny storefront window crammed with more books, a street-level entrance that's easy to miss.

Unnameable Books—recently called Adam's Books, until a similarly named book distributor threatened the store with litigation—is among a small number of independently owned bookstores in the greater New York metropolitan area. One source estimates there are about thirty-five independent bookstores in New York, which seems like a fair number until you consider the fact that New York has a population of nearly eight million people.[1] Opened in late 2006 by Adam Tobin, the bookstore sells a mix of used and new titles, the emphasis for the latter being on books, chapbooks, and literary magazines by local writers and independent presses. Front and center when you walk into the store is a case displaying multiple titles by Brooklyn's Ugly Duckling Presse collective, a nonprofit publisher specializing in poetry and Eastern European poetry in translation. UDP books are letterpressed in the collective's warehouse and, with their surrealist cover art and hand-stitched bindings, they can look like art objects in contrast to the perfectly bound, glossy titles that surround them. There is also a rack dedicated to chapbooks, which are supershort collections of poems or prose usually fewer than twenty pages long, many of which are also letterpressed and hand bound, and a scattering of magazines, including many independently produced titles. Most of these types of books and magazines are difficult to find anywhere outside of independent bookstores, and even while indie presses are multiplying, the onus for getting a book onto bookstore shelves falls increasingly on the shoulders of the author. So the avant-garde poet who's currently unpacking a bag of copies of her own book for Adam to try to sell is doing the same thing the bookstore is doing—struggling to put cutting-edge work into readers' hands. And just as writers increasingly have to manage their own publicity, independent bookstores must do the same, and a two-person operation like Unnameable Books has to rely on word of mouth and personal interaction with customers to generate interest.

Adam himself is behind the counter almost every day of the week. The store is open long hours, until 10 p.m. or midnight most nights of the week, and Adam bears some signs of strain. The store was recently burglarized, and a sign posted near the counter in response to the burglary reads "Please don't steal the books. Thanks." He's affable enough with customers coming in to trade in used books for more used books, but as he switches the CD from baroque music to Yo La Tengo, he yawns widely and asks a visiting friend to run out and bring him some food since he doesn't want to close the store to do so himself. In spite of the tight space, the store has recently begun hosting readings and book parties, and it's slowly gaining a customer base in the increasingly well-off Park Slope community. This success is hard-won; even in Brooklyn—widely thought of as one of the epicenters of indie culture in America—a small bookstore faces daunting obstacles that often stem from the practices of its mainstream counterparts. Nonetheless, book lovers like Adam continue to open independent bookstores. Prior to opening his own store, Adam worked at another independently owned bookstore, Berkeley's Pegasus Books. Like Pegasus, Unnameable Books has reached out to independent publishers that often face distribution problems that prevent them from getting their books and magazines onto the shelves at chain bookstores. This creates a symbiotic relationship between independent booksellers and publishers; they need one another to survive. Adam says keeping things small makes life a bit easier, but to help ease the constraints of the crammed space, he's planning to rent the basement downstairs, to make more room for shelves and reading events by local authors, and he plans to keep the store open late in order to bring in a few more customers. Even if running a business like Unnameable is a struggle, the care shown by business owners like Adam helps to forge a community of readers and writers, and that kind of community, whether it's widespread or localized, is crucial to the survival of independent media.

While Unnameable Books does its best to keep the flames of independent publishing lit, the highly anticipated Pitchfork Music Festival has kicked into gear in Chicago's Lincoln Park, bearing witness to the massive popularity of independent rock. Chicago has been home to a booming indie scene since the eighties, when classic indie acts like Naked Raygun and Tortoise established themselves there. Chicago's affordable rents and the plethora of service-industry jobs available to young, creative types make the city appealing to writers and artists, so indie communities are able to thrive here, and this climate gave rise to *Pitchfork*. *Pitchfork*, the online review site for indie rockers, was launched in 1995 and currently gets about four thousand readers a day.[2] It is both beloved and loathed for its long, complex reviews and unfailingly elitist stance as a tastemaker in the fickle community it serves, where bands of varying visibility rapidly go in and out of style. It's that volatility that makes the number of fervent followers who catalog every new arrival and departure from the scene so remarkable. A *Pitchfork* review can help an indie band gain an international cult following or relegate it to a rarely visited corner of MySpace. It's the sense of community that *Pitchfork* also helps to create that has drawn a huge number of avid music fans to its third annual music festival, where they can revel in offerings that range from an elite squad of indie godfathers, including Stephen Malkmus, Slint, Sonic Youth, Yoko Ono, and Cat Power, to several dozen up-and-comers.

The festival's sponsors this year include eco-friendly purveyor of organic goods Whole Foods Market, indie-friendly download Web site Emusic, and Chipotle, the national burrito chain. Indie journalists who are covering the festival on their blogs chow down on free burritos—after all, rock journalism has never been a high-paying gig. Another attendant reported that "people-watching not surprisingly yielded everything from metallic bike shorts and messenger bags full of books to awkwardly-short dresses and cutoff jean shorts at every length," and Chicago-based rock journalist Jessica Hopper told readers of her blog that "drunk kids careened towards one another, texting, crossing their Bambi-legs in line for the baking hot potties."[3]

The festival crowd demonstrates something of a "this is no country for old men" skew (excepting the seventy-four-year-old Ono and fortyish Malkmus and Slint guys), but this may be part of its inherent appeal for the average *Pitchfork* reader. *Pitchfork* is written mostly by and for people in their twenties and early thirties, and indie rock, even when it's being made by forty-something artists, is mostly sold to people in that demographic. In his *New York Times* review of the festival, John Pareles notes that "*Pitchfork* favors introspective music that's ideal for a lone headphone-wearing computer user," the very cliché of a hipster kid. And those same hipster kids, wearing the same hipster outfits, naturally congregate to see a bunch of what Pareles calls their "beloved cult acts" for a relatively cheap fifty dollars per ticket, good for three days worth of music.

Pitchfork's writers are scattered all over the country, and people come from all over America to attend the festival. Attendants report that there are hookups, joyous reunions of far-flung friends, and late-night after-parties all over the city, all signs that, in spite of some of the journalists' grousing, people are really enjoying themselves. But there are also critiques from attendees posted on blogs and message boards: the lack of enthusiasm from the apparently jaded crowd, the homogenous, clichéd fashion choices, and the plethora of somehow still indie-chic mustaches on guys, and the stream of snarky commentary coming out of the mouths of some concertgoers who have perfected a stance of high irony. Though *Pitchfork* attempts to be inclusive by inviting hip-hop pioneers De La Soul to be a headlining act as well as spotlighting DJ sets and featuring relatively avant-garde acts that play music far outside of indie rock's usual guy-and-guitar parameters, the festival still attracts a crowd that can seem unable to appreciate anything without quietly mocking it.

Stereogum's review of the festival, which ignored the hip-hop performances, elicited an appalled comment from a fan who questioned their seemingly narrow-minded taste, saying, "I know you're all patting yourselves on the back for seeing the *Pitchfork*-approved indie weirdos, but WTF, no love for De La Soul? I guess the sneering bearded hipsters were afraid they might be forced to, like, conform to some 'urban hand waving' or something equally frightening."[4] Stereogum's perception of indie rock as a world unto itself is the embodiment of the disaffected indie rocker cliché, and it's spreading via the Internet, television, and radio as indie rock increasingly finds a foothold in mass media. What often gets ignored, however, as that cliché becomes pervasive is the reason these fans were attracted to indie rock in the first place. Though it may skew young and hip, indie rock has a rich history of being open to musicians who want to make music outside of the often rigid parameters of commercialized rock genres, and that history goes back as far as the folk movement in the fifties. And even if *Pitchfork* can come off as pretentious, the fact is that its writers and the bands who play the festival and the fans who attend are all passionate about indie music. But this balancing act between wanting to celebrate the music and wanting it to be an organic part of a close-knit community is one of the many challenges indie culture faces as it works its way into mainstream society.

Art Murmur, Unnameable Books, and the Pitchfork Music Festival each play a part in the lives of independent artists. But they are more than just events or places to go: for many people who create art independently and for many who have done so for years, indie is a valid, thriving culture, and these events and businesses are part of that culture today. If we understand culture to mean something more than a style of music, a visual aesthetic, or a literary mode and try to define it from its Latin root, *cultura*—"to cultivate"—then we can see how indie artists have traditionally worked together to cultivate many things: credibility, freedom, the ability to promote their own work and to control how it's promoted, self-reliance, open-mindedness, and the freedom to take creative risks. Likewise, if a culture is truly a group of people working and living together, independent artists have traditionally embraced the value of networking, making connections, and striving toward doing their art, their way. If being independent in your choices about what you listen to, look at, read, and watch implies a lack of compromise, then many of the people still making music and art independently would absolutely fit that definition. Indie's ambiguity can partially be chalked up to its emphasis on making its participants feel individual and unique. But before any of us were able to be creatively independent, we had to build on the practice of our independent predecessors. Because indie's history is in many ways a shadow history—one that parallels and reflects mainstream culture but also poises itself as being a subculture of outsiders—the threads connecting the twentieth- and twenty-first-century indie movements are not always readily apparent, especially in this day and age, wherein young artists face a plethora of choices about what kind of art they will make and how to distribute that art. Young fans often encounter art that builds on traditions of independence with which they may not be familiar.

When I began teaching a college course on underground music in 2005, I was struck by the number of students I had who, though they identified as indie rock fans, had little to no knowledge of what it meant to be in an indie rock band. They were unaware of the difference between signing to a major label versus an independent label, and they had never heard of Minor Threat, Black Flag, the Minutemen, or Hüsker Dü. While they were able to argue about formerly indie bands like Green Day and Fall Out Boy, most of my students were unaware of how much Green Day, for example, borrows its sound from Stiff Little Fingers, who self-released its first singles, or how Fall Out Boy builds on the tradition of early emo bands like Rites of Spring, whose lead singer, Guy Picciotto, later went on to join Fugazi. My students had also never seen a zine and couldn't tell the difference between the independently published books we were reading and one put out by a major publishing house. Chalking this up to the generation gap, I set about trying to show them how and why these bands were actually part of a very old tradition, one that extended into literature and visual art. But what has become clear over the years that I have taught the course is not just that my students and I are from slightly different eras, but that their lack of knowledge about indie culture is really a part of a greater cloak of secrecy that indie has sometimes wrapped around itself in order to survive. Yet in spite of indie's secrecy, its legacy is venerable.

Indie's history can be traced back to the fifties and sixties, when many artists established the tenets of networking, making art outside of the mainstream, valuing creativity above profit, and working at the grassroots level, which were revived in the eighties indie scene. In this later version of indie, zines, tape trading, comics, flyer art, skating, and many other creative genres rose up out of the punk underground and were embraced by millions of people seeking a way to express themselves. Indie seemed to be thriving well into the early nineties, but Nirvana's crossover success sparked the realization for many of us involved in the indie scene that indie was going to have to reinvent itself in order to survive. "In the early '90s you did get this whole new culture of creeps sort of sniffing around, this kind of old-school music biz types who looked at the underground music scene not as something interesting in and of itself, but as something that could be co-opted and turned into mainstream music," said Gerard Cosloy, one of the founders in 1989 of indie label Matador Records.[5] If the temptation to "sell out" had proven irresistible to many musicians, indie's embrace of capitalist success was like that baby swimming toward a dollar on the cover of Nirvana's *Nevermind*—a sentient being adrift in a sea of money. Many people who had been in the indie scene left it behind in the nineties in pursuit of dot-com stock options and designer lofts. However, what resulted from the exodus was not a gaping hole, but rather an empty stage on which a new kind of indie culture would be revealed. The first ripples of the new indie culture were more about keeping it close to home than they were about changing the world. In the aftermath of grunge, indie went back to its grass-roots beginnings. Some of the newest subgenres of indie rock that began to leak out from small regional scenes showcased their domestic interests in their names: dream pop, twee pop, bedroom rock, nerdcore. In the early part of this century, premillennium tension gave way to domestication across the board, which in turn led to more closely knit regional networks in cities and towns that hadn't had scenes before, as artists began to experiment with home recording, crafting, and other DIY activities. As the hippies used to say, "revolution begins at home." Given time, however, the seemingly sleepy new indie movement turned into a much, much bigger indicator of cultural change.

By the early part of the twenty-first century, it was easy to believe that indie was back in a big way. All of a sudden, indie art was everywhere. Just visiting the news rack at a decent bookstore revealed a plethora of indie magazines: *Bitch, The Believer, Arthur, Clamor* . . . all titles created by their editors and designers rather than conceptualized by Madison Avenue advertising execs. When my friends and I started *Kitchen Sink Magazine* in 2001, our rationale for wading into such a huge project was threefold: the Bay Area lacked a good arts and culture magazine; all of us were indie musicians, artists, and writers and therefore had creative networks to tap into (in other words, people who would help out for free); and we all wanted to do something different, to change things, to offer a different perspective than mainstream magazines were offering. Many of us had come up out of the eighties punk and indie scenes and were now working full-time jobs that could be soul-crushingly dull, and a magazine seemed like a logical way for us to do something fun that might also promote the local writers, musicians, and artists whose work was too abstract or avant-garde for most publications.

Producing, printing, and distributing a magazine was also a shitload of work. All of our peers in the independent press community shared that consensus. Anyone we knew who ran a book press or a magazine was constantly trying to scrape money together: chasing grants, borrowing from family members, and, in our case, using networking to raise money. *Kitchen Sink* became notorious in the Bay Area for its fund-raising parties. Often held in collectively owned warehouse spaces in the same Oakland neighborhoods where Art Murmur occurs today, we booked up-and-coming indie bands like Deerhoof, Erase Errata, Sean Hayes, and Rogue Wave to play for free, hung some art on the walls, and opened the doors to hundreds (and for some events thousands) of Bay Area citizens who wanted to drink cheap beer and hear good music. Sometimes the parties got out of control—a group of performance artists dressed up as clowns started smashing boxes of plates that were actually part of an art installation at one party, the fire marshals were called on others, and neighbors complained about all of them—but we were making enough money to put out our magazine, people were reading it and getting exposed to new ideas, and in the long run that was all that mattered.

Many of the new indie artists we worked with felt the same way. Even if you were struggling to make ends meet, you made your art. New indie record labels began to emerge, building on the networks established by labels in the eighties punk scene. New technologies made home recording cheaper and easier than ever, thus enabling many musicians to take control of their music. Not only did every indie writer, artist, or band have a Web site and a blog, we were all networking online and in person and constantly providing one another with ideas for staying solvent, distributing our work, and in some cases hooking up and starting relationships with one another. It was entirely possible to feel giddy to be a part of this new indie revolution. Neighborhoods attracted cadres of young artists, independently owned businesses began to move in, and everywhere you looked, you saw someone who looked like you—tattooed, bespectacled, creatively dressed, and sporting all of the signifiers of what felt like the most vital incarnation of indie culture since the end of the eighties. Carey, a young indie musician, describes the appeal of being an independent artist when she says, "I am attracted to the unpredictability of independent culture. The mainstream, in contrast, is never going to surprise me because everyone is simply trying to please as many people as they can in order to make a profit. Independent culture is less concerned with what will appeal to the majority of people, so artists are free to make the art that they enjoy making."

Even the demoralizing turn America took when George W. Bush took office in 2001 for a seemingly interminable term and when the Iraq War began were further fuel for the new indie culture. Bands rediscovered politics, and the sounds and overtly politicized lyrics of earlier acts like Gang of Four, the Minutemen, and even Creedence Clearwater Revival returned with a vengeance. Independent publishers began putting out anti-Bush screeds so rapidly it was hard to keep up. Zines and indie magazines chimed in on politics and encouraged the growing antiwar movement. Even crafters got in on the revolution, creating guerrilla knitting collectives and subversive craft networks. For the first time since the eighties, indie artists had something specific to rage about.

But at the same time that indie got political, it also became undeniably appealing to marketers. The media were willing and able to borrow the most appealing aspects of indie culture, from music to comics and style, and use them to market products that had never previously been thought of as indie. At least part of the blame can be laid on the shoulders of the clever producers of the Fox television show *The O.C.*, who created the character of Seth Cohen, a comic-book-loving, emo-listening, ironic-T-shirt-wearing, skateboarding outsider in a wealthy Orange County community that was so bland, tanned, and toned it made Seth's indie quirks look positively exotic. *The O.C.*'s creator Josh Schwartz, himself a fan of indie music, started booking indie bands like Death Cab for Cutie and Modest Mouse on the show. Simultaneously, Madison Avenue advertising firms started matching indie rock to products. Do you like Volkswagens? You might also like the Flaming Lips. Have an iPod? Why not download (legally, of course) some Spoon songs for the trip to school? Indie became a viral buzzword, and like the memes that encouraged people to post quizzes on their blogs that asked "How Indie Are You?" the nascent indie aesthetic that made magazines, books, and clothes so hip was rapidly sucked up, reimagined, and reproduced for a mass audience. Even indie godfathers Sonic Youth sent ripples of outrage through the blogosphere when they announced they'd be releasing a compilation album through Starbucks' music label, Hear Music. Sonic Youth's Thurston Moore tried to shrug off this decision in *Billboard*, saying, "The compilation came out of the idea that I wanted *Rather Ripped* [Sonic Youth's previous album] to be in Starbucks stores because that's where people were seeing CDs. They aren't going into record stores anymore." When indie rock's founders admit something like that about their fan base, you know that the culture of indie has changed irrevocably.

Similarly, while the Internet enabled indie artists to network and share ideas much more easily than the tape-trade-and-zine-exchange meet-ups of the eighties, it also began to blur the concept of what indie meant. MySpace quickly became popular with indie artists because they could post MP3s and discuss music with other bands, bookers from clubs, and potential fans. The social-networking site also aggregated "friends" by allowing them to list their music, film, and literary preferences. If you were a fan of Godspeed You! Black Emperor, one click would help you find thousands of potential friends, hookups, or acquaintances who also liked the same band. But what else did you have in common with them? Maybe nothing—in an age of "branding," whatever slivers of indie culture people claimed for their own were rapidly becoming not much more than labels and tags. As Jill, a twenty-year-old indie fan, puts it, "Personally, I think there is 'true' indie (i.e., underground music) and mainstream indie (typical Seth Cohen lookalikes gathering at Death Cab for Cutie concerts). I feel like indie is dead. Only a very small fraction of bands bring the true indie feel these days."

This mainstreaming of indie culture, which encouraged increasing availability to larger and larger audiences—enabling its co-opting by advertisers and filmmakers, promoting a narrowing down to the clichéd image of a hipster in skinny jeans and big glasses—is still happening as this introduction is being written. But even as indie gets exploited, it continues to change and reinvent itself, continuously giving rise to the question this book will attempt to answer: What does it mean to be indie? At a time when indie's newest audience is negotiating and reinventing indie culture, finding a definition for something so ambiguous is difficult. Nonetheless, it's not impossible. Snapshots of a culture—significant moments when it altered perspectives, changed ways of seeing or hearing, or spun off into new genres—are important ways of seeing a culture as a whole. Therefore, this book will offer snapshots of historical indie surges to provide context for an exploration of the contemporary indie scene.

A friend who works for an independent arts organization recently wrote that because of mass marketing and corporate threats, indie culture today is "hanging on by a thread." If this is true, and the thread is threatening to snap, it's time to step back and try to understand how, where, and to whom that thread reaches back, and where it might possibly go in the future if we are able to keep it intact. There is also the possibility that a broken thread might not result in the death of indie but instead in new kinds of indie culture—after all, indie never really dies; it continues to reemerge in repeated surges. To borrow a phrase from Ian MacKaye, "The flame never goes out."[6] In these pages, many of the people who created this culture, who nurtured and shaped it and still shape it, will tell their stories. Any valid culture, anything that changes people's perception and way of thinking is made of many, many voices, and the disharmony and occasional harmony of those voices is what makes things interesting and complicated when you're trying to define what that culture means. In the case of indie culture, there may be more disharmony than harmony at times, but when it achieves harmony, it is absolutely sublime. In these pages, an attempt will be made to bring the notes that formed that chord—in all their absurd, funny, deeply moving, and occasionally transcendent ways—back together again.

one

Constantly Risking Absurdity:
Early Independent Networks

Independence is defined by the people who live it. When poet Frank O'Hara exited his job as a curator at the Museum of Modern Art in Manhattan in 1960, traveling downtown to the Cedar Tavern, he would spend the evening throwing back drinks and smoking endless cigarettes in the company of other poets and painters whose work was still considered too odd, too quirky, too abstract for the art and literary establishment. O'Hara's poetry and the poems and visual art being created in his circle stood in stark contrast to the traditional lyric poetry and predictably dull painting of the time. Legendary Beat poet Allen Ginsberg, reading his poem *Howl* at a San Francisco art gallery in 1955, and dancing and chanting at "happenings" in the 1960s, redefined the role of poetry and of poets in popular culture, making himself famous for his brilliance and eccentricity. Unlike the safe subject matter his peers were writing about, Ginsberg's erotic, politically charged, and openly gay poetry shattered conventions and helped usher in the revolutionary thinking of the sixties. The Diggers, the anarchist guerrilla theater and activist group started by Peter Berg and his friends, took the idea of creative independence beyond art into a liberal application as a way of life, and when Hal Reynolds bought a ramshackle house in West Berkeley, named it McGee's Farm, and converted it into a men's consciousness-raising commune, he and his communard friends literally embodied the idea of independence. Openly rejecting the idea of the nuclear family, suburban lifestyles, and consumer culture in favor of group living in urban and very rural areas, the communes started in the sixties took a stand for independence and rebuked long-standing notions of what creativity and family really mean.

Whether it was the shadow of the atomic cloud, or the post–World War II blues that followed, the actual availability of affordable housing in Manhattan and San Francisco, or simply the collective shrugged shoulders of a generation bored out of its skull by the strictures and expectations of an era that telegraphed a relentlessly cheerful message, art, and how art is made, changed in the fifties. This generation ushered in a sea change never before seen in American artistic culture. The line between the creative independent cultures of that decade and the ones that exist today, despite a few twists and turns, is not hard to follow. The distance between the paintings of Grace Hartigan, often featuring words from the poems of her friend Frank O'Hara along with abstract imagery, and the flyer art of punk artist Raymond Pettibon, which similarly pulls together abstracted chunks of texts and vibrant, disturbing images, is not all that great either. Even the spirit of the first clandestine gatherings of folk music fans unearthing and discovering the sounds of the Carter Family, slave ballads, and the silvery voice of folksinger John Jacob Niles can be rediscovered in the freak-folk artists like Devendra Banhart and Joanna Newsom who currently proliferate in the indie rock scene. In both the fifties and sixties, being an artist no longer meant that you needed training, education, or patronage. As Frank O'Hara described his own impulse to write, "going on your nerve" meant making art because you wanted to, and making it in your own way. By creating and following that dictum, the independent artists of that time created the blueprint for indie culture today.

But the new creative culture in the fifties didn't arrive flying its freak flag—it arrived wearing a suit, in the form of the writers and artists of the New York School. Working a day job at the Museum of Modern Art, where he curated exhibitions and wrote poems on his lunch hour, O'Hara's lifestyle was not overtly nonconformist. His friend the visual artist Joe Brainard clued in on the subtle indications of what did set O'Hara apart on their first meeting. "He was walking down Second Avenue. It was a cool early spring evening but he was wearing only a white shirt with the sleeves rolled up to his elbows. And blue jeans. And moccasins. I remember that he seemed very sissy to me. Very theatrical. Decadent. I remember that I liked him instantly."[1] With the words "sissy" and "theatrical," Brainard, using the parlance of his time, keyed into one of the elements that bound the poet's creative network together: homosexuality. O'Hara's close friends and fellow poets John Ashbery and James Schuyler, as well as Brainard, O'Hara's roommate Joe LeSueur, and many of the other artists in their circle were either gay or, for an era when homosexuality was viewed as a disease and a criminal act, unusually gay friendly. Frank O'Hara was born into an Irish Catholic family in Baltimore in 1926, and he grew up in the suburban town of Grafton, Massachusetts. After serving as a sonar man in the navy during World War II, he entered Harvard University on the GI Bill, where he became engrossed in the study of literature, falling in love with the poetry of radical French writers Arthur Rimbaud and Stéphane Mallarmé, and beginning to write poems of his own, which led him to a lifelong friendship with another poet who would become part of his circle in New York: John Ashbery. After graduate school at the University of Michigan, O'Hara relocated to New York in 1951, where he found a desk job working at the Museum of Modern Art, eventually working his way up to becoming the assistant curator of paintings and sculpture. Throughout his years at the MoMA, O'Hara wrote at a frenetic pace, sometimes writing a poem a day for weeks at a stretch. Reflecting the circumstances under which they were written, his poems had a tossed-together quality that casually disguised their insights into life in the city. With his balding head and large, crooked nose, he didn't look imposing, but his larger-than-life personality and voracious appetite for friendship and love drew artists of both genders into his circle. Though the writing and art they made was diverse, the one thing the New York School artists had in common was a desire to break taboos and try new things in their creative work. Aside from his former classmate John Ashbery, O'Hara's coterie included the African American poet LeRoi Jones (who later changed his name to Amiri Baraka) and many female artists and writers, including his close friends Grace Hartigan and Jane Freilicher. In its diversity and openness to creative experimentation, the New York School, as the group would later be dubbed by scholars, also set a precedent for open-mindedness about gender, race, and sexuality.

As far as a shared ethic goes in a distinct group of artists, the members of the New York School were interested in poetry as part of the everyday experience rather than something reserved for cloistered academics. If there's one hallmark of O'Hara's poetry that helps it to resonate with so many people, it's a sense of joy and pleasure in cataloging seemingly banal things and experiences: walks, food, chance meetings with friends, films, the urban landscape. The radical aesthetics of O'Hara and his circle were so new and different that the rigidly structured professorial class of the time often had no idea of how to react to them. At Harvard, O'Hara and Ashbery faced a difficult conundrum in their efforts to create serious yet avant-garde work. Their poems had always been considered to be too light and strange in construction and subject matter for the preferred taste for meter and rhyme espoused in college classrooms. Poking fun at the academic style of poetry in 1969, when he was more established, Ashbery wrote that "American poetry still suffers from the mania for over-interpretation. The technical term for this ailment is *objective correlativitis*. It attacks poets in their late 30s, and is especially prevalent in New England; elms are thought to be carriers."[2]

That same concern with life outside of academia, where art can often become something dry and dissectible, created a bond between poets and painters. In "Larry Rivers: A Memoir," O'Hara writes that many of these relationships between painters and poets stemmed from a mutual sense of being outsiders in their own genres, and some of that sense of outsider-ness grew from their mutual perception of being frivolous in their art: "for most of us non-Academic and indeed non-literary poets in the sense of the American scene at that time, the painters were the only generous audience for our poetry, and most of us read publicly at art galleries or at The Club."[3] Although the same division between academic and avant-garde writers and artists continues to exist today, the differentiation was greater in O'Hara's time.

While poets and painters and musicians and dancers and actors had historically collaborated before the New York School, the difference now was that because these collaborations were taking place outside of the watchful eyes of patrons, professors, or even moms and dads, so the question of "what is a poem" or "what is a painting" mattered hardly as much as the resulting product and the relationships that led to those products. Although almost all of these men and women came from middle-class or upper-middle-class backgrounds, their sexuality and the fearless nature of the art they made were defiant gestures to the communities that had reared them. And in making those gestures, they increasingly found things in common with artists from genres outside of their own.

One of O'Hara's most famous poems, "Why I Am Not a Painter," stemmed from a conversation about painting with his friend the abstract expressionist painter Grace Hartigan. Hartigan told O'Hara that she wanted to paint "a lot of something," and O'Hara, who was in the midst of a series of poems called "Orange," suggested she work with them. O'Hara comments further on this process and shared desire for "a lot of something" in his poem "Why I Am Not a Painter" when he writes that "There should be / So much more," a message to Hartigan about their collaboration and friendship.[4] Hartigan's and O'Hara's efforts became so symbiotic that "when O'Hara saw not only his portrait but also his poems reinterpreted through Hartigan's treatment in the Oranges, it seems likely that he had a similar experience of a number of his selves expanding. In this sense the Oranges represent a true collaboration, with each artist responding productively to the contribution of the other," writes critic Terence Diggory.[5] This sense of a fluid interchange between artists resonated strongly in the sixties, when psychedelics made self-expansion a lot easier and faster than it was in the fifties, when creative types stuck to alcohol, though often in vast quantities, and only occasionally dabbled in pot. The idea that a poet like O'Hara could see and understand himself and his own writing better through the lens of a painter was indicative of a cultural shift. It was easier for slightly older poets like Robert Lowell and Sylvia Plath to write for writing's sake than to collaborate with others, and their tortured confessional poems made O'Hara's subject matter look like a cakewalk in comparison. O'Hara and his friends needed to work with other artists like they needed the inspiration of the city where they lived. O'Hara once wrote that he could never be happy unless there was "a subway handy, or a record store or some other sign that people do not totally *regret* life," a huge contrast to the dour, desperate, and lonely lyrics of Plath and Lowell.[6]

Likewise, the symbiosis between a gay man and a straight female presented a new social opportunity, and this and his other friendships with artists and writers gave O'Hara a sense of purpose. Like many independent artists who followed, O'Hara fostered the idea of community being crucial to creative work. His book *Meditations in an Emergency* was dedicated to Freilicher, and many of his best poems were inspired by her and by Hartigan. O'Hara also formed close and lasting friendships, sometimes sexual, sometimes not, with his fellow gay poets Ashbery and James

Schuyler. Though their poems were stylistically different—O'Hara's were more observational, Ashbery's were more intellectual, and Schuyler's were more lyrical—they still had common ground in being outsiders, and they formed a close-knit circle that also included their straight friend Kenneth Koch, whose funny, odd poems further challenged the confessional aesthetic of the previous generation. All of these writers shared an avant-garde style, which sometimes pushed them to find publication in new venues.

O'Hara's books entered the world in unconventional ways, often through his network of friends rather than through a mainstream publisher. O'Hara published several chapbooks—limited edition short collections of poems—through the Tibor De Nagy gallery, often with illustrations and paintings by his friends. Chapbooks are sometimes dismissed as less significant than full-length books, since they are mostly published by small presses, have small print runs, and feature a shorter selection of poems, but they also play an important role in the history of small-press publishing. For thousands of writers like O'Hara, chapbooks provided a way for his work to be circulated in print. Chapbooks often led to longer collections of work, but because they're bite-sized and often funkily designed, they also paved the way for zines, broadsides, and other micropress releases in the sixties, eighties, and today. City Lights, one of the first significant independent presses, at the time already infamous for the government censorship trial it endured over the publication of Allen Ginsberg's *Howl* in 1956, published O'Hara's *Lunch Poems* in 1964 in its Pocket Poets Series, shortly before his death, and his work was often found in little magazines, broadsides, and mimeographed journals, the new organs of the avant-garde, all published by other writers interested in pushing the boundaries of writing and art. At readings, O'Hara, a lifelong cheerleader for his friends' work, would read not only his own poems but also Ashbery's, Schuyler's, and Koch's. He nurtured relationships with younger poets as well, like Bill Berkson, LeRoi Jones, and Barbara Guest.

Passing on both an artistic and social tradition integral to those who were, like him, dedicated to creating art that challenged the status quo, O'Hara may have looked on the surface like any other Irish Catholic from New England, but he was a creative radical, and his colleagues followed in his footsteps. The fevered pace of much of O'Hara's writing also reflected the distinct tension between creative pursuits and the need to earn a living that would come to define the indie lifestyle for generations of artists to come. Time was precious for someone who did not write for a living, who wrote simply because he had to and wanted to. And in the end, it was O'Hara who would help give rise to the figure who would build a bridge between the fifties experimental art scene and the sixties counterculture: Allen Ginsberg.

Although they crossed paths occasionally at readings and bars in New York, wrote their best-known works in the same era, and were sometimes published in the same magazines, the Beats and the New York School poets had little in common on the surface. Both Allen Ginsberg and Jack Kerouac published their seminal works, *Howl and Other Poems* (1956) and *On the Road* (1957), when they were in their thirties, but their writing and their concerns as writers were less refined, less cultured than that of the New York School. The Beats were grubby, dirty-minded, and noisy; the New York School poets were mannered, sophisticated, and somewhat hushed. O'Hara was thirty, the same age as Ginsberg when they met in 1956, but whereas O'Hara held down a day job and preferred mixing at cocktail parties and galleries, Ginsberg and his compatriots lived a more bohemian lifestyle. Ginsberg flitted in and out of a career in advertising, but he also experimented with drugs very early on, wrote poems based on his hallucinations, had openly gay relationships, and was always attracted to writers who lived both blue-collar and criminal lives. Kerouac was a merchant marine and a hard-drinking macho lumberjack type; Gregory Corso had recently been released from prison and was being supported by the patrons of a lesbian bar when he met Ginsberg; William S. Burroughs was a lifelong heroin addict who accidentally shot his wife in the head. The erudite poets of the New York School may have been adventuresome in their work, but their lives were nothing like this.

O'Hara alone among the New York School poets championed the work of Ginsberg and Gregory Corso. Ginsberg recalled his impression of O'Hara being much different than he had been led to expect based on O'Hara's jacket-and-tie image: "I was amazed that he was so open and wasn't just caught in a narrow New York Manhattan Museum of Modern artworld cocktail ballet scene."[7] To Ginsberg, who had already caused a sensation when *Howl* was published, O'Hara's circle may have seemed a little effete. Whereas Ginsberg flaunted his gayness, O'Hara and company kept theirs not secret but politely occluded. When Ginsberg arrived at a party, he'd begin chanting sutras, break out the pot, and generally cause a ruckus, while O'Hara's crowd were more prone to cocktails and chatter. O'Hara, however, saw past this young man's bravado to the possibility for another artistic connection. As it turned out, they liked many of the same writers, disliked the formalist poetry of the time, and both hung out at the Cedar Tavern, the watering hole of choice for many poets and painters. They shared a publisher in City Lights Books, and both collaborated with artists from genres outside of poetry. O'Hara loved to work with painters, dancers, and composers, and Ginsberg would later collaborate with a number of musicians, including Bob Dylan and the Clash. And both tirelessly advocated for their friends' work, creating networks of artists that became self-reliant and self-promoting, and sketching the blueprint for the kind of creative community that inspired the indie artists that would follow.

Ginsberg was born in 1926 to a Jewish family in Newark, New Jersey. His father was a high school teacher and part-time poet; his mother, who was mentally ill, was a member of the Communist Party and took Allen and his brother to party meetings when they were still children, an experience he would later write about in his poem "Kaddish." In 1949, Ginsberg left New Jersey for Columbia University, where he met Lucien Carr, a fellow student who introduced Ginsberg to Kerouac and Burroughs. Ginsberg had experienced an auditory hallucination of the eighteenth-century visionary poet William Blake reading to him while living in an apartment in Harlem, which inspired him to begin experimenting with new forms in his own poems, and the literary experimentation of his new compatriots, along with their taste for drugs, further enhanced the experimental aspects in Ginsberg's poems. In 1954, he moved to San Francisco, where he became involved in the equally freewheeling West Coast literary scene, and in 1955 he gave the first public reading of his poem *Howl,* an epic, incantatory, raging screed that rails against "Moloch," the god of industrialization, and praises "the best minds of my generation," depicting the same best minds engaged in homosexual acts that were shocking at the time. When *Howl* was published in 1956, its subject matter was so scandalous that its publisher, San Francisco's City Lights Books, was tried for circulating obscene material through the mail. When the book finally made it out of court and onto bookstore shelves, its notoriety was already built in, further enhanced by the publication of Kerouac's *On the Road,* which features a character plainly based on Ginsberg and showcases a similarly reckless crowd of characters. By the late fifties, Ginsberg was poetry's first twentieth-century rock star, and he embraced and ran with that role until his death. After O'Hara was killed on Fire Island in 1964 when he was struck by a dune buggy while walking the beach at night, Ginsberg ascended to levels of notoriety and success the understated poet who was his early mentor never dreamed of. The Beats and Ginsberg in particular displayed a sort of media savvy that wasn't as readily available to the artists of the New York School. While the writers and painters of the New York School had largely been ignored outside of art magazines at that point, the Beats' public flamboyance, hipster lingo, and peripatetic, drug-fueled lifestyles made them picture perfect for a society primed for titillation. The image of the renegade Beat poet was so appealing that by 1959 there was even a Beat clone named Maynard G. Krebs on television, arriving complete with black turtleneck, bongo drums, and goatee on the sitcom *The Many Loves of Dobie Gillis.* Whether the

Beats enjoyed this kind of facetious tribute, the fact was that Ginsberg's persona was a magnet for attention. According to writer Ron Sukenick, Ginsberg had "the image of the quintessential outsider, but he never accepted outsider status," and he "was the first to seize the means of promotion."[8] While he reinvented the idea of fame for a bohemian class that had previously largely existed in the shadows, Ginsberg also lived a resolutely independent lifestyle.

Instead of treating his notoriety as a God-given right, Ginsberg saw it as a license to do whatever he wanted and to constantly explore self-reinvention. Rather than embracing the typical career track of a successful writer in America (tenure at a prestigious school, literary prizes, and a mortgage), he used it to propel himself through a new kind of lifestyle, along the way reinventing the decades he lived in. He traveled constantly, never settling in one place for long; he had an open relationship with his partner Peter Orlovsky; he was a relentless cheerleader and promoter of his fellow Beat writers, much like O'Hara was for the writers of the New York School; he constantly pursued spiritual paths. When Ginsberg finally took an academic job, it wasn't at Princeton or the Iowa Writers' Workshop, it was at the Jack Kerouac School for Disembodied Poetics, an experimental writing program where the curriculum was partially based on the Buddhist teachings of Ginsberg's guru, the Tibetan Buddhist monk Chögyam Trungpa. The reading list for Ginsberg's poetics classes included original mystics like Artaud and Blake, as well as fellow Beats Kerouac, William S. Burroughs, Diane di Prima, and Gary Snyder.[9] The curriculum also included chanting, smoking pot, and hanging out with the professor until all hours of the night.

Ginsberg can be seen in endless film footage of many of the culturally transformative events of the sixties: chatting with Bobby Neuwirth in the background of Bob Dylan's *Dont Look Back*, chanting onstage at San Francisco's 1967 mass gathering the Human Be-In, participating in anti–Vietnam War protests, and being crowned the King of May during the first May Day festival in Czechoslovakia since the beginning of Soviet rule. This knack for grabbing and hanging on to the spotlight reflected the openness of Ginsberg's generation to change and to what sociologist Barbara Ehrenreich calls the Beats' "unconventional politics": "The Beats spoke from an underclass of unassimilated people to an unassimilated corner of the middle-class psyche; and this, as much as the wanton beat of rock and roll, was dangerous."[10] What made it even more dangerous was the fact that this message of alienated youth was being broadcast around the world. And, even more dangerously, it had a soundtrack.

In its earliest incarnations in the midfifties, the Beat subculture paid homage to jazz musicians. Kerouac in particular had a fascination with African American culture, which became a frequent subject of his writing, and identified his own prose style with the fast, improvised jazz of the time, calling his own compositional process "spontaneous bop prosody." In the Greenwich Village Beat scene, however, folk music soon superseded jazz as the music of choice. Coffeehouses sprang up all over the Village and soon became crowded with packs of earnest-looking guitarists strumming archaic-sounding tunes. Easy to play, identifiable with the proletariats Kerouac and the other Beats were engaged by (Kerouac wrote frequently about laborers and called them the "fellaheen," the Arabic word for "peasant"), folk offered the Beats a taste of authentic Americana. Since several well-known folk musicians, including Pete Seeger, were Communists who had been blacklisted in the McCarthy era, they were shellacked in a kind of authentic glamour, real people paying the price for freedom of speech. As the folklorist Alan Lomax put it, "To be folk, you live folk."[11] For the Beats, who were irresistibly drawn to hustlers like their friends Herbert Huncke and Neal Cassady, who represented something untouchably "real," folk music's traditions of protest, sorrow, and complaint fit right in with their vision.

Folk, like Beat culture, quickly went from being an underground, independent movement in the late fifties to something easily marketed and imitated in the early sixties. Just as teenagers could wear black turtleneck sweaters and berets and gather together to read bad pseudo-Beat poetry in coffeehouses, they could also learn to play the guitar with a fairly minimal amount of effort, so "hoots"—loosely structured jam sessions of folk musicians—became a regular weekend activity in most college towns by the early sixties. Popular music at the time was also offering up a lot of trite pap, so a void for "real" music, by and for the people, had opened up. Groups like the Kingston Trio offered a scrubbed-down, fresh-faced, and camera-ready kind of folk: wearing khaki pants and collegiate sweaters, they were a nonthreatening version of the music being discovered and resurrected in coffeehouses and clubs. But even among the nascent folkies, there were those who wanted to put a twist on the idea of folk music. The best known of those artists, a newly self-rechristened Bob Dylan, who years later would bring Ginsberg along to recite poetry onstage during his Rolling Thunder Revue tour, would soon bring his own take on folk into the mainstream and radically change the times, but folk was "symbolic of much more than just the hand-clapping entertainment that the popularizers were implementing"—along with jazz, poetry, avant-garde literature and art, and the expanding subcultures that produced them, its popularity represented a growing hunger in American culture for an alternative.[12]

This hunger for something new not only led to the explosion of subcultural values into the mainstream in the sixties; it also parallels closely the similar upsurges in independent culture in the eighties and late nineties. Just as the culture began to take a vapid turn in the eighties, the punk music scene, zines, underground comics, and skateboarding rose up to offer a self-created alternative: an independently generated response to Reaganomics, *Dynasty*, and big hair. And just as the rumbles of neoconservatism began to sound in the late nineties, and as the Iraq war entered the scene in the early years of the next decade, blogs, indie music, independent publishing, and many other forms of subcultural self-expression likewise experienced a resurgence. But the original independent music, art, and literary movements of the fifties and sixties remain a guide for subsequent manifestations of indie to follow. And, as the Beat

subculture began to dim in the public eye, another independent subculture stepped in to take its place. This time, it
seemed to bring the entire nation with it.

Countless radical groups emerged in the sixties, and all of
them stressed independence in one form or another: seeking independence from the draft had led many young American men
to drop out of society or flee the country; independence from
manufactured pop music led to the creation of underground rock,
where bands sang songs critical of the Vietnam War; independence from mass media views on the war and society led to the
creation of the alternative press papers such as the *Berkeley Barb*
and the *New Left Review,* and of underground comics like Robert
Crumb's *Zap*; and the desire for total independence from the
chaos of society gave rise to experiments in communal living and
living off the grid. Loosely organized and focused on the redistri-
bution of wealth, civil rights, women's rights, and sundry other
causes, fringe groups in the sixties often worked in collaboration
with writers, artists, and musicians to stage happenings, be-ins,
and protests both serious and playful. Anything could become
theater, and theater could be an act of liberation not just for the
actors but for the audience as well. This shift in creativity is perhaps best epitomized by the Diggers, a radical theater company
that strove to create "a benevolent anarchist future for post revolutionary implementation," according to one of its founders, Peter Berg.

In his memoir, *Sleeping Where I Fall*, the actor and former Digger Peter Coyote refers to Berg as "mercurial, charming, coercive,
subliminally menacing, and intellectually uncompromising."[13]
On the phone from his office in San Francisco's Noe Valley,
Berg in 2008 is much the same as Coyote describes him. His discussion of his own history as an independent artist covers a
complex journey from childhood in South Florida and his first
exposure to racism, to participating in the civil rights movement
in the South, to an acting career in New York's radical black theater scene of the early sixties, to San Francisco and the revolu-

tionary creative period of the mid- to late sixties. Berg talks fast and piles on anecdotes, but throughout the conversation, he punctures the narrative with interrogative riffs, checking in to make sure that what he's discussing is clearly understood.

Before the Diggers came together in 1966, Berg, Coyote, and most of their cohorts were members of the San Francisco Mime Troupe. This wasn't run-of-the-mill white-pancake-and-beret-style mime; instead, the troupe reinvented the commedia dell'arte, one of the first forms of street theater, refocusing the commedia for a more politicized, contemporary sixties crowd. Berg quickly became initiated into the fray surrounding the group at the staging of his first commissioned contribution, an adaptation of a late Renaissance play by Giordano Bruno. He went in knowing that the group "sensed that I was into a more rigorous political bag than they were at the time. They hadn't had as much exposure to the black revolutionary scene, and didn't know what anarchism was."[14] The Mime Troupe had already butted heads with the San Francisco police for performing in the parks without a permit, and when the day came to stage Berg's adaptation, things looked bad before the actors even took the stage. "Here's what actually happened," Berg says. "The director came out on the stage and said, 'Ladies and gentlemen, the San Francisco Mime Troupe presents a bust.' The police rushed to the stage, grabbed him, took him away, and this group of three hundred or so individuals followed behind him, saying, 'Don't arrest him; he didn't do anything.'" To Berg and many of the other people involved in the production and in the audience that day (which conveniently included many members of the local alternative press, including the *Berkeley Barb* and the *New Left Review*, guaranteed to spill some ink over the bust), the sight of an actor being led away in handcuffs became a galvanizing moment. Berg reflects that "the phenomenon of theater being a social event, being causal, was fascinating to me." It was fascinating to a lot of other people as well; soon afterward, the local underground rock promoter Bill Graham was coerced into putting together a benefit for the

Mime Troupe's escalating legal fees, at which the speakers included LSD guru Timothy Leary and Allen Ginsberg, and the bands included Frank Zappa's freak brotherhood the Mothers of Invention. "Five thousand people came to this event," Berg says. "They were around the block. Now it was not only political; it was a culturally focused phenomenon."

The event marked the formulation of a new concept for Berg and the other members of the Mime Troupe: guerrilla theater. The idea came to Berg as a way to "use theater to cause something to happen and what happened would be an issue in itself, and it was important for people in the audience not to be told that it was theater. Not to sneak it on them, but to have them perceive it as reality, and have them relate to that reality, to create real change." Tactics for deploying guerrilla performances included staging a scene of a military policeman beating prisoners to death in the midst of a free speech protest on the University of California, Berkeley campus; staging Jean Genet's play *The Screens* in a bus station "just to see what the people in the bus station would do"; and staging a play called *Search and Seizure* during scheduled performances in nightclubs, wherein people portraying five types of drug users would be pulled from the audience and interrogated onstage. Musician Country Joe McDonald found *Search and Seizure* so disturbing that he told Berg that "he was never gonna watch it again, because there was too much paranoia involved with it." Guerrilla theater shook up unwitting audiences; people would openly question the performers, wondering whether the action was real, and sometimes the situation turned dangerous: "This is without money," Berg says, "doesn't have commercial interest anymore—none—it is highly political, and the people that do it have to be ready to be arrested, to be beaten up." For Berg and the other actors, writers, and directors involved, it was also liberating.

Around this time, Berg's colleague Billy Murcott had been reading about the history of anarchy in England and came across the story of a group called the Diggers. Led by Gerard Winstanley, a cloth merchant turned organizer for poor Englishmen and later a notorious pamphleteer, the English Diggers argued that land should be free for the poorest people. Winstanley's best-known Digger pamphlet, "The True Leveller's Standard Advanced," declared that by collectively squatting on land and cultivating it, the English Diggers were staging a protest "shewing the Cause why the Common People of England have begun, and gives Consent to Digge up, Manure, and Sow Corn upon George-Hill in Surrey." Thus they earned the derogative sobriquet of Diggers, which they took as a point of pride. For Berg and the San Francisco revolutionaries, the idea of claiming one's freedom for the sake of the poor was an irresistible concept, and they promptly christened themselves the Diggers and set about creating a world with two principal rules: everything is free, and do your own thing.

The Diggers' first "demonstrative and exhibitory" act of revolution, according to Berg, was to feed people. But "this wasn't to be like the Salvation Army"; feeding people became a performance. Golden Gate Park, located in San Francisco's Haight-Ashbury neighborhood, has a long strip of greenway that juts out of it, known locally as the Panhandle. The Panhandle runs between two of the city's busiest streets: Oak Street and Fell Street, and at rush hour, mornings and evenings, thousands of drivers course by the park on either side. The Diggers took advantage of that traffic, Berg says, and erected a "twelve-foot-square orange frame that we called the Free Frame of Reference, and we aimed the frame so that traffic going by would all have to see the scene of people being fed or feeding themselves through this frame." The idea for the frame came from the artist and composer John Cage, who had said that you could put a frame around anything and make it art. The Diggers even invented Digger Bread—whole wheat bread baked in coffee cans—to make feeding people easier; leaflets with a recipe for Digger Bread included the explicit directions that the bread should always be given away.

So when the Diggers dreamed up the concept of a free store, it only served to underscore dual levels of their philosophy. "It wasn't just going to be a free store; it was going to be a theater," Berg says. Laughing, he continues, "The name of it was Trip

Without a Ticket—that's a dead giveaway, isn't it?" The store was conceived as an act of constant improvised performance. The dressing room was designed by poet Lenore Kandel "to cause people to want to have sex." Customers who walked in and asked for the manager were told that they were the manager. Journalists who walked in asking to interview the Diggers were told to wait, at which point another journalist would be brought over, and they would begin interviewing one another. "This really happened," Berg asserts. "You could put people on remarkably within this context."

The store became the center of the rapidly expanding countercultural scene in San Francisco. Hundreds of people joined up with the Diggers, including well-known alternative writers like Richard Brautigan, Diane di Prima, and Philip Whalen. By 1968, as the scene became bigger and more unruly in the Haight, the police responded, as Berg explains, by making "Haight Street one way; they installed mercury vapor lights so that at night it looked like East Berlin, and they're running paddy wagons up and down the street every half hour and picking up everybody that looks like they're under age." The Diggers responded by moving their entire scene to city hall, where musicians played, poets recited, and more food was given away between the vernal equinox and the summer solstice, at which point the Diggers declared that San Francisco had "entered into eternity, and with that the Digger thing ceased in San Francisco." The Diggers then morphed into the larger and more amorphous Free Family; many members of that group in turn moved to rural northern California's Siskiyou County and founded the Black Bear Ranch commune, which still operates today.

According to Berg, the legacy of the Diggers is complex. They pioneered the idea of guerrilla theater, and they also helped advance the concept of a nonprofit free press, which had begun with the alternative literary journals being printed in the New York School and Beat days. The Digger Communication Company owned and operated a printing press, and not only did they print and distribute books of poetry by Brautigan and other contemporary writers; they were also able to print single-sheet broadsides that responded almost immediately to events happening all over the city. "If someone was shot, we could have a broadside out about it by noon," and during the Invisible Circus, a thirty-six-hour "happening" held at Glide Memorial Church, the Communication Company released broadsides every thirty minutes on average so that an instant archive was created as the event was taking place. Not only did the act presage the instantaneous communication that would come to dominate through the Internet; it also paved the way for zines, the xeroxed print organs of the punk community in the eighties, which helped people to hear about events that were occurring off the radar of the mass media, bonding together members of the community. The Diggers mixed anarchist politics with the arts in an unforeseen manner, and their group's emphasis on collective identity over individual fame is echoed in the many waves of independent creativity that followed in their wake.

Black Bear Ranch, the Diggers-founded commune, took the mission of "everything is free" one step further. When people decided to live communally, they took on more than just the responsibility for shared household chores; they worked to make their lifestyles independent from the nuclear family structure essential to nearly all of their upbringings. The squats and collective artist warehouses of the eighties through today followed the beliefs espoused by the communal revolution of the sixties, that living together and sharing all the responsibility of maintaining a home was a revolutionary act necessary to assert true independence and liberation from social norms.

Hal Reynolds was a communard in the early seventies, and today he still bears a strong resemblance to pictures of him from those days; he's bearded and wears work shirts and has an easygoing manner of speaking that's common to members of the counterculture, especially in the Bay Area. Reynolds was a graduate student at Berkeley in the late sixties and early seventies, and when he and his wife purchased a house in a Berkeley neighborhood already crowded with other communes, it made both budgetary and cultural sense to try living cooperatively with friends. "It was just a huge difference from anything any of us had experienced ourselves as we grew up," he recalls, "the idea of living together with a bunch of people who were *not* your family, not having a nuclear family . . . Everything about it was just radically, radically new."[15] McGee's Farm, as they dubbed their commune, was located in West Berkeley on McGee Avenue, where "everybody was living a cultural political dream. Our neighborhood was about separating yourself or establishing an alternative identity lifestyle." Reynolds and his friends knocked down several walls in order to change the house from two separate flats into a collective living space. He recalls that between five and eight people lived in the house at one time, and "there were more women than men." Naturally, because of this imbalance, the members of McGee's Farm applied their radical domestic ideals to reinventing strict and outdated gender roles.

As young parents, Reynolds and his wife appreciated the idea that child care could become a cooperative effort, and "we started a neighborhood men's group, which is the oldest one I've ever heard of, and among the projects we did was to start a child care for the neighborhood in our garage, and it was run completely by the men. It was part of our ideology that men needed to take more responsibility for child care." In order to get to a point where the men in the commune were prepared to take on the role of primary caregivers, and to increase their self-sufficiency, the male communards took a retreat up to the Russian River near the Marin County coast. It was there that Reynolds began to understand how self-empowering his new life could be. "I remember the experience that I had on that retreat was using a chainsaw for the first time in my life," he reflects. "I was clueless with tools, but part of the ideology of that time was that you were supposed to *do things yourself*, not hire plumbers and carpenters; you were supposed to do it yourself, so I wanted to learn. But a chain saw was so hard; it was such a problem to operate it, so when the men's group was out on the retreat, we brought a chain saw, and everybody got a swing." They also collaborated with other communes in the neighborhood to start a food conspiracy ("everything was called a conspiracy," he notes wryly), and they baked bread and carried it to perform an antisexism skit outside of San Francisco's Playboy Club. Their idea was that they would hand out bread to the men leaving the club, but "the guys coming out were not very interested in our bread." Reynolds laughs and admits that "some of us were on the side peeking at the *Playboy*s; regardless of our stance, it was our chance to read it. But that's what we believed in."

McGee's Farm held together for several years, and Reynolds credits his lifestyle with enabling him to complete his PhD course work at Berkeley: "I did it with the help of the commune," he asserts. But fissures in the placid surface of collective life had already begun to appear. One couple that lived in the house, a former Catholic priest and nun who had recently left the church, bowed out shortly after arriving. "They were moving rapidly, but compared to where we were, they were so much more rigid and organized." Conflicts and any sort of contention led to what Reynolds says with a sigh were "endless house meetings. That was one of the things, I think, that killed us. We tried to keep it for things of gravity, but we were so green and inexperienced that we had too many meetings." On top of the too-frequent meetings that often failed to resolve disagreements about sharing work and responsibility, communication—so essential to maintaining their lifestyle—had begun to break down between the communards. "If there was one single thing that ended the commune," Reynolds reflects, it was when a young woman living there "tried to commit suicide in the bathtub, and somebody discovered her up there lying in a pool of blood. But we were just so shocked that that would happen, and we didn't know about anything being wrong with her." This sense of disconnection from one another created a sense of guilt among the members who had missed the signs of their friend's deep depression. On top of the suicide attempt, members of the commune were becoming disillusioned with the same causes that had brought them together. By the early to mid-seventies, the Vietnam War had dragged on for nearly a decade, and the antiwar movement that had brought people together was losing steam. Reynolds witnessed the collective exhaustion and frustration firsthand: "We went to I don't know how many demonstrations, and the war was still going." Many radicals of his generation began to feel the same way.

As the sixties drifted into the seventies, the cultural climate that gave rise to the radical changes in creativity and lifestyle that spurred O'Hara, Ginsberg, Berg, Reynolds, and countless others toward reinvention took a dark turn. The subcultural movements of the seventies, including punk and hip-hop, reflected a mood that was anathema to the idealistic motivations behind much of the sixties counterculture. Cocaine and heroin replaced pot and LSD; those living once idyllic lifestyles now had to face a recession, gas shortages, and the homecoming of thousands of mentally and physically damaged Vietnam vets. The children born in the sixties who bore witness to many of the cultural shifts of that time looked on their parents' adventures in lifestyle experimentation with a mixture of cautious appreciation and cynical disdain. As they came of age in the seventies, they absorbed the anger of punk, the urban critiques and visual styles of hip-hop, and slowly but surely they fermented the next wave of independent creativity. Just as the Eisenhower era, the Cold War, civil rights, and Vietnam had created a climate that was ripe for redefinition according to a new set of rules, the late seventies and early eighties fostered a seismic shift in American culture. Greed was back, the American government was caught up in shady political scandals, Russian bombs were pointed our way, and a new president would wind up angering and alienating many of the young people who had watched their parents trade in tie-dye for gray flannel suits. When independent culture reemerged in the eighties, it didn't come from the big cities with energetic young populations struggling to artistically reinvent themselves; it came from the suburbs, the smaller cities, and from working-class towns, where picking up a guitar, drawing a comic, stapling a zine, or hosting an underground radio show were just a few of the ways the younger generation could vent the tensions they inherited with the new decade. And by venting, they changed the world all over again.

two

Get in the Van: Punk Roots

Hey mister, don't look down on me
for what I believe in

—Minutemen, "This Ain't No Picnic"[1]

12 Galaxies, a small club located in San Francisco's Mission District, took its name from local eccentric Frank Chu, a professional protester and performance artist who walks around the city wearing a baggy suit and carrying an ever-changing sign currently reading "WELCH / 12 Galaxies / Bretrokenitol persecutions / KGO: Textrochenical coverage / Faxkonutikel / Anabolic Contemptuous / Fibrillations." Nobody's sure exactly what this means, but Chu is a notorious enough local character to have a club named after him, and on a drippy November night in 2007, he's standing inside the club with his sign propped on his shoulder, drinking a beer and hanging out with patrons.

Parked at the curb outside on Mission Street is a big white Econoline van, and wandering back and forth from the van to the club is a burly guy with graying hair, wearing a short-sleeved flannel shirt, battered Converse sneakers, and a canvas Carhartt jacket. A very petite woman of about the same age with cropped hair, wearing big white tennis shoes, dark pants, and a shiny shirt, walks alongside him. The pair eventually meander backstage, and then appear onstage, both carrying electric bass guitars. There's no backing band, no drums, and no vocals beyond occasional comments at the mike between songs. The sound is thunderous, melodic, and so deep that patrons rush to the bar to dip into the large jar of free earplugs. The man plays the bass standing in a legs-apart stance, attacking the strings with his upper body; the woman bounces around the stage in rhythm to the music, launching herself back and forth from the balls of her feet.

Mike Watt and Kira Roessler have been playing music together for more than twenty years, since 1985. They're also a former couple who married and amicably separated and continued to make music together under the name Dos (Spanish for "two," pronounced "dose") after their divorce. They look like average hip folks approaching middle age, but many of the people in the club that night are standing around with giddily awed grins on their faces because these are two legends of punk music, still touring and playing together thirty-plus years after the indie punk revolution began. Watt started the Minutemen in 1980 with his childhood friend guitarist and singer D. Boon and George Hurley, another kid from San Pedro, California, the working-class town where they were all born and raised. Roessler, also a gifted bassist, was one of the many musicians to rotate through the pioneering punk band Black Flag; she played on five of Flag's studio albums. Today, Watt and Roessler tour and play together as often as they can. Watt usually has his hands in five or six other music projects at any given time, and Roessler works full-time as a dialogue editor for feature films. On this night at 12 Galaxies, they play together as easily as old friends, bass lines fusing smoothly. Later, after a set by Sistas in the Pit, an all-female African American power trio (Watt's a big fan), Dos will crash somewhere and drive back to their homes in Southern California the next day. Roessler will head back to work and Watt will prepare to play a series of gigs celebrating his fiftieth birthday.

For Mike Watt, Kira Roessler, and the other punks who created the independent music scene in the eighties, the definition of independence came down to one thing: work. Making music was work. Touring was work. Booking shows was work. Drawing flyers and stapling them up around town was work. Doing interviews with zines was work. But unlike the day jobs where most of these musicians toiled when they weren't making music, this was work you could believe in, work as an act of faith. The artists of the fifties and sixties believed in creative life as work too, but never before had taking your art into your own hands been as much of a statement of your beliefs and a way of life as it became in the eighties. Punk took the creative freedom inherited from previous generations and added a strong dose of rage that made its forebears look wimpy in comparison. That rage eventually created a kind of ethical code for many punks, who built on the idea of support networks from the fifties generation of artists and borrowed the idealism of the sixties generation, but tossed in a healthy dose of cynicism and self-awareness that helped punk to become a self-operating, self-navigating subculture with its own set of ideals and alternative models for doing business. Most of those ideals boiled down to the idea that self-reliance was the key to expression, and punks called this thinking DIY: do it yourself.

As testament to how much that simple decision to do it yourself changed the lives of the people who helped create indie culture in the eighties, the legacy of many of the bands who emerged in that decade is evident today. You can't read an interview with any up-and-coming indie band without seeing the name of one of the groundbreaking bands of that era cited as a major influence, not just in terms of making music, but as models for making music a way of life. Black Flag, Hüsker Dü, the Minutemen, the Replacements, Minor Threat, Fugazi, Sonic Youth, Mission of Burma, and many others tore a path through the heart of America's ideas about what music could be, reinventing the punk genre as they simultaneously created new methods for touring, distributing, and recording their own music. In many cases, those bands—via whatever tangled routes took them into adulthood and middle age—still make music today. And they still do it themselves.

Prior to punk's flowering in the 1980s, most bands were still reliant on the major label system for recording, distributing, and promoting their music. Early American punk bands like the Ramones didn't put out their records on independent labels simply because indie labels barely existed and had no viable methods for distribution. Therefore, punk bands signed to major labels, which sometimes didn't know how to handle these new acts. The Ramones, for example, were cast in a silly, exploitative film about teenagers called *Rock 'n' Roll High School*, which was entertaining enough for its footage of the band looking extremely out of place among the overemotive cast, but the film had little to do with the Ramones' ferocious live shows at legendary punk dive CBGB in New York's Bowery. Major labels have a history of signing bands to contracts that look like guaranteed moneymaking deals but that often wind up with the band actually in debt to the label when labels pay enormous advances that the band struggles to make back. The label also controls the band's image and artwork, has the ability to censor its lyrics, and retains the legal rights to its music even if the band somehow manages to extricate itself from its contract. When punks in the eighties decided to start forming their own record labels in answer to this inherently exploitative scenario, their main motivation was control. If you were signed to an independent label, you had control over how you sounded in the studio, how your album art came out, what the label could and couldn't do to promote and market your music, where you would play shows, and what lyrics you could sing. The odds of your making money were theoretically not as good on an indie label since their distribution was more limited and most radio stations ignored indie releases; however, given the fact that so many bands got screwed by majors, they were often willing to sacrifice the chance to get rich for the chance to do what they wanted. For many musicians who recorded for indie labels in the eighties, the limitations of the scene's intimacy and small size were a fair trade for touring with other bands they were friendly with, sharing resources and equipment, and building a network that would sustain some of them to the present day. For Mike Watt's band the Minutemen and for Mission of Burma from Boston, fame would not arrive while they were helping build those networks but, years later, after they built a legacy that would influence many bands that followed in their wake. After the punk scene peaked in the eighties, Watt would go on to tour and play relentlessly, keeping the Minutemen's music alive, and Mission of Burma would experience its creative comeback years after its breakup, just when playing together again was the last thing the band members imagined.

The fact that Watt has been "jamming econo" for more than thirty years and shows no signs of slowing down is evidence that the punk spirit of DIY remains alive and well today. On top of that, Watt has been a guiding light to countless young musicians, writers, and other folks who have sought out examples of a way to make a life in art. He lives frugally and simply, drives himself to gigs, and is revered by younger musicians and his peers alike for always putting his music first. When people talk about the legacy of the Minutemen, the first thing they often say is that the band was both musically advanced and ahead of its time. "They were just great players," says Tom Watson of the band Slovenly. "They kind of brought this whole other level of musicianship to this underground music scene."[2] Not only was its music prescient in its combination of jazz/funk rhythms and punk noise, the band also helped pioneer an engaged, political kind of songwriting without stooping to the pedantry popular at the time. And they pioneered the idea of "jamming econo": taking the matters of recording, touring, promoting, and making music out of the hands of labels and into their own.

The Minutemen formed at a time when arena rock ruled the airwaves and arena rock's bombastic style and sound reflected the vapid turn American culture was taking in the wake of the post-Vietnam era. On their first extended play album, *Paranoid Time*, the Minutemen refused to make songs in the verse-chorus-verse style that dominated popular and punk music alike. Instead, their songs were short, tightly controlled bursts of noise over lyrics that reflected the rising discontentment with America's growing media culture along with the bleak social mood of the early eighties. In "Paranoid Chant," Boon sang, "I try to talk to girls and I keep thinking of World War III."[3] As Jack Brewer from the band Saccharine Trust puts it, "When you listen to *Paranoid Time*, you realize these weren't just songs; these people were really paranoid."[4] But the message of *Paranoid Time* appealed to many like-minded people in the band's growing audience. When they played the song live and dedicated it to Ronald Reagan, the audience nodded along. The Minutemen's undying self-reliance, defiant musical innovation, and their relationships with the growing independent networks made them one of the linchpins of the rapidly expanding punk subculture.

Watt answers the telephone sounding exactly like the answering-machine recording of him included on Sonic Youth's landmark album *Daydream Nation* ("Thurston? WATT. Hey Thurston, did you find your shit?").[5] His individualistic manner of speech might sound odd to someone unschooled in the slang of his hometown of San Pedro, California, but once you figure out what "econo" means (anything done cheaply, and usually quickly), where he's driving his "boat" (van) next, what he means by a "thudstaff" (bass), and that "conk" can totally be used as a noun ("I got four hours of conk and woke up at eight bells"), it's easy to follow along with Watt's occasionally meandering, engaging conversation.

The idea of DIY ethics wasn't entirely new in the late seventies, when Watt and his friends discovered punk. As Watt reflects, "I found out later that there was a whole thing that was kinda parallel to punk in the 1960s like garage bands and little labels. The labels were more regional. And there was a lot of Do-It-Yourself. So there was a big explosion of little bands. But by the time I'm a teenager [the first gig I go to] is [in] seventy-one,

T. Rex. It's arena rock, and I've never been into a club until punk came."[6] For Watt and the other kids who grew up in the seventies, the up-close-and-personal nature of punk shows empowered them to believe that making music might be a realistic option. Arena rock, the only alternative they knew, segregated performers from the audience. Before Jumbotrons made it possible for the audience to actually see what was going on onstage with any clarity, stadium shows looked like puppet theater to anyone not crammed into the front rows. In contrast, punk shows afforded the audience the ability to stand feet from the stage, and Watt and his friends drank it up. "So I'm listening and aware of that kinda stuff where you can actually see the bass and the strings. The music scene too was way different. There wasn't the Guitar Center and instructional videos. The accessibility was different, especially when you didn't have older brothers like us," Watt states. "We had to just stumble through everything and we had to just jam econo." Punk music was confrontational and fast. Skill didn't matter as much as attitude and emotion. And, most significantly for the people in the audience who witnessed it, punk looked like something you could do. "It was really mind-blowing to see these guys not know what they're doing and playing in public but still writing their own songs," says Watt. "And the empowerment by witnessing such a thing. The empowerment on us. I turned to these two people at a gig and said we could do this."

While the notion of "jamming econo"—making music, recording it, touring, and living as frugally as possible—would later become the indie community's modus operandi, in the early days of the Minutemen, it mostly meant fucking around with guitars. The band's early experiments in jamming econo led to some music that Watt admits was "god awful. Gladly we didn't have any takes from then." Learning to play came down to the way everyone else learned to play: "You just copied songs off records and the idea of playing in front of people was a backyard kegger or something." There was an additional stumbling point for D. Boon and Watt in the early days of playing together: "We didn't fuckin' know you had to be in tune with each other. I don't know what the fuck we were thinking. We thought if you weren't in tune, if you played 'Down on the Corner' and that sounded right, then you were in tune. We didn't know 'Down on the Corner' had to be the same as the other guy's 'Down on the Corner.'" To Watt, the problem with the cultural preference for jamming on Creedence or Zeppelin tunes was completely parallel to the divisiveness created by the arena rock shows. "To the guys who played 'Black Dog,'" Watt recalls, "there's just no connection with the stuff you might have inside and want to get out and use music as an artistic vehicle."

Around the same time that the Minutemen got together, the Los Angeles punk scene was beginning to coalesce. Bands like the Germs, the Plugz, X, the Weirdos, and many others began to join up and play gigs at clubs in and around the sprawling Los Angeles area. As Black Flag and Circle Jerks member Keith Morris puts it, "The scene in Los Angeles was spreading out like if you were to spill a bucket of water. All of a sudden it wasn't just about Hollywood, but it was more about Ventura County. It was more about the Valley. It was more about Orange County. It was more about where we were from, which was South Bay, which was about twenty-five miles south of Los Angeles."[7] The Minutemen's hometown of San Pedro, for example, is a harbor town on a peninsula south of Los Angeles proper, so getting to gigs required a lot of commitment, but the growing punk community made it possible for bands like the Minutemen to share resources no matter what part of the LA area they were from. Not only did bands pool money to rent ethnic halls and out-of-the-way spots like gay discos and Moose Lodges to play gigs; they also toured together, frequently turning to Black Flag member Chuck Dukowski's phone book for a list of places to play and crash all over the country. "Black Flag built that entire tour circuit that we still use now thirty years later," Watt reflects, "which is a trip when I think about it."

Flyers, often illustrated by Raymond Pettibon, started appearing all over the greater Los Angeles area. Black Flag's four-bar logo, also designed by Pettibon, was spray painted on almost every wall. These cryptic signifiers attracted an audience that was just as tired of the posing and preening of arena rock as the bands were. In Los Angeles and elsewhere, people were drawn to the intimacy and unpredictability of punk shows and to the idea that they might also have something to contribute, whether it meant starting a zine, being in a band of their own, or making art. Fanzines like *Flipside* and *Slash* were beginning to emerge, reviewing albums and gigs by the LA punk bands, providing an organ for the growing Southern California punk community. These zines helped to convey a message that something cool and different was happening, and punk fans outside of Los Angeles could hunt zines down via mail-order catalogs and their local record stores, building an audience that would turn up when bands ventured out on tour. SST Records, an indie label founded by Black Flag guitarist Greg Ginn, became the home of many of these same bands and went on to release landmark records by independent bands from all over the country later in the eighties and early nineties, including Dinosaur Jr., Sonic Youth, and Bad Brains. The fact that SST and other indie labels of the time were mainly operated by punk musicians helped mitigate any possible accusations of selling out when bands signed to them, since recording and distribution became a cooperative effort rather than a blatant play at making money.

For the Minutemen, Watt says, part of the impetus for writing songs and for being a part of the punk community was simply "trying to figure out stuff. We put it in our songs. A lot of it was about thinking out loud. And it seemed the scene was open enough to accept shit like that." Their songwriting took a political turn early on, and throughout their career they telegraphed messages about the plight of the working man, something that hit close to home for three guys from the working-class town of San Pedro. In accordance with their antielitist stance, the inherent structure of the band was created so that it never had a leader of any sort. "The arena rock was kind of hierarchical with guitars and singers being way at the top and the other section way down there" says Watt. "Obviously, with the punk movement, everybody's lame, so it's kind of equal footing. So all that hierarchy got thrown out." The Minutemen even made a joke of the anticompetitive nature of their structure as a band by releasing an album called *3-Way Tie (for Last)*. It was just this sense of working as a unit, without a leader, that made their music inherently different from traditional guitar-driven rock. "D. Boon played really heavily with trebly new power chords and left all this room for the bass guitar," says Watt, "and then worked with Georgie to make sure he had all these fills and parts to jam to and add movement to the songs. We had this idea that it was a three-way tie and not some hierarchy or aristocracy of guitar." By subverting the structure of songwriting, the Minutemen not only created a whole new sound; they also sent out a message about working together toward a common goal. Other bands responded to this message by supporting the Minutemen and helping promote the band by covering their songs or talking about them in interviews, which meant that the favor would someday be returned. Reciprocity was both a survival mechanism and a conscious choice, since any band's odds of lasting were better if other bands were on its side.

This resonated powerfully in the punk scene, where resources were so scarce that they had to be shared. Anything that led bands to playing live shows and recording was viewed as part of the job. "We divided the world up into two categories," Watt states, "gigs and flyers. Because the gig was intense. We saw it as so profound, you know, so intense, that this was really the deal. And everything else was just to get . . . people at the gig 'cause that seemed like where you had the most control over how you're being perceived, because you're playing for the people you know." Many times, those people were members of other bands, zine writers, and the others who made up the punk community. And the Minutemen's relentless touring and work ethic made them heroes in their own community. In the 2005 documentary *We Jam Econo: The Story of the Minutemen*, more than fifty different punk musicians from the era take turns discussing their admiration for the band, praising its music and repeating the idea that the philosophy of "jamming econo" changed how bands operated. The band recorded fast, during late-night sessions when studio time was cheaper, enlisting their friends to engineer, and their output was prolific: four albums and eight EPs between 1980 and 1985.

Like many independent bands who would follow them, the Minutemen came to a crossroads in the mideighties. Their 1985 EP *Project: Mersh* ("mersh" being Watt-speak for commercial) was an ironic take on "popular" music: the songs actually lasted more than two minutes, and the cover, drawn by Boon, depicts three record executives stating, "I got it! We'll have them write hit songs!"[8] While this crass attempt at "selling out" was intended as parody, the record was released at a time when success was really knocking at the Minutemen's door. Their inimitable 1984 album *Double Nickels on the Dime* sold fourteen thousand copies the year of its release, a highly respectable number for an independent band at the time, and they even filmed a music video for "This Ain't No Picnic," which aired on MTV.[9] By late 1985, the Minutemen had also played a number of gigs with REM, another underground band that was beginning to break through into the mainstream, and the two bands were planning a more extensive tour for 1986. On December 22, 1985, however, both the Minutemen's career and Watt's life took a sudden and devastating turn for the worse. D. Boon, riding in the back of a van, was killed in an accident. Having based the band's entire ethic on the "three-way tie," Watt and Hurley knew they couldn't continue without Boon.

Nonetheless, for a band that lasted only a few years, the Minutemen's legacy is profound. "Jamming econo" is still a way of life for most independent bands, as well as for zinesters, publishers, labels, crafters, and anyone else who makes art independently. Although prior iterations of indie culture had also managed to muddle through on the cheap, the Minutemen's career served as a powerful reminder that independence could also be an ethic for the way you lived your life. Although Watt was devastated by Boon's death and had to be coaxed back into playing music by his friends in Sonic Youth, music has been the core of his life ever since, and the legacy of the Minutemen has continued to grow since Boon's death. All of their albums are still available, a rarity for many early indie bands, and their music continues to inspire bands today. Watt remains active within the indie music community. With the exception of fIREHOSE, the band Watt founded with Hurley and Minutemen fan Ed Crawford in 1986 and played with for eight years, Watt has preferred not to be locked down with one group. He currently plays with a dizzying variety of different groups in many genres of music (including his current obsession: Okinawan folk music from Japan), and he remains a student of music, striving to learn. His current gig as bassist with the reunited protopunk legends The Stooges has been a humbling and empowering experience; finally getting to be the young guy in the band, Watt sees the gig as another chance to expand his musical experience.

After all this time, Watt still sees himself as a punk, because to him punk is anything he wants it to be. "That's why the movement was so important," he says. "I've never been ashamed of it or tried to say I outgrew it, because I really feel in debt to that scene because it changed everything for me."

✳

On the other side of the country, the emergence and popularity of punk gave bands the courage to continue down the path of musical innovation in the late 1970s and early '80s. Punk was still establishing itself as a subculture at that juncture, but enough musicians had discovered it via networks of zines, record stores, and shows that the genre was rapidly evolving. In contrast to LA's gritty, working-class, get-in-the-van style of punk, many East Coast indie bands played an artier, brainier sort of music. Mission of Burma, a band from Boston that released its records on the tiny Ace of Hearts label, was relatively unknown in the eighties, but, like the Minutemen, Burma created a sonic legacy that stretched the existing boundaries of punk music, and its influence is still heard in the indie rock of today. Burma's best-known songs range from Clint Conley's anthemic, hooky "Forget" and "Academy Fight Song" to Roger Miller's avant-pop compositions, including "Max Ernst" and "This Is Not a Photograph." Burma's initial career lasted only four years—one year short of the Minutemen's—but

Burma's experimentation with new modes of playing guitar, bass, and drums and its early incorporation of tape loops and other noise-manipulating techniques changed the way many of its listeners thought about what music could be.

Boston's music scene in the late seventies was somewhat different from the burgeoning punk scene in LA, where a variety of different indie scenes coexisted. Unlike LA's suburban sprawl, Boston's smaller size, along with its heavy concentration of colleges, helped Boston musicians build a small but faithful audience that was open to radical new sounds. Burma's bassist and cosongwriter Clint Conley says that "Boston sort of made its rep on what was basically a juked-up Chuck Berry sound."[10] Though a gutsy, violent hardcore punk scene did find traction in the area, including the bands Gang Green, Negative FX, and SS Decontrol, Burma swam in slightly different waters. "There was a small group of bands here that were sort of loosely associated with the art colleges," Conley remembers. "We played lofts and art galleries and the pretentious spaces as well as the clubs. There were some other like-minded bands like the Girls and Human Sexual Response and La Peste that never made much of an impression outside of the city, but that were really great bands." Roger Miller, Burma's guitarist and other songwriter, concurs that the Boston scene wasn't limited to one kind of noise: "In 1979 in the loft scene in Boston you'd have performance art and rock bands all at one show."[11] That cross-pollination between genres made Burma's experimental sound less surprising than it could have been in a more small-minded community, and the band quickly built a loyal local following. "Boston was a pretty good place for us," says Conley, "because there are a ton of students, and they're sort of a forward-thinking group in general, so you had a fairly progressive mentality and a large curious audience that worked for us."

Conley describes the emotional uplift of his early Burma days with a kind of messianic fervor familiar to many people who were part of the indie scene at this time. "It was just the most exciting thing," he says about the early days of writing songs for Burma. "It was just like huffing gasoline or something. We were always just *cranked up*." The group's innovative sound was further enhanced by the contributions of member Martin Swope, who integrated live tape loops into the band's songs. While this additional layer of noise may have made for mesmerizing shows and recordings, it also resulted in music that was less accessible to some audiences. This may sound oppositional to punk's anyone-can-do-it vibe, but Burma's antipopulist stance fits right in with most forward-thinking creativity because the band was conscious that it was blazing a trail. Conley admits that "our music was of such limited appeal, and we knew it, but it didn't matter to us in the least. It was a badge of honor, purely fueled by righteous conviction that we were on to something, so fuck the world. And it really was like a *burning conviction*—you'd wake up in the morning and feel it." For Miller, the independent music scene of the late seventies and early eighties was nothing short of revolutionary, and the fact that Burma and many other bands of their caliber were confined to the fringes was just par for the course. "Part of the nature of revolution is that things have to be held down until they MUST explode," Miller argues. "In the '50s rock and roll took over AM. In the '60s, the psychedelic edge moved to FM while AM became drab Top 40. When FM morphed into 'Classic Rock,' punk was born on college radio in the US. But then college radio began to be monitored by major labels, and where else was there to go?"

In spite of Burma's enthusiasm and innovation, they constantly struggled to get heard. In the late seventies, the touring networks that were beginning to be forged by West Coast and DC bands were still tiny and often out of the way, and the zine network was also in its infancy. Needless to say, this was also before the Internet and the college radio boom. Both Miller and Mike Watt agree that college radio at that juncture was not the left-of-dial indie paradise it would later become ("I remember calling radio stations for SST in the earlier eighties," Watt recalls, "and they'd be playing Journey and shit, and the people would be looking to get corporate jobs on the major labels"). For Burma, building any kind of audience—even a small, localized one—meant a lot of hard work. Conley recalls that "it was one set of ears at a time; it wasn't get on the radio and get massive exposure. We'd just keep playing these gigs that we had a blast at even though there were a lot of apathetic audiences who didn't understand, but that just sort of stoked us more. It made us more convinced that we were right and they were wrong." That sort of righteous fervor and sense of purpose was enough to get Burma through a series of tours during which they might play to audiences as small as five or six people—and maybe even fewer than that. Miller argues that "Mission of Burma always felt like we were doing the correct thing, at least for ourselves. Oddly we were never that put off by the general unacceptance of our music in 1979–1983. We just figured that was the way it was, part of the game."

Burma also lucked out with their record label. Ace of Hearts, run by local scenester Rick Harte, was tiny, but Harte worked hard to put out high-quality records. "Rick Harte caught on to us early on and put out our records in a nice way, nice studios," Conley recalls, "and he took great care with those recordings, so we were very fortunate to have run into him." Nonetheless, Ace of Hearts ran up against the same problems SST and the handful of other independent labels that existed at that time were having with distribution. The records were coming out, but without much in the way of radio play and only minimal numbers of people at gigs, orders arrived at a trickle and had to be fulfilled by a staff that was usually unpaid or barely paid. Burma would sometimes travel out of town and be greeted by audiences saying, "We've heard about your single . . . where is it?"[12] Even as West Coast bands grew to depend on one another for help with landing gigs, places to crash, and the other logistical aspects of being an independent musician, because they were so under the radar Burma struggled with the same issues. But "struggle was built into it with the channels of distribution and making records, and we knew that from the get-go," says Conley. That awareness of what lay ahead, however, didn't prepare Burma for what was going to happen to one of its members.

One hallmark of Burma's live shows was crushing, punishing

volume. They were known to turn the sound up so high that you could feel it in the bones of your face. Those same rattling facial bones, however, connect directly to the minuscule bones in the ear. Miller had for many years been suffering from tinnitus, a constant ringing in the ears. Over the four years of Mission of Burma's career, what had started as a chronic annoyance advanced into a crippling condition. Miller was hearing tones at all hours of the day and night, and even when he performed in headphones designed for target practice, the tinnitus still interfered. On top of this, Burma's first full-length album *Vs.* had garnered them many positive reviews but had still done little to improve the problem they had on tour of often playing to nearly empty rooms. Conley also admits, "I was the least comfortable performing of the three of us in the olden days," and he battled his stage fright with alcohol. The band called it quits in 1983, and all signs at that time indicated that Burma would enter into indie rock history as one of the many bands who never "made it," their records becoming collector's items and their legacy dependent on vinyl and CDs and the rapidly fading memories of a few people who'd managed to catch them play live. "When we folded in 1983," Miller reflects, "we all thought, well, that's it: that was fun."

Nineteen years later, the unexpected: Mission of Burma started playing together again. Miller was still suffering from tinnitus, though he continued to make music with the groups Birdsongs of the Mesozoic and Alloy Orchestra, a group that plays live soundtracks for silent films; Conley had essentially retired from playing music after producing Yo La Tengo's first album and was working as a producer for public television. Peter Prescott, the band's drummer, had been playing in and around the Boston scene. But the total absence of any rumors about a Burma reunion made their getting back together all the more surprising. "I in particular approached the idea of playing again with the most trepidation," says Conley, "maybe because I'd been out of music longer than those guys." However, Burma's reputation had continued to grow in the interim. Their albums were rereleased in the late eighties by Rykodisc, and this created a new wave of interest in Burma's sound. Bands from REM, who frequently covered Conley's anthem of discontent "Academy Fight Song," to the Pixies, Nirvana, and many more cited Burma as an influence. As Miller puts it, "When the subterranean interest in Burma began to become obvious, and then the reissues in the late '80s were so highly praised, we were kind of taken aback. You know, how can this be?"

Whatever confluence of circumstances caused the interest in Burma to revive, it peaked when it was announced that the group would be releasing a new album, *ONOFFON*, on Matador Records in 2004. "When we first started playing again in 2002/2003," Miller recalls, "our audience was mostly people 'from the day,' people close to our age." "In the first round of gigs there were certainly a lot of gray ponytails and paunches out there, and god bless 'em," adds Conley. But as the band kept playing and releasing albums (*The Obliterati* followed in 2006), something interesting happened: Burma gained an entirely new audience. "When we first came back," Conley reflects, "it came with a ready-made story, 'long neglected band, tragically overlooked'—the template was right there for every writer. And we were like, whatever." Miller is likewise frank about the reincarnation of Burma: "When we released *The Obliterati*, a strange thing happened: our audiences grew again. But this time the front three rows were all people in their 20s or 30s! I'm getting used to the whole thing, but if I stand back and look at it objectively, it is quite interesting, if not downright odd." Whether or not the narrative of Burma's rise, decline, and resurrection was what brought them a new audience of indie rockers too young to have heard them the first time around, the fact is that the band continues to make music relevant to a contemporary audience.

Like many other bands from indie's early era, Mission of Burma's influence took many years to reveal itself. They had what is best described as a cult following in their first incarnation, but their music actually grew in popularity and influence after they broke up. The Minutemen's music had a similar trajectory. After Boon's death, Watt's relentless work ethic helped keep the band's music in circulation. Because the early indie scene was so small, even innovative bands that had a strong community surrounding them still sold only a handful of records compared to successful indie bands today. Thus, the current popularity of Mission of Burma surprises no one more than the band members. Miller and Conley's reaction to their new circumstances as indie heroes is judicious. Conley laughs when he admits, "We find ourselves at festivals with these young hipster bands, and they'd be all jaded and road weary, and we're like, *Look at this! Golly, free soda, and they want to feed us too!* It's ridiculous. We feel like we fell down the rabbit hole." As to the oft-repeated idea that Mission of Burma was ahead of its time, Miller says, "We weren't ahead of our time at all—audiences were just slow! Our main feeling at the time was of being 'outside' the time. We just didn't belong. I suppose we were comfortable with that." But any discussion of Burma's prescience and comeback leads to some reflection on their place in the current indie rock scene. Miller comments that indie rock may be stuck in a rut: "With rock since post-punk . . . almost anything now can be seen as a combination/variation on what existed by the mid-'80s. It's an odd time." Conley agrees. "In general, I kind of think that it's not a good sign that we fit in with people right now," he admits. "I don't think that's a sign of health on the macro level for indie rock. If it's in the same place it was in twenty-five years ago, what does that say? It seems to be plying the same waters." Although Conley and Miller argue that their music wasn't ahead of its time, just "outside" it, their ability to slide right back into the current indie rock scene and attract greater popularity this time around attests to the durability of innovative music.

In the early eighties, the indie scene was small enough that publicizing new music depended on word of mouth, what Conley refers to as "one set of ears at a time." But across the country, young people hooked in to the punk and indie community saw the music as more than just a revolutionary shift in sound; music was an opportunity for expression, for growth, and for experimentation, as evidenced by the growing number of scenes in off-the-radar towns. For many, music was also a way to reach out and find similarly minded people. As the fanzine culture began to grow along with the music community, reports of bands doing inconceivable things like starting their own labels and touring on minuscule budgets inspired untold numbers of people to think, "Fuck it," and try to do the same. In many cases, those new groups of musicians, writers, artists, and scenesters didn't come from New York or LA, where punk had been created—they came from out-of-the-way towns that existed in the shadow of their bigger and more glamorous neighbors. The Berkeley, California, scene took the lessons of the Minutemen and Mission of Burma seriously: work hard, play fast and loud, have faith in what you're doing, and someone will prick up their ears and listen.

three

Homegrown:

Indie Regionalism in Berkeley

It's a smart town and a dumb town. Cosmopolitan.
Provincial. Boring. Wild. Bizarre. Staid. Small. Big.
(Un)predictable. (Un)American. Magnanimous. Self-
absorbed. Self-sufficient.

Richie, *Cometbus #30*[1]

On May 25, 1989, Operation Ivy played its final show at 924 Gilman Street Project in Berkeley, California. More than a thousand fans showed up and packed into the sweaty warehouse space, licensed to hold three hundred people. The side doors, usually closed to avoid disturbing the neighbors, had to be propped open so people in the audience and onstage wouldn't pass out from the heat. The band had just released its first and only LP, *Energy,* but it was common knowledge in the tightly knit East Bay punk community that the group was calling it quits for a variety of the same reasons that had killed other short-lived but well-intentioned punk bands: incessant touring on no money, interband conflict, growing audiences that demanded more and more of them, all of the battle scars of life lived in the underground. Rather than letting their career as a band drag on to the point of irrelevance or (for the band members) self-destruction, Op Ivy decided to take its final bow. May 25 would be the band's chance to say good-bye to its community in the same space where it had played its first show a year and a half earlier. The opening band, Green Day, unknowns from the nearby suburban town of Pinole, had at one point been accused of not being punk enough to play at the stalwartly punk Gilman. May 25 could have been just another night in any medium-sized town in America, but the confluence of acts, people in the audience, and venue would later add a layer of significance to the evening: punk was beginning its transformation into something newer and different, and small scenes like Berkeley's would have a big impact on the course of that change.

In the years since the Minutemen and Mission of Burma had wrapped up their careers, the networks those bands and others had helped establish continued to grow and thrive. Not only was punk spreading; its sound and aesthetics were changing as they went, reflecting the cultures and demographics of the farther-flung cities and towns across America, where people had sniffed out punk and DIY notions of creative work. By the mideighties, many smaller cities had scenes of their own, and thanks to zines like *Maximumrocknroll* and *Flipside,* which were available through mail-order record catalogs and subscriptions, a kid isolated somewhere like Albuquerque, New Mexico, for example, might find out from scene reports in a zine that there were punk shows happening every week in the basement of the local church. And that same kid might start a band or a zine of her own and open her doors to a touring band so they could have a place to crash. But several of these smaller regional scenes that began to flourish in the mid- to late eighties also changed the larger subculture of DIY. They did so by embracing DIY ethics and by reinventing the idea of what punk meant, injecting it with homegrown sounds, and the nerdy humor and creativity that's often necessary when you live some distance from the main centers of cultural activity.

Berkeley, California, has always been known as a college town, and in particular it is home to a university with a history of experimental learning and political engagement. It exists in the shadow of a major city and in the eighties played host to a music and art scene that would radically transform and affect the way punk culture was perceived and created for the next decade, sowing the seeds of many of the manifestations of indie music, writing, art, and craft that would eventually become what we recognize as indie culture today. If one of the operative tenets of indie culture is its sense of otherness, of existing a step outside of everything else, Berkeley in the late eighties and early nineties exemplified that otherness and embraced it.

People from outside of the Bay Area tend to cling to the idea that Berkeley is full of dope-smoking, LSD-munching, idealistic hair farmers who dropped out in the sixties and never quite woke up, the kind of people who tool around in VW vans and Volvo station wagons, nodding off at intersections while listening to NPR. While it's true that the city retains a fair number of citizens who fit that description pretty closely, it also contains a fairly diverse population for its size. The city is divided geographically by class: the rich live in historical craftsman homes that cling to the lush hills, and although many of their houses are poised precariously on the Hayward fault line, property values remain frighteningly high. The middle class and poor live in the flats, which fan out from the bottom of the hills all the way to the lip of San Francisco Bay. Houses in the flats are mostly shotgun-style affairs, with cramped backyards and drafty windows. 924 Gilman, the warehouse club where Operation Ivy played its final show and generations of punks came of age, is in the mixed industrial neighborhood of West Berkeley, one of the last bastions of semiaffordable housing remaining in the city and the setting for almost all of Berkeley's violent crime.

Much of Berkeley's cultural life naturally revolves around the University of California, which swelled in the eighties to an institution of more than thirty thousand students (the city's total population hovers around fifty thousand), but the constant influx of bright young minds has little to do with the native population of Berkeley, the kids who were born and raised there, some of whom grew up with the same hippy parents who created the Berkeley cliché. The town-and-gown division that affects many college towns affects Berkeley as well. The majority of Berkeley kids don't attend the university; some of them grow up without ever setting foot on campus. Those kids, however, and kids from the surrounding towns of Oakland, Albany, El Cerrito, and other farther-flung suburban towns like Concord, Pinole, El Sobrante, and Vallejo, were the ones who created the local punk scene in the eighties. Some of them were reacting directly to what they perceived as the hippy generation's abandonment of its independent values. Some of them embraced the city's tradition of activism, engaging in a politically charged version of punk that addressed issues ranging from racism to homophobia to the guerrilla insurgence in Central America. Others were simply bored. Clubs in San Francisco were typically reserved for those twenty-one and up, and travel to and from the city was difficult without a car, because the local train system stops running at midnight. Likewise, Berkeley's nightlife left something to be desired; for years, the only options for live music were either the world music center Ashkenaz, which featured Deadhead DJ nights and Balkan folk dancing, bars with live music like Larry Blakes, which refused to book punk bands for fear of vandalism or violence, or dance clubs where New Wave still ruled. Berkeley's punk scene grew organically out of the city's essential character, a place where so many contradictory impulses played out daily.

Jesse Michaels, Operation Ivy's singer and lyricist, is one of those Berkeley kids. Michaels comes from a highly literary background (his father was the late writer Leonard Michaels, and his stepmother is the poet Brenda Hillman), and Michaels was engaged in music and visual art from a very young age. "The atmosphere of Berkeley affected young people by being a place where creativity was rewarded," he says. "This sounds like a simple thing and a cliché, but having lived in other parts of the country I know that it is a remarkable and unusual thing."[2] The city's general tolerance for freakishness in young people allowed them free rein for self-expression, whereas punk modes of creativity in more conservative climates might have gotten a teenager into a lot of trouble. Michaels affirms this notion when he says, "the same teenager would be socially elevated [in Berkeley] provided they had a certain amount of charm." But even as charmingly weird as some of them were, most Berkeley punks didn't quite fit into the leather-jacket-and-mohawk cliché that had come to represent punk by the mideighties (to be fair, many leather jackets and liberty spikes were seen in Berkeley, but there were also punk kids in checkerboard Vans, cords, flannel, and other varieties of thrift-store geek chic). Many local bands, like Crimpshrine, The Mr. T Experience, Sweet Baby, and 924 Gilman's "house band" Isocracy tended toward a style that came to define Gilman's, and by extension Berkeley's, sound. Michaels recalls that "bands were silly and being unpretentious and a little bit nerdy, which became its own aesthetic." Likewise, many local bands also engaged in political rhetoric and activism that echoes the political engagement of earlier punk bands like the Minutemen, which was unsurprising to Michaels since "Berkeley's political consciousness, which is everywhere apparent, has always been a part of its bands' lyrics."

The nexus of Berkeley's scene in the 1980s and '90s, 924 Gilman Street, simply called Gilman by locals, was founded in 1986 by Tim Yohannan, the editor of the influential punk zine and radio show *Maximumrocknroll* (*MRR*). Yohannan, who was already in his forties by the time he opened Gilman, worked a blue-collar job at the Lawrence Hall of Science, near the main Berkeley campus, and was something of an indie Renaissance man. In addition to his pursuits with *MRR* and Gilman, he also founded Blacklist Mail Order, a distribution company for zines, and the Epicenter record store and community center in San Francisco. As zine writer and musician Aaron Cometbus put it in the zine *Slingshot* in 1988, "His hard work provided the radio show we could all listen to while doing the dishes, the magazine we could be bored by, the club we could stand outside, the place to mail-order our shitty fanzines, the record label to put out our shitty local bands, and the record store where we could play free pool and use the bathroom . . . it was the scenery and soundtrack for our community and the framework for keeping that community alive and self-sufficient."[3] *MRR*—both the zine and the radio show—also became a community voice at a time when the community as such was scattered, without the ease of communication aided by technology. Gavin McNett wrote in the online magazine *Salon* that "the *MRR* explosion was the first truly global, grass-roots youth phenomenon in history, and it did for some of us what the Web would later do for the culture at large: It removed the limitations of place and substituted for them an unplumbable pool of information and discourse."[4] *MRR* continued to play an important role in the subculture for years, and was particularly important to the Bay Area scene since, as Cometbus points out, it helped give local punks places to gravitate to, but Yohannan's tenure at Gilman was ultimately short-lived.

In 1985 and 1986, Yohannan began doing the footwork for opening an all-ages, collectively run club. Finding the location wasn't that hard—collective member Kamala P described the neighborhood at the time by commenting that "our closest residential neighbors were a block away and the only two businesses open after 6:00 PM were an independent movie theater and a burrito place. It was a perfect location, we would not offend anyone here with our looks or noise."[5] But even with such ideal circumstances, the *MRR* crew still had to contend with bureaucratic red tape. Thankfully, Berkeley's liberal reputation still enjoyed a practical reality in the eighties. Yohannan wrote that "overall, the city was pretty supportive. The mayor at the time, Gus Newport, was totally supportive."[6] While the city's support would wax and wane (mostly wane) over the subsequent twenty-plus years of Gilman's existence, in the beginning the club was a kind of idyllic communist fantasy: collectively run, all ages, with people pitching in voluntarily to build the place, do sound, run the door, take out the garbage, book bands, and take care of everything else that the place required. During the first couple of years, however, Yohannan's reputation as a control freak began to play out. Michaels states it bluntly: "Tim Yohannan was a total commie, and although I liked him personally, I never completely trusted his motives or agreed with his dogmatic, party-line approach to everything. Growing up in Berkeley I was naturally left-leaning, but I was as distrustful of left-wing ideologues as I was of their right-wing counterparts."

Another early member of the Gilman collective was Lawrence Livermore, who, like Yohannan, was slightly older than most of the people joining the Gilman world. Livermore would also make a significant contribution to the community. A native of Detroit, Livermore (which, by the way, is his "punk name," borrowed from the name of the government laboratory for nuclear research in the Bay Area suburbs) migrated to California in the early eighties and wound up living in Laytonville, a tiny town in Mendocino County, three hours north of the Bay Area. In 1984, Livermore had started his own zine, *Lookout,* and, by 1987, only a year into Gilman's existence, Livermore decided to start his own label by the same name. "Originally," he says, "this was actually when Gilman had just opened and before we realized how many great bands were going to come out of it—I'd envisioned [Lookout Records] mainly as a way of putting out a record for my own band, also called, strangely enough, the Lookouts."[7] Aside from upholding the by now long-standing punk tradition of putting out your own band's record, Livermore had begun to feel a vested interest in many of the bands who played Gilman regularly, including Operation Ivy, Isocracy, Crimpshrine, and Corrupted Morals. "At the time, I sincerely believed that these bands were as good as or better than anything I was hearing on the radio or in the mainstream clubs," Livermore adds, "but I also realized that nobody who was in a position to help them put out records was likely to see things that way, so I decided to do it myself."

Between *MRR*'s scene reports, Livermore's own zine and column in *MRR*, other local zines like *Cometbus* and *Absolutely Zippo,* and local bands hitting the road to tour, word about the growing Berkeley scene began to spread. "Zines were the MySpace of those days, pretty much essential," reflects Livermore. "The Berkeley scene as kids from other parts of the country saw it existed more in zines than in real life at first. It was almost a case of life imitating art: we wrote about things as though there was this amazing scene going on in Berkeley, and the next thing we knew, kids from all over were starting to show up wanting to be a part of it. Which in turn made things really start happening." According to Jesse Michaels, the scene was indeed attractive to locals and outsiders alike: "In Gilman you had a place where you could go that didn't get shut down, that was less violent than other clubs (usually), that was friendlier to people that didn't quite fit into the previous wave of punk, and that was in Berkeley in a relatively safe neighborhood. It soon became its own entity entirely removed from the stuff that had come before." But that growth outpaced what the collective's founders were able to keep up with, and the club hemorrhaged money for the first couple of years it existed. Likewise, Yohannan's contentious personality and strict rules rubbed many people the wrong way. When Yohannan and *MRR* pulled out of the club in 1988, he looked back with some bitterness about the reality that he'd helped create. "I felt like the place had not lived up to its potential," he said in a 1996 interview. "There were certain amazing moments, but overall it wasn't doing what I thought it should . . . my feeling was, the scene didn't deserve a place this cool, and if people weren't really going to make it 'theirs,' and they're just going to act like consumers, then I didn't want to kill myself for that."[8] This terminal push and pull between intentions and execution, between DIY and its audience, would often plague indie artists and purveyors as the culture began to expand. Though it may have looked from the outside like Gilman was over just as it was getting started, new volunteers soon stepped in, and the collective fell into a new group's hands in 1988. This was the first of many, many rotations in volunteers to come, but the rapid response to Gilman's potential demise was testimony to its growing importance both in the local community and on a national scale.

Arguably, the biggest contribution Gilman made in its early days was as a vehicle for the music that came out of it. Though punk networks did exist in the mid- to late eighties, they were still tentative, small-time collectives, even ten years after early independent bands set out on tour. According to Livermore, "When Operation Ivy went on their first and only tour in 1988, having released only one 7" EP and being virtually unknown outside the Bay Area, it almost felt as though they were setting off into terra incognita, much like 15th- and 16th-century explorers who were still reckoning with the possibility that they might fall off the edge of the world." Before punks or pundits for that matter used the term "flyover states," punk bands were staging cross-country tours in vans and somehow not starving to death or ending up stranded in an *Easy Rider*–esque nightmare of redneck middle America. Though much of what Livermore describes about the terra incognita of Op Ivy's tour was true, Michaels reveals that punks had a survival mechanism for dealing with being stuck in the middle of nowhere: they just looked for each other. "At that time if you went out of town and saw somebody dressed in punk rock clothing," he says, "you could walk up to them and talk to them simply because you had a sense of affiliation with a unique culture which existed in opposition to pressure." Though there is something fantastical about the idea of the one punk kid in some out-of-the-way town spotting another punk kid and striking up a conversation, the fact is that in the eighties, those things really happened. Thousands of friendships and relationships of all sorts were spawned in the *MRR* classified section, all based simply on the fact that you liked the same stuff as someone from across the country or around the world. And if you were from the East Bay, you had a certain cachet of cool. Once East Bay bands began to hit the road and pick up like-minded fans along the way, word about the scene, already spreading through zines and records, began to reach farther than ever before.

Livermore and his Lookout cohorts were in the right place at the right time to tap into the growing East Bay scene, as his early inklings that some of the bands coming out of Gilman were on to something potentially great came to fruition. In the beginning, the label ran for several years out of a rent-controlled room near the Berkeley campus, managed mainly by Livermore and a staff of two or three other people. Chris Appelgren, one of these people, argued that the relationship between Gilman and Lookout was irreplaceable, a kind of symbiosis between music and place: "Lookout Records would not exist today if not for Gilman. It might have lasted for a short period of time, but the inspiration and source of all the bands wouldn't have been there if not for Gilman."[9] But Livermore's ethics, reflective of the spirit of fairness endemic to DIY, were also a big part of Lookout's success. "I'd like to think that we treated the bands pretty well compared with most labels," he recalls. "We paid them regularly, based strictly on a share of any profits, and were generally available to explain what was going on and why, which in turn produced quite a bit of loyalty and good word of mouth when it came to attracting new bands to the label." That fair treatment not only created a sense of loyalty between the bands and the label; it helped to create a kind of mutual identity: bands felt invested in the label, and in the community of other artists on the label, rather than just becoming one-hit wonders or moneymaking machines. This balanced relationship was a hallmark for many other independent labels, particularly for those labels from smaller scenes like Berkeley's. Chapel Hill's Merge, Chicago's Touch and Go, and Olympia's K Records, and Kill Rock Stars would all forge close relationships with their bands as indie's audience grew in the nineties. Lookout's roster primarily consisted of Gilman stalwarts, but that close proximity of label to artists helped to bond the community. Livermore acknowledges that Lookout also helped financially by creating jobs at the growing label and an outlet for vendors like Cinder Block, a T-shirt manufacturer that "eventually became a bigger business than nearly all of the record labels it served." "More importantly than any economic contribution," he argues, "was the opportunity and inspiration that was provided for musicians and artists in general by knowing that there was a viable outlet for their creativity."

UC Berkeley's radio station, KALX, played a huge part in helping to promote the scene at Gilman. Blessed with an unusually strong transmitter for a college radio station, KALX reaches beyond the local area and has a long history of promoting local bands. Many Lookout and Gilman bands played live in the studio; the station also broadcast many live shows from the venue, and many local musicians were also DJs, which accounts in part for the station's support. Frank Portman, aka Dr. Frank of the band The Mr. T Experience, held down a regular KALX slot for years. MTX even recorded a song called "God Bless Lawrence Livermore" and another tune, called "At Gilman Street," that encapsulates the entire scene in about two minutes: "It's democracy . . . it's a bunch of geeks, it's a load of freaks."[10] For a few years, Berkeley felt pretty close to idyllic for Bay Area punks. Out of the many bands that came up through the Gilman and Lookout scenes, Operation Ivy exemplified many of East Bay punk's best qualities, even in its short life span.

✻

Operation Ivy was founded by Tim Armstrong (aka Lint), Matt McCall (later Matt Freeman), Jesse Michaels, and Dave Mello in 1987. Armstrong and McCall were both from Albany, a pocket-sized town between Berkeley and El Cerrito; Michaels had recently returned to the area after spending a few years in Pittsburgh. All four members had done time in various other bands and had known each other from around the East Bay scene. The band started practicing together only briefly before they played their first public gigs; primarily, their early shows were performed in friends' backyards and even once in an Albany laundromat. Michaels told Aaron Cometbus in a *Cometbus* zine interview from 1989 that the local response to Operation Ivy, even from the earliest shows, was stronger than anyone had expected. "Everything blew up immediately, people knew the lyrics at our second show and were singing along."[11] Operation Ivy's sound, a combination of punk guitars and ska rhythms, was different from the purer pop-punk of other local bands, and ska—one of the oldest forms of outsider music to be adapted by rock musicians—had fallen out of fashion at that time, but Michaels's lyrics were the biggest draw for many of the band's early fans. "It was a moment when the things I wrote about in my lyrics were actually happening," Michaels told Aaron Cometbus. "There was a sense of community, there was [sic] radically different people getting along with each other, and above all these was excitement and urgency." Part of that urgency, at least for many of those who discovered Op Ivy's music, was the urgency of finding an identity in the increasingly consumerist and conservative culture of the late eighties. Michaels's lyrics tapped directly into the struggle many people have with self-expression in the midst of the quest for both community and an individual identity. In the song "Here We Go Again," he sings: "Conditioned to self-interest with emotions locked away / If that's what they call normal I'd rather be insane."[12] Other Op Ivy songs addressed the idea of alienation even more directly; in "Just Another Crowd," Michaels sings, "Feelings under covers like books on a shelf / if we're scared of one another / must be scared of ourself."[13]

After playing locally and recording the *Hectic* EP on Lookout in early 1988, Operation Ivy set out for a tour in a 1967 Chrysler Newport. Dave Mello told Aaron Cometbus, "They always made me ride on the hump on the backseat."[14] Armstrong recalled in *Flipside* that "we would play anywhere, anytime, any kind of show we could get, we saved all our money and ate really cheaply, cheese sandwiches every night."[15] In the best punk tradition, the band played a series of shows to audiences ranging from packed houses to empty rooms, but they were surprised to find that their reputation preceded them in many places even though they had only one seven-inch record to their name. This was testament to the mythology of Berkeley that continued to build and to the unique appeal of the band's sound and message. Whatever combination of talent, timing, content, and sound it takes for a band to grow a reputation during and after its lifetime, Operation Ivy had it from the beginning. When they returned home after the tour, their audiences were bigger—and more fanatical—than before. Many locals felt a kind of possessive ownership of the band, donning Op Ivy T-shirts with Michaels's distinctively drawn band logo of a skanking man, or simply painting the name of the band on the backs of their jackets in Wite-Out. As the band wrote songs and put together live shows, fans just as rapidly learned what was coming; hence, the singing-along phenomenon Michaels described to Aaron Cometbus. While this kind of reputation and fan base might be welcome news to any band from a small scene like Berkeley's, for Op Ivy the results of that adulation were mixed. In his lyrics, Michaels grappled with the pressure of the audience on the performer; the "impersonal mob" he sang about in "The Crowd" was not just the face of consumerism and mainstream culture but also the face of the local audience, to which he pleaded, in the face of pressure to conform to community expectations: "we need a gathering instead."

Despite the kinds of warning messages about the dangers of conformity embedded in their lyrics, Op Ivy's audience continued to grow, and that audience quickly bifurcated into people who liked the message and people who liked the music. Part of the surge in its following had to do with Michaels's charisma; the band, which consisted of extremely talented and original musicians, added to his appeal. Billie Joe Armstrong (no relation to Tim Armstrong) of the band Green Day told Larry Livermore in 2001 that many local musicians who witnessed Op Ivy's growing popularity believed the band would be able to manage the balance between audience expectations and band intentions: "I always thought [Michaels] had that sort of sensibility, that he could work both sides of the fence, the people who were into him because they had great music, and the people who were into them because of the things they stood for."[16] But by the time the release of the *Energy* LP was pending, tensions between band members were fraying their connection. Rumor had it that Michaels pulled the plug, but years later he told the *San Francisco Chronicle* that the decision to end the band was made for the sake of his own sanity and development. "I made the choice that I didn't want to grow up in the spotlight. I just had things to work out. I'm a sensitive person, and notoriety isn't something that came very easy for me."[17] After their final gigs on May 25 and 26 (after their last Gilman show, they played a final set in a friend's backyard), the band members scattered and looked for other bands and activities to occupy their time.

In the midnineties, Tim Armstrong and Matt McCall would go on to form the band Rancid and toy with mainstream success, and Michaels would turn to visual art for self-expression. Even as the band members went their separate ways, Operation Ivy's reputation proved to have staying power: if anything, the band attracted greater popularity in the decades to follow than it had ever enjoyed as a unit. Livermore estimated on his blog that Operation Ivy's *Energy* LP has sold close to a million records in the two decades since its 1989 release, a feat achieved on the power of word of mouth alone. That the ideals the band stood for—ethics, community, DIY, originality—have also managed to survive in Berkeley and at Gilman is perhaps even more remarkable given the pressure the local scene was under in the early nineties.

In 1987, Livermore took an interest in another local band. Green Day was less politically engaged than Op Ivy, but it had a tremendous advantage over many other bands: its music was catchy as fuck. The band's bratty attitude, combined with its pop punk sound, made it extremely identifiable to young audiences, not just in the Bay Area or in the punk community but all around the country. Soon after the release of Green Day's second Lookout LP, *Kerplunk*, major labels started sniffing around and showing an interest in signing the band, a phenomenon that had begun with the first wave of independent bands in the eighties. When bands like Hüsker Dü and the Replacements signed with majors back then, it turned out to be a disaster for both the bands and their labels; neither sold well on a major, and their independent labels, Twin/Tone and SST, disintegrated after the bands' defections. Green Day eventually signed with Reprise Records, a division of Warner Brothers, and released the *Dookie* LP in 1994. When the album went on to sell ten million copies, interest in Green Day's Lookout releases begat an enormous flow of cash into the record company's coffers. For an independent stalwart like Livermore, this turned out to be very bad news.

"Strange as it may seem," Livermore says, "growing too fast and making far more money than you expected can be nearly as much of a challenge to a business as not growing and not making enough money." Lookout, which had always operated on a shoestring, was logistically unprepared for this level of success. "Once Green Day made it big on Warner Brothers, our income multiplied by a factor of 10 within the space of a year or two," Livermore reflects. "There was a great deal of pressure on us regarding what we were going to do with this sudden influx of money." Part of the problem with handling the money came down to the people who now worked for the label. Livermore had always run his company in the spirit of other independent businesses: go with the people who share your philosophy and taste. "I had personally hired every employee, based not so much on experience or skill in the record business as on what I perceived to be shared values," he says. "But once we started expanding, others besides myself were doing some of the hiring, and I gradually became aware of feeling like an outsider in my own company." The differentiation between the "new" and "old" Lookout came down to a sense of trying to be "professional," which for the new employees meant "running it more like a traditional label in the sense that we would spend far more money on releases in hopes of breaking through to the mainstream." Not only was this antithetical to the Berkeley punk spirit; it was antithetical to Livermore's personal values. For a time, he attempted to handle the change by backing off: "I let others try doing things their way, reasoning that either they'd be successful and I could learn something from them, or that they wouldn't, and, suitably chastened, would revert to the old-school Lookout way of doing things."

But anyone who's been involved in the arts knows that once something goes mainstream, things can never go back to how they were before. By 1996, Livermore had been dragged into a protracted, public battle with the band Screeching Weasel over money, and this was the last straw for him. "My decision to leave was an emotional one," he says, "and not at all well-reasoned, and the circumstances under which I left were far from ideal, and may even have contributed to Lookout's near-demise some years later." In Lookout's early days, Livermore, often unable to pay his staff, had instead offered his partners, David Hayes and Chris Appelgren, a profit-sharing plan. When Livermore left the label, Hayes decided to leave as well, and Appelgren bought them out based on the company's accumulated earnings at that point. Livermore relocated to London and eventually to New York, but after his departure, Lookout spiraled into a series of errors in judgment that decimated the once successful independent label. Rather than putting the label's cash into signing new bands and cultivating a roster as Livermore had, the new owners instead spent money on marketing—in one case, the queercore band Pansy Division shot a video that cost "more than the recording budgets for its first three records combined," according to the *East Bay Express*.[18] Even worse, the label started failing to pay royalties to longtime bands, according to Livermore, which, he says, "in turn led to most of the label's best bands leaving under bad terms, something which hit me hard as well, since I had signed most of those bands, and, on leaving Lookout, I had assured them that under the new ownership, they'd be taken care of just as they always had." Green Day pulled its back catalog from Lookout in 2005, and Operation Ivy, which continues to sell copies of its sole LP twenty years after its release, followed suit in 2007. Interestingly, both bands chose to rerelease their back catalogs not on major labels but on independent labels founded by members of both bands: Billie Joe Armstrong's Adeline Records and Tim Armstrong's Hellcat Records. This defection effectively ended Lookout Records for good. The label laid off most of its staff, sold the building where its offices were located, and now sells only a few items via its Web site. "So," says Livermore, "not a happy ending, you might say, nor one which I had foreseen." But he also points out that most Lookout bands found homes on other labels, and in some cases new labels were created "to take up the slack left by Lookout's failure." In spite of Lookout's demise, Livermore is optimistic about the future of independent punk rock, "because nowadays it's based on a more substantial foundation rather than the gold rush, get-rich-quick mentality that had crept in by the mid-90s." And he says that "despite the bittersweet ending, [Lookout was] the experience of a lifetime for me."

Jesse Michaels is similarly reflective about the legacy of Operation Ivy. "I really try not to think of the band historically," he says. "I think it's a dangerous habit for any artist ever to think of their work or their image or anything like that in the third person. You have to stay *in it* or you become a kind of walking ghost, psychologically. This is not melodramatic; I have seen it happen to people and it's disturbing. The only way to describe it is they become 'otherated.'" Michaels has dealt with this by channeling his creative energy into other projects. He's had a longtime interest in visual art, which is now his primary pursuit (he says that art is "very liberating because it's not connected with a youth culture, with the expectations I'm used to, with anything popular or 'cool' or stupid in that way"), and he formed a few short-lived bands in the post–Op Ivy years as well. For the most part, however, he feels that his life in the band was "what I did from day to day. Now it's what I deal with through lawyers, and it's a strange thing where people I've never met write me e-mails, but I refuse to entertain a public superego where I reflect on what it all means."

924 Gilman Street Project continues to host punk bands from the Bay Area and from all over the world to this day, though many of the people involved in it back in the day have moved on. There's a sense of being an old fart if you're in your thirties or forties and go to a Gilman show; the place can feel a bit haunted, as if your younger identity was somehow buried somewhere in the layers of graffiti on the walls. But Gilman still has a legacy, and it can still change the lives of people who discover it; in the anthology of Gilman stories *924 Gilman: The Story So Far,* Mike K wrote, "I used to be resolved to the fact that history was a larger than life

process. Before Gilman, my friends and I did not have much hope that we could seriously redirect the course of our lives, let alone larger events."[19] After Tim Yohannan died of cancer in 1998, *Maximumrocknroll* continued to publish, and it still arrives monthly on newsstands and in the mailboxes of punk rockers and true believers. Many people involved in the Berkeley scene would argue that it hit its peak before Green Day and never really recovered its identity after that, but the Bay Area still remains home to hundreds of independent bands, zines, magazines, distributors, and various other DIY business and individuals who were inspired by what they saw at that warehouse in West Berkeley. Aside from the bands who provided the soundtrack to our lives, those who made the greatest impact on the notion of empowerment through independent creativity were writers like Aaron Cometbus and Robert Eggplant, who created the zines *Cometbus* and *Absolutely Zippo*. In these zines, along with *MRR, Flipside*, and countless other zines, people were writing about everything: music, politics, scenery, the way it felt to be in the center of things or on the fringes. Both zines and small presses played a huge role in the creation of independent culture throughout the eighties and nineties. And in punk and indie networks in the Bay Area and all over the country, small presses and their distributors, poets, fiction writers, and journalists were all continuing in a tradition of independent publishing that closely mirrored the alternative press movement of the sixties. In the calm before the storm that signaled a sea change in the indie community in the early nineties, writing and publishing gave a voice to anyone anywhere who had access to a copy machine and felt like they had something to say.

four

Xerox, Staple, Repeat:
The Evolution of
Independent Literature

For most people, indie is most easily recognizable when it comes to music. Listeners keyed into the difference between low-fi on one end of the spectrum and high-tech on the other can hear an independent band and instantly get that it's making music outside of the mainstream. Indie musicians recording on four-tracks in their garages turn out albums that are grimy, distorted, and stripped down to the bones. The differentiation was an auditory marker that survived from the punk era into the early nineties, when smaller, regional music scenes like Berkeley's made a mark that stretched past the city limits. Thanks to the growing number of independent labels and distributors, and because bands looked on touring as an essential part of their lifestyle, indie bands were able to carry the message of DIY across the country via their very existence. In many cases, a band's arrival in any town or city where it parked its van was also preceded by word of mouth—rumors about shows in neighboring or far-flung cities, urban legends concerning band members' more salacious proclivities, and stories from band members themselves about life on the road. These could include tales of sleeping on the urine-soaked floor of a squat, eating uncooked Top Ramen noodles out of the package, playing gigs for rooms full of unsuspecting rednecks or worshipful fans, and packing themselves into cars permeated with the heady fragrance of unshowered bandmates. In most cases, the gossip and news that fueled indie communities arrived in the myriad incarnations of zines. For the zinesters who grabbed a pile of their zines and toted them around to record stores, bookstores, galleries, shows, and cafés, making and distributing independent literature was the equivalent to bands driving their own vans to gigs: it was a matter of necessity and a way of building community one person at a time.

Many debates have ensued about what a zine is or ought to be since people first began making them, but in a literal sense, a zine is usually a self-produced magazine, most often hand bound with a stapler, its content often reflective of the idiosyncracies of its writers. As independent culture evolved further, zines played an increasingly important role in getting the word out about the music people were listening to, as well as politics, local issues, and DIY lifestyle tips. Some of the most interesting zines, the ones that people sought out whenever a new issue arrived, were simply diaries of life in the underground, providing a written narrative of life on the fringe.

While zines have been around in one form or another for as long as mimeograph and copy machines have existed, their impact on independent culture was perhaps felt most strongly around the same time that early independent bands like the Minutemen and Minor Threat began playing music in the early eighties. Before technology enabled people to easily forge online connections (and to engage in often rancorous debates) about the shared interests that form the basis for independent networks, zines were the organ of the community. The biggest titles, like *Maximumrocknroll, Flipside,* and *Factsheet 5,* had national distribution and eventually attracted an international audience as well, but thousands of smaller titles also offered readers an inside perspective on punk and independent life. In a zine, writers who lacked the desire to conform to the often stringent standards of mainstream magazine writing could get away with ranting, raving, or quietly meditating on music and community, while also chronicling the minutiae of their day-to-day lives. Relationships, travel, dead-end jobs, school, the town you lived in, and your friends and family all became topical in the pages of a zine. There were no editors, no assignments, no query letters to be rejected, which helped expedite the passage of information from the writer to the printed page, even if that page sported numerous typos. If DIY had made music available to people who'd previously believed that being in a band was off-limits or beyond their capacity, zines and small presses made writing as a vehicle for self-expression and even self-transformation and communication with like-minded people accessible to anyone. You didn't even need a typewriter (this being the precomputer era); a zine could be handwritten and illustrated, stapled together at your kitchen table, and walked over to the local record store to be sold on consignment. In their homespun, left of the dial takes on life in America, zines were the literary version of the lyrical and musical messages being sent out by bands in the eighties and early nineties.

Before zine culture established a foothold in the landscape of American literature, earlier iterations of independent publishing, including literary magazines, small presses, and the distributors who enabled these microproduced books and journals to make inroads into bookstores and libraries, paved the way for the DIY publishing revolution of the eighties and nineties. Located just steps from 924 Gilman Street in West Berkeley, Small Press Distribution's offices and warehouse are the heart that pumps the arteries that allow thousands of independently produced titles—primarily poetry and fiction—to make their way into readers' hands every year. Founded in 1969, SPD began distributing books at a time when avant-garde poetry and fiction were experiencing a resurgence on the fringes of literary culture. For SPD then and now, finding a way to pass the literature produced by those communities into the hands of readers became an important mission. Since book distribution is primarily handled by large corporations that aren't interested in avant-garde literature in tiny print runs, SPD's smaller circulation options help enable small presses to actually get their books into stores. In the late sixties and early seventies, writers in the Bay Area and New York began experimenting with an even more visionary, experimental sort of writing than any generation before, and the underground literary scene was home to many writers who would not only go on to write groundbreaking work but also found small presses and literary journals—all of which were run by the writers themselves, and, like zines and small presses that followed them, were often run collectively. As Laura Moriarty, SPD's deputy director and a longtime member of the Bay Area literary community, puts it, in the late sixties there were "many avant gardes" in American literature, referring to the many independent presses and journals nationwide. The primary goal of most of the publishers that SPD distributes has been to give a voice to challenging writing. Since other small press distributors have historically been few and far between, SPD has long-standing relationships with many of the presses it represents. Many of the earliest independent presses and journals still exist today, and many others have sprung up in their wake, but just as indie labels like Lookout Records gave voice to bands like Operation Ivy, independent publishing empowered people to publish work that might not otherwise make it into print.

The foundation of these journals and presses wasn't just a hobby; it was a necessity. In the sixties, American literature was sharply divided between academically sanctioned creative writing and creative writing that emerged from outsider groups, like the New York School poets and Beats. This extreme division became even more apparent when you examined the literary magazines being made on either side of the fence: academic journals were impeccable, perfectly bound (the spine is stitched and glued, producing a squared spine on which text can be written), professionally typeset, and professionally printed on heavy paper; mimeo magazines were haphazardly assembled, usually around a kitchen table, in conjunction with the copious consumption of a lot of wine. According to *A Secret Location on the Lower East Side*, which chronicles the evolution of the small press literary community, joining up with friends to put that magazine together meant that you had comrades who were active participants in the production of the final product. "Collating, stapling, and mailing parties helped speed up production, but, more significantly, they helped galvanize a literary group."[1] But it was this process of working together to produce a funky handmade object that actually allowed underground writers to feel a kind of ownership over their work, an instinct that academic publishing never quite satisfied. Mimeo publishing also offered writers instant gratification. Before desktop publishing, it could take months and even years before a journal featuring one of your poems would arrive in a bookstore or at the library. Mimeo in the sixties replaced that arduous process: "For the price of a few reams of paper and a handful of stencils, a poet could produce, by mimeograph, a magazine or booklet in a small edition over the course of several days."[2]

As independent culture evolved into a literary culture as well as a musical one, more and more cities in America would add their imprint. Soon, independent publishing and the early "mimeo revolution" would open the door for the even more freewheeling and wide-ranging variety of zines that would emerge in the eighties and nineties.

Aside from the journals coming out of the Bay Area and New York, literary scenes began to evolve across the United States: Black Mountain College in North Carolina was an important nexus for many writers who would embrace mimeo publishing, and writers in Chicago, Providence, Ohio, Michigan, and Iowa would also join the small press publishing world. Distribution was scarcer in those days, so most small press magazines were sold at readings or carried to a local bookstore by the writers themselves. In spite of the small-scale distribution, the growth of small presses would turn out to have mixed blessings for some people involved because America was still culturally conservative. LeRoi Jones's (later Amiri Baraka) mimeo magazine *The Floating Bear*, which he designed with the poet Diane di Prima to be "an engine for quick and informal communication, particularly for younger and unpublished experimental poets," was the subject of censorship in 1961, when Jones was charged with sending obscene material through the mail.[3] The case never made it to trial, but Jones requested a grand jury hearing, "at which he stayed on for much of two days discussing the difficulties in distinguishing pornography from literature."[4] Jones was never indicted, but the case is an example of the evocative power of something that many perceived to be a cheap and disposable form of literature. Among the writers in that issue of *The Floating Bear* were Jones himself and Beat legend William S. Burroughs. Aside from Baraka and Burroughs, many other important writers would go on to join the mimeo revolution, in many cases founding their own magazines and presses. Jack Spicer's *J*, Robert Creeley's *Black Mountain Review*, Nathaniel Mackey's *Hambone*, Ted Berrigan's *C Press*, Ed Sanders's *Fuck You: A Magazine of the Arts*, Anne Waldman's *Angel Hair*, Ron Silliman's *Tottel's*, and Lyn Hejinian's Tuumba Press were just a few among many other writer-owned and -operated journals and presses that emerged between the early sixties and mideighties. Hejinian provides what might be the quintessential anecdote about starting a press when she describes asking for a job in a print shop in Willits, California, and being told by the owner that "printing ain't for girls."[5] Hejinian subsequently moved to Berkeley, where she purchased a press from a newspaper ad, "bought paper from a local warehouse and used the trim size that was the most economical," and started printing books. Becoming a publisher was really that easy after all.

In contrast to some of the other forms of independent culture, small press publishing offered an almost equal opportunity for women to participate. In addition to journals and presses run by women like Waldman and Hejinian and others, women contributed to the independent press world in many other ways.

Laura Moriarty, who currently works as the deputy director of Small Press Distribution, was previously the archivist for the Poetry Center at San Francisco State University, which houses a collection of video and sound recordings of readings. Moriarty recalls her early days as a member of the experimental literary community in the late sixties and seventies as a time when camaraderie was created via the radical lifestyle choices writers were making. "This was a time when very few of the poets were graduate students," she says, which is in sharp contrast to the current vogue for MFA programs.[6] "A few of them were, but most of them were being alternative and really occupying that kind of bohemian space in the scene. And so the world that they really put all their energy into was the scene." In the Bay Area and in other parts of America, the literary world was ripe for experimentation and freedom, and Moriarty and her friends took advantage of that freedom to write and to become publishers as well. "In the sixties, there were people around here that were related to printing, small printing presses," she recalls, and "in the seventies, we were sitting around setting our own type and pretending to be Anaïs Nin. It was great," she adds with a laugh.

Much like the low-budget but highly creative punk community that would emerge a few years later, the experimental and small press community allowed people to simply write without concern for careerism or opportunism. "I was working completely in the bohemian fringes of being a waitress for about ten years, and really enjoying it, actually," Moriarty recollects. "Living in San Francisco, never getting up before noon, writing all night, working two or three days a week and quitting every summer, I was living like a rich person even though I was penniless." At that juncture, SPD, which Moriarty and other members of her circle frequented, was a "Tiny, tiny, tiny, tiny place. SPD started with five presses in 1969. It's a couple of people working part-time, no benefits, and making very tiny money, and these people are all very active in the local scene." That setting was growing exponentially by the late sixties. In addition to SPD, the Bay Area was also home to multiple reading series at many local cafés and galleries, all of which helped bring individual writers together. On the Lower East Side of New York, a parallel movement of writers and publishers evolved around reading series at Le Metro, Les Deux Mégots, and eventually at St. Mark's Church in-the-Bowery. The Lower East Side poetry scene was as intimate as the Bay Area's. At readings, what might have been considered heckling at a more staid venue was yet another form of community building, since "many people . . . knew each other and commented on one another's work during the readings."[7] This was at the same time that the Diggers hit upon operating their own press in order to distribute bulletins about political events, be-ins, and happenings; poets and writers from other genres were similarly empowering themselves and their communities via cheap and easy access to the written word.

Like Laura Moriarty, Ron Silliman took a circuitous route through the counterculture to his career as a writer and advocate for small press publishing. Born in the East Bay, he didn't begin college right after high school but "spent the intervening period hanging out with folks on Telegraph Avenue exploring career opportunities and recreational pharmaceuticals." Silliman eventually attended San Francisco State in the late sixties but "went back to [UC] Berkeley after every professor I liked [at SF State] either got fired or arrested during the strike in sixty-eight, back in the days when my professor would carry a pistol onto campus. It was so out of control."[8] Silliman wound up dropping out of Berkeley and moving back to San Francisco in the early seventies, where he began participating in group poetry readings that often involved collaborative performances with artists from other genres. "We put together a series called Visual Eyes," he remembers, "and the idea was a performance by one of the performance artists for conceptual people in the area and one reading each night." Silliman and other poets would read, and "Tom Marioni, at one point, stood on a ladder, peeing into buckets," along with other conceptual performance art. The series took place at the Farm, an urban farm in the Mission District, and Silliman "actually read down in the barn area, and I had pigs and geese accompanying me in my readings. Geese are nature's saxophone." A bit later, Silliman and his cohorts began another reading series called the Grand Piano, which wound up attracting much larger crowds than they had been led to expect for an experimental poetry series. Silliman chalks this up to the "blank canvas" of San Francisco in the waning days of the hippie era: "We didn't have to push against any great resistance," he reflects. "When we first started doing the Grand Piano series, our audiences were huge for the first year and half or so, just literally out of curiosity. It was clear that something different was happening, so all these people would come and check it out." In New York, on the other hand, writers "felt like mice working in the shadows of preexisting conditions," such as the New York School of poets and the visual arts scene they had often mingled with, "and therefore [they were] working in opposition to something that was local and not particularly welcoming their new input. There was none of that in SF."

Like many other writers in the Bay Area and around the country at that time, Silliman took the next logical step and decided to start editing a small press journal. A friend convinced Silliman to take matters into his own hands rather than sending out Silliman's work to journals he didn't like because their content was too staid. He found the role suited him, "[it] gave me an opportunity to correspond with people I was interested in, and get work from them, talk to them about their work, show them my work, publish my work alongside their work." With the aid of a Rolodex loaned by another friend who had contact with many of the significant experimental writers of the time, Silliman started soliciting work. Soon, he had more than enough material for an issue of a journal. At the time, Silliman, like many others in the counterculture, was unemployed and living off food stamps and student loans, so figuring out a way to get the money together to take the work to a printer proved an early obstacle. Eventually, Silliman gave up on the idea of spending money for printing and opted instead to go the DIY route. "I took the work that I had and typed it up into a semiconsistent format and literally trotted on to one of the copy shops on Telegraph and Durant [in Berkeley] and printed up thirty-five copies and stapled them in the corner, gave them a completely different name than the one I had been thinking about, and started sending that around." The resulting mimeo journal, *Tottel's*, became a useful resource for the growing experimental writing community. Silliman would publish the work of one person, who would in turn recommend another writer friend, and so the network grew.

For Moriarty, Silliman, and others who were beginning to forge networks of publishing, readings, and friendship, the idea of a community of like-minded writers, publishers, and editors was essential to their endeavors. In the seventies, according to Silliman, writers who shared in this aesthetic vision began to move to the Bay Area, "and suddenly there were all these people who could talk to each other, who all knew we were really too young to be simply like another branch of new American poetry." Not only was their writing different, but this new breed also had very different ideas about how to make one's way through the literary world and how to live a literary life almost completely in opposition to the staid nature of literary culture at the time. These writers in many ways lived like indie musicians would in the eighties: on the cheap, stringing together various part-time jobs, depending on one another for opportunities to publish and read rather than turning to someone outside of their network. That inherent sense of cooperation led to the formation of a very tightly knit community that still exists today. Moriarty says that choosing books to stock at SPD today still comes down to this precedent. "When a book comes in here, that's what I look for," she says. "I don't care what it looks like. I don't care if it's good—it doesn't have to be what I think of as good. It has to be out of a literary community. As long as it's out of a community, we don't care what they do." And finding a community doesn't need to be difficult: "When I teach," she asserts, "I tell my students you are part of a community whether you know it or not. It may not be my community, but you need to think of who you like, you need to Google that person and go to their readings and find out who they read. It's not rocket science."

Today, both Moriarty and Silliman are advocates for many of

the technological tools that have emerged that easily enable writers to forge communities and take the publishing process into their own hands. Moriarty has published eleven books, all with small presses, and, in addition to his poetry writing, Silliman maintains a popular poetics blog that frequently spurs epic, free-wheeling conversations about small press publishing, independent journals, and experimental writing. Blogs, print-on-demand publishing, desktop-publishing software, and the Internet have all had a massive effect on the way in which independently produced books and writing arrive in the world. The writers of the sixties and seventies who took matters into their own hands when it came to publishing also laid a foundation for the zine community that emerged in the eighties. While zines may appear to be somewhat less strictly literary than most small press poetry and fiction, they take many of their motivational cues from the writers who stood at mimeograph machines making journals and hauled printing presses up their front steps in the sixties and seventies. If you felt you had something to say and odds were against someone paying you to say it in a book or a magazine, you might as well take matters into your own hands.

*

To see evidence of what zine culture represents today in a town with a strong independent community, your best bet is to head to Portland, Oregon, home to the monolithic independent bookstore Powell's Books (which encompasses an entire block on Burnside Street, one of Portland's main thoroughfares). Tucked away on a triangular-shaped block just a short walk from Powell's, Reading Frenzy is a self-described "independent press emporium" that sells hundreds of zines in store and online, along with a scattering of small press books, the latter mostly Oregon based. The store, like most of the zines and books it carries, is tiny; on a typically damp Portland morning when five or six regular customers are in the store, they have to jostle for standing space. Reading Frenzy opened in 1994 in an even smaller space of only 150 square feet, and much like SPD in its early days, it carried only a handful of titles. The variety of titles has grown exponentially. Today, you can pick up copies of a Portland-produced literary journal called *Yeti* that comes packaged with a custom-mixed CD, a wide array of crafting zines, and a small press book about anarchist road trips from CrimethInc, a self-described "ex-workers' collective" press based in Salem, Oregon, in addition to a few hundred other titles.

Reading Frenzy's presence plays a significant part in Portland's indie culture; according to the young woman with asymmetrical hair who's staffing the counter on a Saturday morning in 2008, the store has had the same owner since its inception, and when she's not there, it's run by volunteers. Reading Frenzy sponsors concerts, readings, and art shows and actively promotes the work of local artists and writers. The owner and a partner run a small press of their own out of the office upstairs. In addition to the stock of zines, comics, and books, the store also sells prints, knick-knacks, and candy (lollipops and gum are displayed in a rotating postcard rack along with cards by local artists like Olympia's Nikki McClure, whose X-acto knife cutout art has its own cult following). At its core, though, Reading Frenzy is really about reading. Over the course of an hour or so, about a dozen people—a mix of young hipsters and older hippies, reflective of Portland's demographics—come in, pick up zines, read, drink coffee, and chat quietly. Everyone buys something before they leave, and it's fairly likely, given the nature of zines to inspire the production of more zines, that at least a few of Reading Frenzy's clients will soon be xeroxing a zine of their own, if they aren't already.

Like the small press publishing culture of the sixties and seventies, the zine culture of the eighties and nineties operated on the basic tenets of DIY. Prior to the punk zines that emerged in the eighties, the earliest fanzines, produced in the thirties and forties, were the product of another marginalized community: science fiction fans. What was missing for people who read science fiction at that time was any sort of critical discourse about it; professional critics tended to ignore science fiction, so "its analysis was left to the fan."[9] Science fiction fanzines became a tool for communication among readers at a time when technology was even more primitive than it would be in the sixties and seventies. Many of these early science fiction zines were produced on a minimal budget like their latter-day peers, so "most fanzines accordingly take the form we find today," as xeroxed and folded and stapled sheaves of paper.[10] By the seventies, the growing punk community, like the science fiction and small press communities before it, felt similarly ignored in terms of critical attention to the music it was producing. "As the [word] 'fan' was by and large dropped off 'zine' and their number increased exponentially," writes Stephen Duncombe, "a culture of zines developed."[11] The word "culture" is crucial here. Just as Mike Watt, Ian MacKaye, and other early members of the American punk scene felt a kinship with other punk musicians even if they superficially had little in common except for being young, independent minded, and broke, zine writers in the early days ranged from young punks to people old enough to have been radically engaged in the sixties who continued to carry that torch and needed a place to vent about the turn the country was taking back toward conservative values. All of these people, and the wide range of zinesters in between, were real writers and taken seriously in the zine world, which didn't care if they'd dropped out of high school or attended the Iowa Writers' Workshop. Among the many zines to emerge in the eighties, *Factsheet 5* would eventually become one of the most important titles in bringing the sprawling zine community together.

Founded by Mike Gunderloy, who was both an anarchist and a science fiction fan himself, *Factsheet* began as a literal sheet. Gunderloy perceived a need for a central document that would bring together reviews of the different zines he was reading. He had been writing to friends about them when, as he told writer Stephen Duncombe, "Finally, I said this is stupid, I've written the same thing five times to five different people, I'll publish it . . . that was *Factsheet Five #1*."[12] *Factsheet's* first issue consisted of reviews of six or so zines on that single sheet of paper; by the time Gunderloy passed the title on to another editor in 1991, it was reviewing "over a thousand zines" per issue, along with reviews of "books, records, tapes, t-shirts, computer software and other independent media."[13] Along the way, Gunderloy created an essential document of the growing zine community. And, in spite of the disparate nature of many of the zines included in an issue of *Factsheet*, which could range from zines about music to zines about travel, literature, politics, media, and sex, zine writers and publishers really did see themselves as part of a community. "Reading [*Factsheet*]," according to Duncombe, "you definitely got the sense that you were *inside* of something."[14]

That very notion of being an insider, even if your interests were different, was reason enough for Gunderloy to spend increasing amounts of time on each issue of *Factsheet*. This in turn created a pressure that he admits became unbearable. On his personal Web site, there's a short essay called "About Factsheet Five" that sums up the consequences of the high-stress atmosphere of publishing *Factsheet* thusly (with Gunderloy writing about himself in the third person): "Ironically, just as success seemed to be looming, Gunderloy had a nervous breakdown and quit the magazine. Since then, he has steadfastly refused to discuss the small press, and having sold out, has become a computer programmer."[15] After Gunderloy's departure, *Factsheet* was taken over by editor Seth Friedman and changed radically; under Friedman's aegis, *Factsheet* became a slicker production overall and more accessible to readers outside of the zine circle. This gambit, however, didn't pay off in the long run; *Factsheet* now exists only as a Web page that hasn't been updated in several years.

Gunderloy's burnout can be partly attributed to the enormous expansion of the zine network in the eighties and early nineties. If *Factsheet* was reviewing a thousand zines a month, it was still only skimming the top of the pile. Duncombe estimated in 1992 that there were somewhere between ten thousand and twenty thousand zines being published in America, but exact numbers are impossible to determine because of the DIY nature of zines. Since most of them were self-distributed, it never became entirely clear just how many people were cranking out zines, but it was clear to anyone paying attention that there were more zines than ever before by the late eighties. The vast variety of topics and writers made for a lively conversation between writers and readers in the underground, but some zines had both a longer shelf life than their compatriots and a wider audience. In the punk rock circles that had first embraced zines in the seventies, *Maximumrocknroll,* a participant in the early days of the Gilman Project, came to play a central role in helping shape the punk community.

MRR offered up hundreds of reviews of albums, seven-inch records, tapes, and shows in every issue, and it also had a variety of columns, scene reports, and classified ads that reflected the multifaceted international punk community. If, as Mike Watt says, punk is what you make of it, *MRR,* in its best issues, mirrored that diversity. And it steadfastly retained its identity as a zine, not a magazine, even as its size and circulation grew. Today, *MRR* is still printed on newsprint—the cheapest paper stock available—and still has a stapled spine, one of the hallmarks of a zine.

But zines of *MRR*'s size and scope were few and far between. For the most part, the average zine was a much smaller-scale production. Many were one-offs that lasted for only one issue, intentionally; others were published for longer time periods but were handed around among groups of friends and never circulated beyond that. Rather than limiting their content, however, smaller print runs and tighter budgets actually encouraged zine writers to be even more creative. Outside of the realms of music and politics, some of the most interesting zines of the eighties and nineties were personal ones. One of the better-known personal zines, *Cometbus,* is written (handwritten, in fact—it has never appeared in typeface) by Aaron Cometbus (aka Aaron Elliot), a drummer for the bands Crimpshrine, Sweet Baby, and Pinhead Gunpowder. *Cometbus*—which he has been writing for more than twenty years—chronicles not only Cometbus's life as a musician but as a punk: dumpster diving, relationships, traveling on little to no money, scraping to get by. Its visual aesthetic— black-and-white, copier-distorted images, Cometbus's unique, all caps handwriting—became a blueprint for many zines that followed. The zine's candid honesty and sense of humor compelled many people to track the author's adventures as he moved around the country, and the zine quickly gained a large cult following.

Cometbus's wanderings were driven by what he refers to as the "impatience" of punks in the eighties. Prior to starting *Cometbus*, he put together a zine in 1981 with Jesse Michaels of the band Operation Ivy. "Punks just weren't as self-conscious then, as a culture," Cometbus writes.[16] "We put out a new fanzine every week! And in the spirit of constant rebirth, we chose a new name for each issue." After Michaels departed to spend some time living in Pittsburgh, Cometbus began working on the zine by himself. He told *Punk Planet* in 2002 that when he started reading zines, "there was an emphasis on localism—fanzines were about their local scenes."[17] But before *MRR* came along, the Bay Area lacked a zine with that kind of focus on local bands, so bands, "especially small local bands with dumb names who never made it very far," became the primary focus of his first venture.[18] Soon Cometbus began to see the limitations of writing about music. Although record reviews and show stories were all well and good, for Cometbus, this missed the entire point of punk. His mission with the zine became "trying to tap directly into the passion and struggle and adventures of punk," and that struggle for him was better reflected in short narratives about his own journey through the underground. The backdrop to many of those early stories was Berkeley; however, he soon began casting a wider net and traveling across the United States in true punk style—staying in squats, seeking out co-op cafés, falling in love, and constantly trying "to fully engage and explore. To document, challenge, demand, or maybe just appreciate." Those themes tied *Cometbus*'s fifty issues, spanning 1983 to 2006, together. The zine was never really "about" anything other than what its author put into it, yet Cometbus's writing was powerful enough and the stories he told so interesting that people outside of the East Bay punk scene went out of their way to find the zine. "I think of fanzines as being an intrinsically punk thing," he told *MRR* in 2000, "but also existing separately.

I'm able to reach a huge cross-section of people and also be very true and specific to one community and culture."[19] At times, the stories Cometbus told were actually so interesting that people found them far-fetched and mistook them for fiction. He laughed this off in the *MRR* interview, when he argued that "I can say I burned down a house and stole a car and all these other things and people will assume it's fictionalized. That's fine, but it's not."[20]

Cometbus's most recent issue, number fifty, appeared in 2006. Two anthologies of back issues have been published so far, and Cometbus has also self-published three books that collect thematically linked stories from the zine. While *Cometbus* is just one example out of the thousands and thousands of titles that were published in the eighties and nineties, it encapsulates many of the best things about the zine culture of that time. With their freedom of expression, emphasis on low-budget creativity, and function as a networking device for people scattered across the country, zines became a truly independent mode of creativity funded, created, and distributed by the artist or artists whose words appeared between the hand-bound covers. Some zines later evolved into record labels and full-blown magazines with national distribution and (to many readers' dismay) advertising, but most of them remained just as they had begun: as xeroxed documents of individuals making their way on the fringes of American culture. When the independent music scene stepped into the glare of the mass media spotlight in the early nineties, zines, as the print manifestation of that community, were forced into the spotlight as well, for better or worse. Some zines of that era—particularly those that came out of the riot grrrl movement—were the subject of misunderstanding and misreading. But before certain examples could be culturally exploited in venues like *Time* magazine, zines, small presses, and the whole history of independent publishing opened the door to another important print documentation of independent culture: independent comics. Just as zines had often been a visual as well as a written medium, with an emphasis on illustrations that were often more gutsy and raw than attractive, independently produced comics changed the entire topical and stylistic nature of what comics could be. For many of the artists who produced these groundbreaking comics, the freedom of drawing and writing and then distributing whatever you wanted was something you could experience only outside of the margins of the mainstream because you can draw and write whatever privately. The grubby hippies who stood at mimeo machines in the sixties, cranking a handle and inhaling the sweet-smelling fumes of their own ideas made manifest in print, would totally dig that notion.

five

Like a Velvet Glove Cast in Iron: The Independent Comics Revolution

If the zine world of the eighties and nineties was home to freethinkers, buskers, outlaws, and the occasional nutcase, the subculture of comics had historically also been home to its own collection of oddball personalities. Before the advent of independent comics, comic books had traditionally been the provenance of superheroes, those ubermuscular caricatures of human beings, with their puffed-up chests and matching egos, family-friendly fare like the gang from the Archies, perennially stuck in the fifties, and the safe stuff typically found in the Sunday funnies. Underneath the superheroes and squeaky-clean depictions of families and teens, however, a long line of cartoonists who ventured into stranger, more surreal, and more sexual and violent territory within the comics medium stretches back into the earliest years of comics' existence. Winsor McCay's *Little Nemo in Slumberland* snuck into the pages of newspapers early in the twentieth century, depicting a surreal dreamscape instead of the typical bubbly drawings and corny escapades, sometimes appearing alongside George Herriman's *Krazy Kat*, a subversive tale of unrequited love between an asexual cat and a brick-tossing mouse. In the sixties, underground comic artists like R. Crumb would take from these predecessors, creating an even stranger version of comics that strongly emphasized sex, drugs, and other accoutrements of the sixties lifestyle. These comics (or comix, as some of the underground artists preferred) were independently produced and printed and could usually be found alongside roach clips and rolling papers in head shops.

Before the advent of the sixties underground artists, the innocent, neutralized content of most comics was in part due to the enforcement of the Comics Code. In 1954, Dr. Fredric Wertham published a sensationalist tome entitled *Seduction of the Innocent* that warned of the youth-corrupting potential of comic books. Wertham focused his argument on what he referred to as "injury to the eye," caused by the violence in comics.[1] The book is now out of print and highly prized by collectors, but its greatest legacy was the creation of the Comics Code, sparked by the Senate Subcommittee on Juvenile Delinquency, which decreed that "members of the [comics] industry must see to it that gains made in this medium are not lost and that violations of standards of good taste, which might tend toward corruption of the comic book as an instructive and wholesome form of entertainment, will be eliminated."[2] Included among the things that had to be stripped from comics in order for them to earn the comics code seal (and therefore to be sold in stores) were nudity, depictions of drug use, depictions of crime as anything but a "sordid and unpleasant activity," the use of the words "horror" or "terror" in the title, profanity, "sexual abnormality" (which at the time implicitly included homosexuality), and the depiction of women's bodies with any exaggeration of body parts, along with forty-one other forbidden items. Some comics publishers went out of business because of the code; others simply started censoring everything for the sake of survival.

By the time the underground comix movement began in

the sixties, comix artists' response to the code could easily be summed up in three words: fuck that shit. These artists gleefully broke every rule in the code. Just as the Diggers redefined the sixties as a time when people could seize their own creative freedom and "do their own thing," and small press publishers and mimeo magazines put the power of publishing directly into writers' hands, underground comix played a similar role within the art form's larger culture and history. A fringe medium in the first place, before they transitioned into something artier, the audience for comics was typically limited to adolescent boys and the semiguilty adults who kept up the habit they formed in childhood. And before comics had their own trade journals and magazines, much of the hype about a new title or artist was passed on through word of mouth. So when artists like R. Crumb, Vaughn Bodé, Art Spiegelman, Trina Robbins, David Geiser, and S. Clay Wilson began drawing comics, the unorthodox nature of much of their work, along with the same spirit of collaboration that was inherent to subcultural art, brought them together, and a community of underground comix was born. The content and feel of many of the comix being produced were perfectly in synch with the music, art, and writing of the time. Explicitly sexual, surrealistic in both illustration style and plotting, and extremely frank about depicting drug use (to the point that it was surprising *not* to see a doobie being lit up or a character bad-tripping on acid in any given issue), comix served as a mirror of the changing realities of life in the underground, more than any other art form at the time, even though they went against the grain of what was deemed acceptable for public consumption.

R. Crumb's *Zap Comix* became one of the first underground titles to open other artists' and consumers' eyes to the potential of the medium. Crumb had been reading and drawing comics from a very young age, and he and his brother "were connoisseurs by age eleven. By then it was obvious to us that most comics were hacked out crap."[3] Crumb and his brother Charles would soon discover the world of comics fandom via letters from fanzine editors that appeared in other fanzines. Once the Crumbs started corresponding with fanzine editors, writers, and other teen comics artists, they discovered a network that "broke us out of the isolation of our own little world of comics and changed our lives."[4] After high school, Crumb took a straightlaced job with American Greetings, the gift card company, but managed to cultivate the seeds of revolution that had spawned in his psyche by working on his own comics in his spare time. Fritz the Cat, one of his first characters, presaged some of the sexual/perverse themes that would become a trademark of Crumb's work. One issue depicted the titular black-turtleneck-clad and smirking cat undressing a female companion only to pick fleas off of her; another showed him getting it on with his own sister. After giving up on the greeting card gambit and traveling in Europe in the midsixties, Crumb returned to the states and found that "that whole hipster counterculture thing had coalesced even more," and he soon began some hard-core indulgence in the day's drug of choice.[5] LSD caused Crumb's drawing style to change; realism was warped into a world of exaggerated body shapes and exploding heads, a natural offshoot of the drug's effects on the artist's already sensitive brain. By 1967, Crumb was living in San Francisco, epicenter of the counterculture, and his strips "contained the hopeful spirit of the times, drawn in a lovable 'big foot' style. The stuff caught on."[6] Don Donahue, the typesetter and layout artist for the Bay Area underground organ the *Berkeley Barb*, had around this time met up with a printer named Charles Plymell, who shared his interest in creating an underground tabloid. The two men ran into some of Crumb's work at a friend's house and were startled when the three men met to discover that they were all the same age. "I thought he must be an old man," Donahue remembered. "Maybe he'd been drawing for comics back in the 20s or 30s and he went berserk or something."[7]

Donahue, Plymell, and Crumb joined forces and began collaborating on publishing *Zap #1*, released in February 1968. In the spirit of independent publishing, the comic was folded and stapled at Crumb's kitchen table. It was easy enough to hand out copies to the hippies who were flooding Haight Street, but initially, Crumb and his cohorts had problems getting shopkeepers—even hippie shopkeepers—to sell the comic. Even though underground newspapers, mimeo magazines, and Digger broadsides were a common sight at this juncture, comics were just . . . different. And even though hippies believed themselves to be open-minded, many of them just didn't "get" comics. Soon enough, however, the *Zap* creators found an alternative means of distribution, one that opened underground comix up to a whole new audience, while also allowing them to evade the strictures of the Comics Code. Head shops, which specialized in selling all the accoutrements of drug use along with clothing, records, and alternative newspapers, were much more open-minded about distributing and selling comics like *Zap*. In 1968, shortly after the release of *Zap #1*, psychedelic poster artist Victor Moscoso helped the *Zap* crew secure distribution via the Print Mint, which was already distributing poster art via its mail order catalogs. "The posters and the comix were the one-two graphic punch of the counterculture movement," Moscoso declared, and the independent distribution system already in place for posters was able to get the comics into head shops and underground-friendly bookstores.[8] With its juxtaposition of old-fashioned comics against raunchy and psychedelic images and subject matter, *Zap* filled a void for the visual expression of countercultural lifestyles. Comics were "a whole medium of expression that had been neglected for so long . . . and nobody had done much with it," Donahue recalled.[9] "And all of a sudden someone did start doing something with it, and then there was this explosion."

Because underground comix were sold in underground shops and via underground mail order catalogs, publishers and artists were able to evade the notice of those who would typically enforce the Comics Code. Sure enough, shortly after *Zap #1*'s appearance, a flood of underground comix arrived. It's arguable whether or not *Zap* was really the *first* underground comic—titles like Jack Jackson's *God Nose* and Joel Beck's *Lenny of Laredo* may have preceded it, but most comics artists who were around at the time generally agree that Crumb was the artist who "reinvented the form," according to Bill Griffith, who created the long-running comic *Zippy the Pinhead*.[10] In 1968, as *Zap* swung into gear, Crumb agreed to do one mainstream gig: he illustrated an album cover for the local band Big Brother and the Holding Company, featuring as its lead singer the boozy-voiced Janis Joplin, who, with her feathery wardrobe and defiant stance on social issues of the day, was fast emerging as a heroine of the counterculture. The cover featured a wheel of hippie imagery, including a smoking frog, a swami, a one-eyed man, and a voluptuous, reclining Joplin. When Big Brother's *Cheap Thrills* became a best seller, it quickly catapulted Crumb's art into the national spotlight, and, just as quickly, he cringed and ducked from the attention. Other underground comix artists shared Crumb's disdain for the mainstream, but their collective style so perfectly captured the mind-set and illicit lifestyles of the times that their aesthetic—wiped clean of its code-breaking taint—was imitated and replicated for a mass audience. A strip that had appeared in *Zap #1*, entitled "Keep on Truckin'," inspired a slew of merchandise, including T-shirts, bumper stickers, and posters, all manufactured without Crumb's permission. An animated film based on his comic Fritz the Cat was so distasteful to Crumb that he killed off the character in a strip that showed an ice pick being driven through Fritz's head.

These kinds of acts of defiance, along with his stalwart support of the underground comix community, made Crumb into a countercultural hero in his own right, but his depiction of women brought him a more mixed sort of attention. Crumb's long-standing attraction to women of a certain body type—big assed, big breasted, and generally of Amazonian stature—was perfectly fine with most women of that body type, who had long hoped that someone would celebrate their figure, which had fallen out of fashion long ago. On the other hand, his tendency to push the envelope, depicting actions like having his character Flakey Foont remove Devil Girl's head and then have sex with her headless body or the image of himself vomiting on his wife's head during their first LSD trip, led to some understandable criticism from the growing feminist movement. Crumb's ability to simultaneously celebrate and exploit women mirrored the reality of many women's lives in the counterculture at that time. Earth mothers and groupies alike were expected to be sexually available at all times while also taking care of the kids, cooking the food, and, if needed, stapling the comics together. Female comics artists would struggle to reverse this problematic dichotomy in the next wave of independent comics that began to arrive in the eighties.

※

Arguably, the underground comix movement's biggest contribution to the later generation of indie comics was not just in its taboo-busting subject matter and freewheeling illustration style but in its insistence on creator control. According to comics journalist Douglas Wolk, the sixties underground artists' first step in this direction entailed "breaking every taboo they could possibly find."[11] Breaking free of creative taboos allowed artists to assert creative control over their work because they had proven their independence from both the Comics Code and staid notions about what comics could be. This maneuver helped solidify the growing network of independent comics that were artistically sophisticated and established a new business model. "Creator ownership is what really made all this possible," argues Wolk, "because you didn't have to serve somebody else who owned what you had. You owned it; you could do whatever the hell you wanted with it. And that meant that there was this flowering of visual style in comics. There was this flowering of writerly style too."

Among the many artists who came from sixties comics and continued to have an impact on the underground comix community into the nineties were Crumb (with *Zap* and his later anthology *Weirdo*) and Art Spiegelman, who, with his wife, Françoise Mouly, founded the comics anthology *RAW* in 1980. Spiegelman, like Crumb, had been involved in the San Francisco underground comix scene in the sixties; he collaborated with Bill Griffith on a comic called *Arcade*.[12] Before he went on to write the Holocaust-based *Maus*, the first comic to win a Pulitzer,

Spiegelman's greatest contribution to independent comics was in discovering and featuring many of the important comics artists of the eighties and nineties in *RAW*. "I think Art's the greatest editor in the history of comics," Fantagraphics founder Gary Groth said in 1999, and the impact of *RAW* helped reinforce that opinion.[13] *RAW* featured work by artists like Charles Burns, Gary Panter, and Kaz, who "went on to be the big names of the eighties and nineties," according to Wolk. "Their sense of design looks like everything in the world that you have innate now." *RAW* was visually striking as well as being cutting-edge in its content; one of the first oversized comics, it stood out on store shelves and was embraced by a more highbrow crowd as Spiegelman's reputation grew. "To the whole intellectual northeastern Ivy League *New York Times*–New York literary crowd," comic artist Peter Bagge said, "he's the guy."[14]

Changes in the comics business and how comics were distributed had helped to make creator control an even greater possibility in the early seventies, when antiparaphernalia laws led to the closing of many head shops, where underground comix had traditionally been sold. But within a few years of the decimation of these stores, the comics-direct market began to emerge. According to Wolk, "In the midseventies, a guy named Phil Sealing and various other people noticed there were a bunch of stores that sort of were specializing in selling comic books, and they came up with the idea of distributing comics directly to those stores." For small comics publishers and self-published titles, this was crucial to their survival because it cut out the possibility of returns, which are financially damaging to a publisher of any size, but particularly hard on small presses, which operate on a hand-to-mouth basis. The comics-direct people "cut deals with the comic book companies in which these comic stores would get a lower wholesale price, and they would get copies of all the comics sooner, and in exchange the comics would be nonreturnable—whatever you ordered you had to eat," says Wolk. This maneuver "made small press comics financially much more possible than they'd really ever been, because once you got the orders from your distributors, for whatever your small press, twenty-four-page black-and-white comic was, you could print up that many copies, send them off, and ninety days later, you'd get a check."

By the time the eighties rolled around, this system of direct distribution had led to a full-on revival of underground comics, and foremost among the publishers that had the greatest impact on this revival was the Seattle-based, stalwartly independent Fantagraphics. Founded by Gary Groth and his partner Kim Thompson in the midseventies as a vehicle for publishing Groth's *Comics Journal*—one of the first trade magazines about comics—Fantagraphics soon began publishing original comics by other artists as well. The same wave of conservative values that had sparked the punk movement pushed people like Groth to create their own venues for publishing work that would never be touched by either of the big comics publishers of that time, DC Comics and Marvel, both known mostly for serial superhero comics. DC and Marvel focused on work with content that would appeal to a mass audience and make money, which was never the point of underground comix. The Comics Code's influence was waning in the eighties, because new publishers like Fantagraphics sold directly to comics shops, which meant their titles didn't have to pass muster with the Comics Code Authority, but Marvel and DC still toed the conservative line. Groth argued from early on that comics had too long been ghettoized by big business. "For 50 years," he said in a 1987 interview, "comic books have been a junk medium created by hacks or enthusiastic adolescents who are taken advantage of by businessmen who don't care about making any sort of intelligent or literate contribution to American culture."[15] Groth realized that this mistreatment of both comics and comics artists sprang from the same system that had forced underground artists in the sixties to seek alternative distribution via head shops and that the new movement of direct distribution was helping to provide a venue for more and more alternative comics making it into comic shops. "Until specialty shops became a force in the 70s and you began to see alternative comics," he said, "you didn't have what's going on now—a rejection of and contempt for mass culture values and a need to put your own values on paper."[16]

One of Fantagraphics' first comics, which appeared in 1982, successfully managed to mirror not only Groth's idea of "contempt for mass culture," but it also reflected subsets of society—and a cast of characters—very rarely glimpsed before in any medium, including comics. Written and illustrated by Jaime and Gilbert Hernandez, with occasional contributions from their brother Mario, *Love and Rockets* was, for many of its readers, the first comic that looked and felt like their lives. According to Jaime Hernandez, "Comic books were one of those things I was basically born into. Our mother being a comics fan herself as a kid actually encouraged Mario to buy them."[17] The Hernandez brothers grew up in Oxnard, California, a primarily Chicano city south of Ventura. Jaime became immersed in the punk and lowrider cultures, and this filtered into the comics he and his brothers were drawing. He recalled that SoCal punk was important to him "at the time I started writing these characters so it made sense to put them right in the thick of it. It also helped that almost none of that particular scene was portrayed in comics or anywhere else (unless you count [cheesy TV cop shows where the heroes busted up punk clubs] *Quincy*, *CHiPS*, or *C.P.O. Sharkey*) so we sort of made it our duty. To portray it truthfully, that is."[18]

For many readers who picked up early issues of *Love and Rockets*, the primary attraction was the epic friendship and romance between Jaime's two main characters, Maggie and Hopey. For female readers, the identification with these characters was sometimes so strong that the series skipped right over being aspirational and went directly into being almost uncomfortably realistic (except the occasional stylistic digression into sci-fi, though Jaime dropped those plotlines fairly early on). Maggie and Hopey were young, underemployed girls from a remote town somewhere in Southern California called Hoppers. While they fell for one another at a young age, they also slept around and fell in love with a variety of characters of both genders. They were also, like their creator, a part of the punk scene, and Hopey played bass—

badly—in a series of punk bands, while Maggie struggled to make ends meet as a mechanic and later at a series of blue-collar jobs. The resonance of Maggie and Hopey's on-off romance and daily doses of ennui and confusion were powerful for many other young people (male and female). Not only were these women struggling to express themselves; they were also struggling with many of the same issues of love, money, relocation, stir-craziness, and identity conflicts that people of their generation were living through every day. Jaime called their stories "Locas," Spanish for "crazy women," but Maggie and Hopey were the good kind of crazy. Plus, they were beautifully drawn in Jaime's high-contrast, thick-lined style. Even when Maggie began to realistically gain weight as she aged, and as Hopey's mischievous face grew sharp, Hernandez always made them look amazing. The entire package was irresistible, and it drew in an entirely new audience of female readers as well as gay, lesbian, and bisexual readers, who had often felt objectified and marginalized by their portrayal in comics up until that point.

Gilbert's story lines, mostly set in a fictional Central American town called Palomar, were artistically distinct from his brother's style, but they too featured a cast of powerful women. Palomar stories focused mainly on the extended family of Luba, an extremely large-breasted, strong-willed, and very fertile woman (she has at least seven children, all by different men), who dominates most of the Palomar story lines just as her impressive physique dominates men's perspective of her. But reducing Luba to a busty earth mother cliché would be a mistake—Luba is not to be fucked with. She wields a hammer when anyone crosses her and eventually becomes mayor of Palomar. The series featured both political storytelling, befitting the impoverished Latin American setting of the series, as well as surrealistic storytelling, often in a nonlinear narrative structure. There's also a ton of sex. At one point, Gilbert did another series called *Birdland*, which was part of Fantagraphics' Eros line of "adult" titles, and *Birdland* was the kind of dirty, dirty comic that absolutely had to be tucked away in the back of the store. The Eros imprint was formed partly as a survival strategy for

Fantagraphics. Even as alternative comics titles like *Love and Rockets* began to attract press attention in the late eighties and early nineties, Groth and Thompson's admitted lack of business sense often found the publisher on the brink of financial disaster. "Porn came to us in a vision," Thompson was quoted as saying, and Groth echoed this when he bluntly stated: "I like sex. I don't like superheroes."[19] Gilbert Hernandez's work was already so laden with sex that the shift to what was pretty much a straight-ahead porn story with a few plot points inserted (pardon the pun) here and there didn't seem unnatural, and even though many Fantagraphics fans found the Eros line to be a crass bid for money, it saved the company from bankruptcy during a financially rough time.

Two of Fantagaphics' other titles were likewise in touch with the cultural zeitgeist of the early nineties. As grunge captured the public imagination and the klieg lights of the media turned toward Seattle, Peter Bagge's *Hate* appeared, a quasi-autobiographical comic about a Seattle protoslacker named Buddy Bradley and his valiant attempts to fuck around. Bagge's exaggerated, over-the-top drawing style mirrored the drunken musical exploits of Buddy and his pals, chronicling some of Buddy's exploits that looked suspiciously like the adventures of a lot of grunge musicians. Douglas Wolk recalls that *Hate*'s venture into Buddy's music career was a point of interest for many readers who were also musicians themselves. "There were bands that thought there would be nothing cooler than to have the cover of their record drawn by Peter Bagge," he recalls, "and at the same time you had *Hate* ripping off the Seattle music scene, which it only really did for a few issues, but that's the part that everybody remembers." In particular, an oft-reprinted panel illustrating a clichéd-looking hairy grunge band rocking out and singing "You scream, I scream, we all scream for HEROIN!" encapsulated *Hate*'s affectionate mockery of the Seattle scene. "Seriously, that 'We all scream for heroin' panel is Peter Bagge's career boiled down into the perfect image," Wolk laughs. Bagge was no dummy, however, and he recognized the transcendence of the grunge/slacker moment a few years later when, according to Wolk, "as I recall he actually did another version of it where they're saying 'I scream, you scream, we all scream for major label record contracts!'"

Aside from *Love and Rockets* and *Hate*, the other Fantagraphics comic that transformed the potential and style of independent comics in the late eighties and early nineties was Daniel Clowes's *Eightball*, a spin-off series based on Clowes's *Lloyd Llewellyn* comic, which appeared as a one-off in *Love and Rockets*, issue 13. A film noir–style detective character, Lloyd Llewellyn established many of the hallmarks of Clowes's creepy, dark, off-kilter style of illustration and storytelling. With *Eightball*, which first began appearing in 1989, Clowes went beyond the noir plots and began adding in a freak show variety of characters, including the cast of *Eightball*'s first serialized story, "Like a Velvet Glove Cast in Iron." With its plot about a man whose wife has mysteriously begun appearing in bondage films, its detours into religious cults, conspiracy theorists, and the appearance of a strange fish girl, the "Velvet Glove" story felt a lot like the films of director David Lynch. Starting in 1993, Clowes's next serialized *Eightball* story was even more in touch with the cultural moment. *Ghost World*'s main characters are two disaffected, hip teenage girls who live in a town increasingly transformed by the encroaching march of strip malls, chain diners trafficking in fifties nostalgia, and other markers of bland American capitalism. Enid and Becky skewer, mock, and provide a cynical, smart commentary on their hometown at the same time as they experience achingly honest moments of sexual confusion and self-doubt. Like *Love and Rocket*'s Hopey and Maggie, Enid and Becky were a reflection of many female (and male) comics readers, and *Ghost World*, which ran in *Eightball* from 1993 to 1997, quickly attracted a big audience, many of whom had never really been into comics before. I worked in an Oakland comic book shop from 1993 to 1994, and many of the local musicians I knew and played with would wander in weekly looking for new issues of *Eightball*, *Hate*, and *Love and Rockets*. These were the kinds of guys and girls who would never be caught dead picking up an issue of *X Men* or *Wonder Woman*, yet their enthusiasm and excitement about the Fantagraphics lineup was contagious. Just like punk music and zines had grown and thrived via word of mouth, the same phenomenon applied to underground comics.

For Clowes, however, being a part of the new wave of cutting-edge cartoonists with a growing audience that had never picked up a comic before didn't necessarily translate to feeling like he was part of a gang. When asked if the theme of alienation often reflected in his comics has always been part of his own life, he had this to say: "I remember this feeling of going to a baseball game as a kid. I was like the hugest fan, but I was this isolated fan—I'd listen on the AM radio in my room—I went to a game, and it was just all these drunk, fat guys from Chicago, and I remember thinking, Is this my people?"[20] Clowes relates a similar anecdote about loving the Beatles, then discovering that everyone at school liked them too, and thinking, "Eh, I can't like the Beatles." This mixed fascination with and disdain for popular culture, along with his innate preference to discover things on his own, are all character traits he shares with the people (and creatures) who populate his art. Clowes, who was born in 1961, grew up in Chicago and moved to New York to attend school at the Pratt Institute, an art college. After that, he decided to pursue a career in commercial illustration, "with the hopes of someday doing some kind of weird comics, but there was just no market for it at the time." Soon enough, he discovered a SoHo zine shop and "this whole world of weird personal zine stuff that didn't exist in any other place or time." Clowes also discovered *RAW* magazine around the same time, and he says, "It was just mind-blowing to see these five or six artists I'd never heard of in my life that were amazing, and totally on my wavelength, and all completely different, yet all formed by that same collective media experience that we all grew up in." Though Clowes came into the orbit of writers and musicians working on the legendary *Punk* magazine (some of *Punk*'s editor's friends were doing comics), Clowes didn't feel like he quite fit in with that crowd either. "I think that sometimes it's not such a good thing to be in a real scene like that," he reflects, "especially when you're young and somebody doesn't like something you do; you actually do listen to them. I felt like I had such a luxury of living in a total vacuum. There was no Internet. There was no way to get any feedback at all." He shrugs and continues, "I just went with my own thing. That's why it was so developed. It made for more idiosyncratic stuff."

When Clowes began drawing and writing his first Lloyd Llewellyn stories, the number of independent comics publishers was minimal at best. Aside from Fantagraphics and a few creator-owned publishers, there were precious few venues that would touch work as odd as Clowes's. Clowes instinctively felt that "*RAW* and *Weirdo* were not right for *Lloyd Llewellyn*, and I didn't want to have it be my first attempt to get into those. I just went to the comic store, and was like, 'Oh, I've heard of this *Love and Rockets* thing. I guess these guys are publishers,' and I sent it to them blind." About a month later, he got a call from a representative of that publisher, Fantagraphics, who told him that the Llewellyn stories were "what we're looking for. Would you like to do a book?" Groth suggested putting some of Clowes's work in *Love and Rockets*—at that point their signature comic—for promotion. Clowes was initially resistant to having his work appear in the Hernandez brothers' already iconic series: "I didn't want to be in that context of something that everybody loves and it's really great, and here's my very first thing. I was like twenty-two years old. I didn't really feel like 'take the world by storm with this one!' I wanted to figure out what I was doing because that was the first long comic I'd ever done in my life." Clowes approached the prospect of doing a long-form comic with a bit of the dread you might see in one of his characters: "To have someone just give you your goal [for] ten years down the road was a weird feeling. The first years of my career were like, me, on the stage with no audience, doing my bit, just sort of honing it based on my own ear, but not at all based on any response." Clowes admits that making art in that kind of bubble was actually good for his work, so when he began working on *Lloyd Llewellyn*, the comics' combination of noirish narrative alongside Clowes's insightful and darkly funny narrative fit right together.

In spite of Clowes's early doubts, *Lloyd Llewellyn* turned into a cult classic, and *Eightball* was even more of a success, eventually becoming one of Fantagraphics' best-selling titles. *Eightball* had the good fortune to come along at a time when Fantagraphics was learning how to successfully promote its artists. Fantagraphics' publicist Larry Reed had an inkling that Clowes, Bagge, and the Hernandez brothers, like the underground artists who had preceded them in the sixties, might actually find their audience outside of comic shops. "He came in and he saw *Hate* and *Eightball* and *Love and Rockets*, there's a market for that out there, and it's not in a comic store," Clowes recalls. "He really focused on the three of us and just pushed that, and got us into record stores and just this whole other world and all of a sudden *Rolling Stone*'s writing about us, and it was just a whole new world." Whole new world was right. Fantagraphics titles were the hippest, newest thing to emerge from the independent culture in the early to midnineties. Between Clowes, Bagge, and the Hernandez brothers, readers were able to get a taste of everything from sex to rock and roll to slackerdom to mystery stories and everything in between. Clowes is both grateful for his good fortune and cognizant of its being helped along by Reed's promotional tactics. "I realized this guy just saw what was there and took it to the right marketplace. And from then on, it's kind of always been in that other world, and he's really the guy I owe all that to."

For Clowes and his cohort, the new world of mainstream recognition and relative success (relative in the sense that he was able to pay his rent, as he notes) came with a few sacrifices and changes in the comics community. A big part of that shift came when Fantagraphics began repackaging the comics as graphic novels: bound collections that could be sold in any respectable bookstore. Calling comics "graphic novels" also opened them up to an audience that accepted the idea of comics as "real" literature more easily than it swallowed the concept of a comic book, which can carry an air of disposability except for an audience of collectors. The initial split between underground comics and mainstream ones became less and less noticeable as underground artists began gaining greater recognition outside of the underground comics culture. "This artist named Mary Flemer started this Web site where she's putting up her twenty-something years of photos from the San Diego Comicon," Clowes says, referring to the country's biggest comic book convention, which began in the early seventies. "And the early ones are so charming, and you see there's nobody there, and it's really sparse. You sort of see us sitting sadly waiting for somebody to come by. And as it gets closer to nowadays, it's just more and more media, and it's so densely packed that she can barely get the photos, just in between Klingons. It's just so unpleasant now, and it really used to be a lot of fun. It was like our own little scene, and now it's like everybody's invited or something."

Arguments often ensue among comics enthusiasts about what constitutes an underground comic after the underground has been discovered by the mainstream—much in the same way that one might question whether a band like Green Day can really be called "punk" after they left the Gilman scene behind. It becomes a battle of semantics, as Douglas Wolk notes. "At some point, you have Robert Crumb on the cover of the *New Yorker*; is it a blow to the counterculture? Or is it the counterculture becoming the pill that the greater culture eats and becomes?" Wolk argues that any shift from the underground to the mainstream within comics is actually a good thing because it reinforces the benefits of creator ownership, which is something the original underground comix artists fought hard for. "Eventually the mainstream swallows a lot of the style that's being developed in the underground, but the underground just keeps expanding," Wolk asserts. "There's endless possibilities for people to devise something that's kind of cool-looking. And you can't do that if you don't own it." Creator ownership and independent comix did radically alter the comics landscape throughout the nineties and into the following decade. Not only did Fantagraphics artists and titles break through into the mainstream, but comic artists' work began appearing in formerly staid venues like the *New Yorker* and the *New York Times*. Spiegelman and Crumb led the way, but they were quickly followed by a large, unruly cast of artists. Graphic novels like Spiegelman's *Maus*, Clowes's *Ghost World*, Craig Thompson's *Blankets*, and Marjane Satrapi's *Persepolis* all made the move from comic book stores to getting written up in the *New York Review of Books*. While this seismic shift in the potential audiences for comics was definitely a good thing for artists who could now rely on comics to pay the rent, it did change the culture of underground comics, for good and bad.

Clowes is conscious of this shift. His script for the film adaptation of *Ghost World* was nominated for an Academy Award, and he regularly does illustration work for the *New Yorker*, along with his colleagues Adrian Tomine, Charles Burns, and others. In 2008, he began to collaborate on a film project with the renegade director Michel Gondry, who made *Eternal Sunshine of the Spotless Mind* and *The Science of Sleep*. Clowes's comics sell well, and while he's not wealthy, he makes ends meet from his art alone. We met for a conversation just after his serial comic *Mister Wonderful* had finished its run in the *New York Times* magazine over the course of several months, following in the footsteps of the magazine's publication of serial comics by several other alternative comics artists, including Jaime Hernandez, Megan Kelso, and Chris Ware. When I asked him if this had caused a shift in his audience, he said it hadn't yet. "Back in the old days if I did an issue of *Eightball*, I'd have my little address in there, and I'd get thirty, forty letters a week, every week," he says. "With the *New York Times*, I think if they'd had a comments thing attached to it, I would've gotten a lot, but as it was, I only heard from people who knew me or knew my e-mail address." Clowes imagines that when *Mister Wonderful* is released as a graphic novel, people will respond "like it's a brand new thing. There's all these different audiences now," he admits, "and they really don't interact at all."

Comics may have entered the mainstream, but many of their creators still work on the fringes. In this way, they closely parallel the evolution of zines and independent publishing. Both art forms share the print medium and both began to attract bigger and different audiences in the moment of the same cultural shift of the late eighties and early to midnineties. Both comics and zines are, in some ways, anonymous art—unlike music, the creators are a bit more obfuscated because they stand behind their words and pictures. But comics had always been part of a small, insular community, one with its own set of rules, rituals, and definitions of success. In the same moment that the underground comics world was being peeled open for the whole world to see, a layer of fog was burning off in the air above the Pacific Northwest. In Seattle, where Peter Bagge's Buddy Bradley character cracked jokes about selling out, musicians were about to face the biggest hype machine the independent underground had yet encountered, and it started within their own community. In Seattle's neighboring town of Olympia, a more fiercely independent movement of music, zines, and art was also percolating. The independent nation—music, comics, zines, art, all of it—was about to enter the culture wars and challenge staid notions of what it meant to be independent along the way.

We're Gonna Have to Be the Band: Olympia, Riot Grrrl, and the Great Independent Crossover

In 1977, a fifteen-year-old named Calvin Johnson began volunteering at the Evergreen State College radio station in Olympia, Washington. A tall, lanky kid with a flattop haircut and a penchant for cardigan sweaters, he had a taste for unusual music that had led him to this place, through a high school outreach program. According to Johnson, before signing up for shifts at KAOS, he was already a fan of underground music, but it was hard to find those kinds of records locally since the local record stores—Rainy Day Records and Budget Tapes and Records—didn't have strong independent collections at that time. KAOS offered a simple solution to this scarcity, because "it provided me with an opportunity to hear music. There was a lot of music underground that I didn't have access to because it wasn't accessible through normal channels like the radio. And you could read about the music, but there wasn't any way to hear it."[1] Before the Internet and CDs were available, tracking down records in out-of-the-way towns like Olympia posed a problem. "You would just read about the Velvet Underground or the Stooges," Johnson recalls, "but you would have no way to actually hear them." In addition to making these connections, KAOS also managed to do for him what any good college radio station should do: expand his musical palette. "The radio station had a good record library that included a lot of music from the past and present that I was really interested in, so I ate it up," he says. "But I also found a lot of other music that I didn't know about or had been vaguely curious about, soul and reggae and things like that." Johnson would incorporate this mash-up of musical sources, including punk, reggae, soul, and even DC's underground go-go scene, into his own style as he moved on from his DJ gig to making his own music.

Olympia, situated almost exactly halfway between Portland and Seattle, has long had a working-class vibe. Downtown Olympia, an area of just a few blocks, looks like a run-down version of Mayberry: the fifties-style diners are a little worse for wear, the town's numerous bars are filled with drinkers even in the middle of the day, and the oppressive, year-round rainy weather forces people indoors, sometimes giving Olympia's streets the feel of a ghost town. But Olympia is also home to a thriving counterculture, partially thanks to the presence of the Evergreen State College, which was founded in 1967. Evergreen's presence helped downtown Olympia to gain good bookstores, record stores, vintage clothing shops, cafés, and tattoo shops in addition to its more blue-collar establishments. Notorious for the fact that it didn't assign grades but instead relied on narrative evaluations of students, Evergreen boasted an unofficial motto of "Omnia Extares" (let it all hang out), and the campus had a freewheeling culture. The school's small size made for an intimate environment where word of mouth about music and local culture spread quickly, reflecting, in a way, Olympia's long-established creative community. In fact, college radio had played a large part in bringing Olympia's early independent scene together, starting as early as

1975, when Evergreen's radio station, KAOS, initiated a huge emphasis on independent music in its play lists. The program director, John Foster, decreed that 80 percent of the music played on the station had to be from independent labels, calling this the "green line policy"; green marker lines were drawn across independent records to easily distinguish them from those on mainstream labels. According to indie historian and journalist Michael Azerrad, "That whole idea was revolutionary at the time because nobody was making the distinction between major and independent, and after a while he started this addition to the program guide of KAOS which reviewed independent label records and things like that, and that was called *OP*."[2] *OP* became an important zine for small-scale releases of music on cassettes and vinyl, and each issue had a letter theme: *A* contained reviews of artists whose names began with *A*, and so on and so on through the release of *Z*, at which point Foster declared he was done and left to join the Peace Corps.

With KAOS as the auditory voice and *OP* as the written voice of Olympia's nascent punk scene in the late seventies and early eighties, local bands cropped up and started putting on shows. Kill Rock Stars records founder Slim Moon recalled that "in the Olympia rock scene from the moment I moved here, it was always understood that punk rock was about, if you can think of it and it's a good thing to do then just do it. There's no rules."[3] Olympia's geographical isolation from the larger cities of Portland and Seattle helped to ferment its unique take on DIY, and the posthippie education many locals were receiving at Evergreen further encouraged musical experimentation. Steve Fisk, who would later go on to become one of indie music's most important recording engineers, noted that in Olympia in the early indie days, "We were all the older punk rockers or wannabes or whatever that had the cool records, the radio show. John had the magazine, everybody had bands, and we wanted a scene, and we wanted to be, like, legitimate."[4] The problem was, local kids just didn't appear to be interested in local music. Soon enough, however, a fifteen-year-old would enter the picture who would go on to become the so-called mayor of Olympia, bridging the gap between generations. The founder of one of the city's main record labels, producer of festivals, lead singer of one of its most notoriously lo-fi bands, Beat Happening, and an undyingly enthusiastic and quirky local cheerleader, Calvin Johnson was from the beginning the kind of guy who made a noticeable impact on the people around him. "In many ways," says Fisk, "Calvin was like our lone youth."

Born in 1962, Johnson lived in Olympia for the first four years of his life, but it was during his adolescence, when his family spent a few years in Washington DC that he would encounter the DC punk scene, which at the time was home to Minor Threat and other bands that placed a strong emphasis on DIY business practices. DC bands ran their own labels, booked their own shows, and drove themselves on tours. DC punk also placed a lyrical emphasis on straight edge, the no-drinking, no-drugs philosophy that Johnson eventually decided to follow as well. Ian MacKaye of Minor Threat (and later of Fugazi) remembered meeting an unknown, eighteen-year-old Johnson in 1980, and "Calvin had a pink bandana or something tied around his ankle that didn't seem right, particularly given that era."[5] From the beginning, Johnson's take on punk was similar to the idea put across by his idiosyncratic accessorizing: he wasn't interested in playing fast and hard; he was interested in simplicity, innocence, and shaking up accepted ideas about gender norms. After leaving DC Johnson returned to Olympia, and "it really took me a while to get in touch with any kind of underground culture in Olympia. But KAOS was helpful in that way because when I discovered KAOS, I became more aware about punk rock, some of the underground rock that was going on."

Like many other indie music fanatics, Johnson had long harbored the desire to play in a band of his own. Beat Happening started playing as a group around 1983 and included Johnson, Heather Lewis, and Bret Lunsford. Lewis had come to attend Evergreen from suburban New York and had previously played with Johnson in the Supreme Cool Beings and Laura, Heather, and Calvin; Lunsford was from the nearby town of Anacortes,

Washington. None of the three was trained as a musician. With the kind of hubris that would come to characterize many Olympia bands and many of the indie pop bands that followed in their footsteps, Beat Happening figured that the sheer desire to make music was far more important than any kind of perceptible skill. Whereas other punk bands would cover this deficit by playing faster and louder, Beat Happening tuned the volume down and slowed the tempo. The band's lineup consisted of Lunsford on guitar, Lewis on drums, and Johnson on vocals. They didn't own any equipment at the beginning except for a Sears guitar purchased at a thrift store. Lewis would play drums on cardboard boxes, yogurt containers, and any other hard and somewhat resonant object that was lying around. Beat Happening's sound reflected this primitive instrumentation, but its primary characteristic was Johnson's voice: a monotone, deep-sea baritone that came up from under the listener like a car with its bass cranked up creeping down the street, sprawling out over pounding drums and jangling rudimentary guitar riffs. In contrast to Johnson's singing style were Beat Happening's lyrics. Johnson sang about young love, escaping from parents, and other seemingly time-worn troubles, but undercurrents of sexuality and occasional menace ran underneath that placid surface. In one of their best-known songs, "Indian Summer," Johnson sings, "Breakfast in cemetery / Boy tasting wild cherry," a sex-and-death combo opening line that leads into the sweet/sour chorus of "We'll come back for Indian summer / and go our separate ways."[6] Imagine these words sung in a droning deep voice, and you can get a sense of the weird, unorthodox cast to what Beat Happening was doing.

Around the time that he founded Beat Happening, Johnson was also helping out with a local fanzine called *Sub Pop*. Issues of the zine with the motto "Decentralize Pop Culture" came with cassette compilations attached (focused primarily on Northwest bands). Cassettes had popped up on the scene in the eighties and had multiple advantages over vinyl as a recording medium: they were cheaper to produce, they could be dubbed at home rather than sent to a manufacturer for pressing, and they could be customized into mix tapes, to pass the creator's tastes from hand to hand. Since his band needed recordings in order to get gigs and gain a following, the idea of producing cassettes appealed greatly to Johnson. He started his own label, K Records, in 1982, initially focusing on cassette-only releases. According to the K Records Web site, in the early eighties, "The cassette was just beginning to make sense as a format; up to this point, LPs dominated the music consumer landscape. The Walkman and ghetto blaster were just emerging, as cassette technology made giant advances in audio fidelity."[7] For a scene that played with sound as much as it played with image, the idea of a "cassette revolution" was ideal. Tapes might not have lasted as long as records, but they were portable, cheap, and easy to personalize. K releases featured covers with primitive drawings of dancing stick figures and childlike handwriting. With their stripped-down sound, multigender musicians, and the DIY visual aesthetic displayed on their cassettes, Beat Happening was clearly up to something new.

The band steadily gained a strong local following during the next few years, and K Records became a local phenomenon, known for putting out unique records by a dizzying variety of bands. By the late eighties, every local band wanted to be on K, and thanks to Johnson's innate charisma, everyone wanted to be his friend. Fans of the band jokingly referred to themselves as "Calvinists," and a young musician named Kurt Cobain, who had recently started traveling to Olympia from his hometown of Aberdeen to attend shows, was so taken with Johnson that he had the K Records logo (a shield surrounding the letter K) tattooed on his arm. When Beat Happening began recording and touring around the Northwest, however, young audiences were either completely taken with them or completely disgusted. Very few people fell in the middle. Johnson loved to perform a snake-hipped, sexy dance onstage while wearing his usual skin-tight white T-shirts. With his fifties flattop haircut, Johnson was a curiosity at a time when punk's Doc Martens and leather were still signifiers of independence. Was this punk? If so, what the fuck kind of punk was it? Kathleen Hanna recalls that at the time punks in nearby Seattle felt that "K Records was twee music."[8] The fact that the band had a female member complicated matters; female drummers were few and far between, and Lewis's cropped hair and big eyeglasses kept her from being perceived as a sex kitten and also mimicked Johnson's fey style in a reversal of expectations.

Beat Happening's unique take on gender images was only a small part of the local style, which included this kind of complicated gender play, as well as a general openness to the participation of women both onstage and off. Many local women affected a kind of thrift-store librarian chic: smock dresses, black lace-up shoes, home haircuts, and chunky eyeglasses. When they mixed with nerdy cool local male scenesters clad in cardigans, the resulting subculture looked almost nothing like other pockets of indie culture in America, where the eighties punk style of ripped pants and leather was still predominant even into the early nineties. Olympia's isolation and small size had a lot to do with the foundations of this new community; according to Johnson, Olympia has "a definable regional flavor perhaps. But each scene has its own kind of world that it creates and exists in." Johnson also notes that Evergreen's physical distance from the downtown Olympia scene, where most K artists and friends lived and congregated, means that Olympia isn't a real college town like Athens, Georgia. "In terms of underground culture it provides weirdos who were affected by the school and [the sort of person who] sticks around . . . and hangs out downtown," he says of Evergreen. As this new downtown scene grew throughout the late eighties and early nineties, K bands began attracting attention outside of the Pacific Northwest. Some of this attention came from K's International Pop Underground series of seven-inch singles, which Johnson began releasing in 1987. The IPU singles often featured bands that were "closely allied with K and have toured with K artists," including bands from abroad as well as American indie bands making guest appearances on K, which helped strengthen K's reputation as the coolest label around.[9] By 1991, the K network was truly international, and to celebrate their friendships with artists outside of Olympia, Johnson and his business partner, Candice Peterson, decided to throw a party.

The International Pop Underground Convention took place over a week in August 1991. With a relatively simple game plan, Johnson and Peterson thought up a list of bands they liked and asked them to come to Olympia and play. Since K had released singles by so many indie bands and so many bands had collaborated and toured with K artists, most of the bands they asked agreed to play. When it came to the actual logistics, though, things were more complicated due to the fact that everything had to be arranged and booked via mail and phone. As Peterson stated, "it was really hard work."[10] But Johnson remained laid-back about the planning of the event. "It never occurred to me that it wouldn't happen," he told filmmaker Heather Rose Dominic. "I'd just assumed that it would. And pretty much everyone that I wanted to have play, I just had to say, hey, I'm doing this thing, and everyone's like yeah."[11] Among the "yeahs" who answered Johnson's calls were some of the most significant independent bands of the eighties and early nineties: Fugazi, Nation of Ulysses, Mecca Normal, the Fastbacks, the Spinanes, L7, and many more. Events that echoed K's quirky-cool style happened in tandem with the music shows: a cake walk, a *Planet of the Apes* movie marathon, and a round of musical chairs set the tone for the thousand or so guests who poured into downtown Olympia. The word about the convention spread via zines, pen pals, and college radio shows, the same indie network that had been building for years. And the entire week's operation was pure DIY: everyone pitched in, so there was no hired security at shows, and everything was staffed by volunteers who were loosely organized by Peterson and Johnson, including Fugazi's Ian MacKaye, who sat and took tickets one night at the Capital Theater. Years later, Nitsu Abebe summarized much of the spirit of the IPU convention and of the Olympia scene when he wrote that "the music being made wasn't even necessarily the point; the real joy was creating a pop world that was decentralized, local, personal, and handmade, one where a primitive bedroom recording could be enjoyed not just by your friends but by a whole community."[12] One particular night at the IPU, however, would go on to leave the most lasting impression for the performers and attendants.

*

"Girl Night," an abbreviated version of the event's full title, "Love Rock Revolution Girl Style Now," was a show organized by K musician Lois Maffeo along with Michelle Noel, a KAOS DJ, and Margaret Doherty, the owner of an Olympia vintage clothing store. Conceived as a chance to give women the main stage, it held a prime spot on August 20, the first night of the IPU convention. Even in a female-inclusive community like Olympia's, female musicians were still few and far between, and Doherty recalled in 2001 that "Girl Night" "was really about getting the young women in the audience who were sitting on the edge of, 'Maybe I'm gonna play in a band; maybe I'm gonna pick up a guitar; maybe I'm gonna write a song about how I feel'—to make them go, 'Yeah, I think I am, 'cause it's legitimate, and I don't have to do it well right from the start.'"[13] Bands that night ranged from the musically bare-bones Mecca Normal to the darkly melodic Spinanes; rowdy, primitive-sounding Bratmobile; heavy metal–influenced 7 Year Bitch; and a brand-new band called Heavens to Betsy, whose round-cheeked and banshee-voiced lead singer, Corin Tucker, would go on to form the influential all-female band Sleater-Kinney. Women took their turns at the mike delivering manifestos, spoken word, and a capella music performances. For many in the audience and onstage, the evening catalyzed the recognition of a nascent community that had begun to cohere in Olympia's scene. If the IPU was a spark that helped ignite the forthcoming flurry of mainstream interest in indie music, "Love Rock Revolution Girl Style Now" was the bomb that exploded long-standing notions about women's roles within the indie scene, setting off a series of similar events and clearing the way through the twee sweetness of K culture for one of the most vital and often misunderstood underground movements of the nineties: riot grrrl.

In order to understand how riot grrrl evolved in Olympia, it's crucial to acknowledge that before riot grrrl existed, women had long been relegated to supporting roles in the independent music community. Madigan Shive of the band Bonfire Madigan described an all too familiar scenario from a typical punk show when she recalled that "there would be girls all around the corners holding these jackets, and there would be boys with their shirts off playing the hardcore music, and I remember hearing another person there go, those are the coat hangers."[14] Even pioneering female musicians like Kira Roessler of Black Flag and Kim Gordon of Sonic Youth were bass players, not lead guitarists or lead singers, which forced them into the background behind charismatic male performers. Women did do important work behind the scenes in indie, running clubs, music labels, and mail-order services, writing for zines, and publishing books, but within the realm of music they still assumed primarily supportive roles. The violence that had become commonplace at punk shows in the eighties may be partly to blame for this; Corin Tucker recalled that "it was hard to go to shows and be a girl, going to shows was a really violent atmosphere to be in if you were a woman."[15] This kind of violence may not have been as much of an issue at a Beat Happening show as it was at a Black Flag show in LA, but even women in Olympia felt they were being shunned by their male counterparts, especially when it came to playing in a band.

Another trailblazing mind behind the riot grrrl movement also found inspiration in Olympia's subculture. Kathleen Hanna had arrived in Olympia in the late eighties, another aspiring Evergreen artist but one who loved to jump into the fray. "I wanted to live downtown—I was from Portland, and you know, not a big city, but kind of a city, and I wanted to be downtown, as opposed to living in the woods like most people." Her new digs put Hanna into the orbit of Calvin Johnson and the rest of the K records crowd, and she soon found inspiration in their DIY attitude. "I actually got to see the music scene," she recalls, "and for me if there's not much to do, you have to make your own entertainment . . . there's not art shows you want to go see so if you want to see good art you've got to bring it there and make it happen." Hanna arrived in Olympia with a background in feminism already in place. Her mother had volunteered assisting victims of domestic violence when Hanna was a child, and had taken her once to a rally where Gloria Steinem spoke; both Hanna and her mother were fans of Steinem's *Ms.* magazine. These early forays into gender politics influenced all of Hanna's creative work. As a photography student at Evergreen, Hanna found that even in Evergreen's enlightened environment, certain kinds of art could still cause a ruckus. Her photo exhibit about sexism was taken down by school administrators, which led to her "first foray into activism," as Hanna tussled with Evergreen over the censorship of her art.[16] Eventually, she and a group of friends opened their own art gallery, Reko Muse, in downtown Olympia. Money was tight, so Hanna recruited local bands to play at the gallery to help raise funds. "Everything was so immediate," she reflects. "It was 'Oh, we need to raise money for this thing we're doing. Let's start a band and have a benefit.'" Shows at Reko Muse put her in touch with a number of local musicians, including Tobi Vail, who was producing a zine called *Jigsaw* and playing in a number of different bands. Hanna, Vail, and their friend Kathi Wilcox soon began collaborating on a zine called *Bikini Kill*, and by early 1991 the three women, along with guitarist Billy Karren, were playing together in a band of the same name.

Bikini Kill's approach to music, according to Hanna, was highly colored by the locally espoused idea that musicianship mattered much less than passion; in fact, one of Beat Happening's slogans was "learn NOT to play your instrument." "That's all it was," Hanna recalls, "taking the idea of punk rock and not thinking of punk rock as a genre, but thinking of punk rock as an idea, and then you can apply it to different styles of music you're making up." Just as Mike Watt of the Minutemen thought of punk as a musical objection to the highly skilled arena rock bands of the seventies, Bikini Kill and other local female bands believed that simply playing an instrument was the most significant gesture of defiance they could make. And local musicians provided the inspiration for that. "Beat Happening is an incredibly sexy band," Hanna asserts. "What they sounded like to me was incredibly sexy, and I wanted to be a part of it. And it was also the thing of demystifying rock and roll—I mean, I went to shows when I was in high school too; in Portland, I went to see hardcore speed metal and reggae—and because I went to small shows, I didn't go to stadium shows, I already had this idea that the musicians weren't a thousand million miles away, and in Olympia that got brought home even more because they were literally five feet in front of you, and people played at parties at people's houses, and the separation between you as an audience member and them as a musician was so small already, that it wasn't a huge step to be on the stage. [It was easy to think that] we need a band; we don't have a band; well we're gonna have to be the band."

From the beginning, Bikini Kill was bound to make an impression. All of its members were charismatic and fiercely intelligent despite their amateurish musicianship. "The fact that we weren't taking guitar lessons and getting really good before we let anybody see us was really perceived as the hugest 'fuck you,'" Hanna recalls. "What I think was remarkable about us was the fact that we were women and we were doing that, [which] made it ten times harder. Because the other thing that we were surrounded with was [that] there's already the stigma that you're a total fake-ass if you're a woman. The fact that we were saying, not only are we women who are singing militant feminist lyrics, but also we're not gonna play by your rules, and we're not gonna be oppositional to the idea that we suck before we even started." The zines that Hanna, Vail, Wilcox, and others in the community were putting out reflected their unique take on being female in the male-dominated worlds of indie and punk music, where DIY took on a whole new context as it was enacted by women. Bikini Kill's lyrics—provocative, in your face, and occasionally confessional—celebrated the band's unique point of view. Hanna recalls that Evergreen, where "the education was all about making things happen yourself," had a big influence on her wanting to express herself through music: "I feel like that [atmosphere] at least for me and some of my friends really influenced me to think, 'Oh, there should be like a girl band singing about feminism—why isn't there? We should make that happen.'"

Bikini Kill recorded a demo tape fairly quickly so that they could begin booking gigs, and their self-titled EP was released in 1992 on the Kill Rock Stars label, run by Slim Moon, a local musician and man about town. Moon remarks in a Kill Rock Stars time line that at that point, the label was in its infancy, but Calvin Johnson, unafraid of competition and happy to expand the playing field, was prodding him to start releasing albums. Moon was unprepared when Bikini Kill approached him about doing a recording, but "they felt they could trust me because I was their friend. I didn't know they were going to get into this vortex of riot grrrl popularity with national press and everything."[17] After the release of their first EP, Bikini Kill began gaining bigger audiences, and they frequently collaborated with Bratmobile, a band from Oregon with a zine of its own called *Girl Germs*. After seeing one or both of these bands perform, more young women became inspired to start bands and zines of their own. Riot grrrl represented the first time in the history of indie culture that women joined forces to try and change some of the status quo sexism that's been a part of women's lives for centuries and has also infected indie throughout its history. The second issue of the *Bikini Kill* zine included Hanna's "Riot Grrrl Manifesto," which made eighteen declarative statements about the purpose of the movement, including the idea that "we wanna make it easier for girls to see/hear each other's work so that we can share strategies . . ."; "we are patently aware that the punk rock 'you can do anything idea' is crucial to the coming angry grrrl rock revolution"; and "we are angry at a society that tells us girl=dumb, girl=bad, girl=weak."[18] Hanna's manifesto helped inspire women to start riot grrrl groups in their hometowns. Zine networks made it possible for women to communicate about both political and personal issues, and chapter meetings where women could get together and hash out ideas for instigating change proliferated across the United States and Europe. By

1992, enough women were participating in riot grrrl bands, zines, and chapters that the first riot grrrl convention was held in Washington DC. Yet Hanna and other women involved in the movement resisted giving it a simplistic definition. They felt that distilling riot grrrl down to a pat statement didn't reflect the diversity of women involved in it, and they were also aware that the more simplistic the movement appeared to be from the outside, the more easily it might be co-opted and distorted.

Reception to Bikini Kill's first album was the beginning of a series of mixed blessings for the group. Their tour of the United Kingdom with the band Huggy Bear was hugely successful and garnered both bands attention from the powerful UK music media. By the time they returned to Olympia, the cozy familiarity of their community had turned into something a bit more sinister. "It was really strange for us to go places, and there's such a mythology about Olympia as an area," Hanna remembers, "that we used to open every show with 'We're Bikini Kill from Olympia, Washington,' because we were really proud of it, and we were also really into the idea of kind of addressing the thing that all good bands aren't from LA or New York." That kind of regional thinking was par for the course for Vail, who had been born and raised in Olympia, and it felt comfortable enough for Hanna as well. But "people in a small town talk all the time, so it was really hard to deal with people coming up to you in the grocery store and saying really mean shit to you."

The mainstream press had latched on to Bikini Kill as the prime example of the riot grrrl movement made flesh. Part of the band's mixed reception at home had to do with that attention. Though they openly resisted being labeled as the leaders of riot grrrl, the band members were still singled out in the increasing number of articles being written about the phenomenon that had captured the minds of a sizable contingent of young women across the nation, including features in unlikely magazines such as *Newsweek, Seventeen,* and *Sassy.* The *Newsweek* feature was particularly controversial because it was the first national article to focus on the movement, but it made sweeping, stereotypical generalizations about the type of girls attracted to the scene ("They've set out to make the world safe for their kind of girlhood: sexy, assertive and loud"), and ultimately dismissed riot grrrl as a passing fad for sheltered kids ("There's no telling whether [their] catchy passion . . . will evaporate when it hits the adult real world").[19] Nonetheless, Olympia remained in a kind of bubble, and locals didn't pay much mind to what was going on in the outside world. "What really changed things," says Hanna, "was when Olympia got a magazine store downtown, and people all of a sudden knew we were famous—this was pre-Internet. So all of a sudden there's this fucking magazine store, the bane of my existence—you could go to England and be in every single magazine, and no one knew. Then all of a sudden, the magazine store came, and then everyone knew that we were big for like our ten seconds in England." When locals in Olympia who already harbored resentment about the band simply because they were women got wind of media attention like this, it made Olympia feel a lot less friendly than it had in the warm and fuzzy days of the IPU convention. Hanna recalls that after touring, "We came back and everyone hated us. We had new shoes on, but at the same time because we were feminists, it made people's anger about the fame even more exaggerated."

The negative attention didn't stop at home. Though they did receive a fair amount of press, Bikini Kill always inspired a range of reactions from critics. Even in a mostly positive review of their first album in the *Village Voice*, Charles Aaron referred to Hanna as the band's "lead ranter" and claimed that the scenario of a girl waking up to her innate rights in the song "Double Dare Ya" "exists only in the minds of a handful of boho progeny with access to copy machines and feminist reading lists."[20] But the song's lyrics are actually straightforward: Hanna sings, "You're a big girl now / you've got no reason not to fight."[21] Not many women require a degree in women's studies to understand Hanna's message. Aaron goes on, claiming that the band was "pretentious enough to shout about 'revolution' and then Xerox it," and they "savvily provoke the media hype with headline ready slogans."[22]

In the media glare, Bikini Kill's lyrics could sometimes come across as reductive, but the narrative of riot grrrl—the story that almost every woman experiences of being marginalized, silenced, and objectified—was a story that needed to be told. In the end, the mixed blessings of fame didn't hinder the fact that the movement's message of female empowerment was massively appealing to thousands of young women. By the midnineties, there were thousands of "girl zines" being produced in America and abroad, and along with the zines, thousands of girls were picking up instruments and learning to play for the first time. Carla Costa, the former publisher of *Kitchen Sink* magazine and a longtime friend of mine, recalls that she discovered riot grrrl while growing up near Providence, Rhode Island, "probably around 1993. I was thirteen going on fourteen, and I'd heard about random bands through other bands. Listening to Sonic Youth and Babes in Toyland, I started to get a sense that there was a network, especially with Sonic Youth who had antennas out into different genres."[23] Carla and her high school best friend went into the local record store looking for a *Pussy Whipped* album they'd read about in *Ray Gun* magazine, and they were greeted by a clerk who took one look at them with their bleached hair and thrift-store dresses and said, "Hey, riot grrrls." "We didn't know what we were," she says. "We had the barrettes because of Babes in Toyland" (whose singer Kat Bjelland created the "kinder whore" style popular with indie girls at the time: baby doll dresses or vintage nightgowns worn over ripped tights, Mary Jane shoes, runny mascara and eyeliner, and matted, bleached white hair studded with randomly placed barrettes). Soon after that, Carla discovered the United Kingdom's Huggy Bear via pen pals in England and Ireland, then started taking guitar lessons along with her friend and making zines "because there were no cool people in our town." Networking via mail became a crucial means of getting in touch with other riot grrrls. "We started getting a lot of things through the mail," she says. "Once you got the Bikini Kill records, you sent away for the KRS catalogue," so you could find similar bands, "which led you to the K records catalogue."

Even as Carla was discovering the growing international network of riot grrrls, she was aware that its moment might already be passing. "We felt like we came in at a point when it was the last time that you could really find a subculture," she recalls. "You had to send away for mail-order catalogs. It was still a club, and we had to work hard to access the information." The moment of transition from hard-won network to a lost cause is easy for Carla to pinpoint: "I had a definitive sense of when riot grrrl was over, and it started with the 'angry women in rock' covers," which were soon a common sight in glossy magazines like *Rolling Stone* and *Spin*, and "Courtney Love distorting everything it was. Mainstream media had no way to distinguish her or Liz Phair or Meredith Brooks from riot grrrl. You started to see aesthetics of riot grrrl being warped, like the image and persona and theories became whitewashed and spread too thin." Carla recalls with irony the sight of angry young rocker girls appearing on an episode of Oprah Winfrey's talk show, and "the episode of Roseanne's sitcom where the Sandra Bernhard character took everyone to a Bikini Kill show." By 1992, aware of the growing distortions, many riot grrrls refused to talk to the mainstream press, but that didn't stop hungry media from further exploiting the scene for its shock value. "All of a sudden, we were seeing people we knew in every magazine across the country," Bratmobile's Allison Wolfe said. "It was kind of exciting, but it also felt threatening."[24] Carla has similarly mixed feelings about riot grrrl's crossover. "When the exploitation happened with riot grrrl, it was such a loss because indie was such a boys' club. There wasn't going to be a way for girls to have their own club anymore." In the wake of this kind of unwanted attention, Bikini Kill left Olympia for a new home in Washington DC in 1992 and split up a few years later.

Riot grrrl's explosion into the American mainstream happened almost in tandem with the nationwide emergence of another Northwest music scene, one that seemed from the beginning to court the attention that riot grrrl was attempting to shun. Thirty days after the IPU convention, Nirvana's *Nevermind* was released on major label Geffen Records, and any focus that had been paid to Olympia paled in comparison to the floodlights suddenly shining on Seattle. Nirvana's first home, the Sub Pop label, was run by Bruce Pavitt, an Evergreen graduate who, along with his partner Jonathan Poneman, had conceived the label as an offshoot of his zine of the same name. Although Calvin Johnson had at one point helped out with the *Sub Pop* zine when it was based in Olympia, Sub Pop the label and K Records had almost nothing in common except for the fact that they were both based out of Washington, and Johnson and Pavitt had worked on the zine together. K releases looked like homemade objects, with their line drawings of cats and hand-penned liner notes. Sub Pop singles and LPs, on the other hand, helped promote the label's growing mythology of the Northwest mad woodsman-cum-rocker, with their striking black and white photos of flailing, long-haired dudes rocking the fuck out on stages with cans of beer at their feet. K was gender neutral; Sub Pop was balls out. The music on Sub Pop further emphasized the label's stoned aggression, focusing on bands like Mudhoney, TAD, Screaming Trees, and Nirvana—all noisy, sludgy, and dirty. At some point, this mix was labeled "grunge" (a term first used by the notorious rock critic Lester Bangs in the seventies), and that term, along with the savvy marketing of the label's owners, added up to a package no label A&R guy could resist. Sure enough, Geffen led Nirvana away in 1990. Pavitt and Poneman courted this kind of attention with what could be perceived as a tongue-in-cheek sense of humor, but their ability to package and hype their label demonstrated a seriously canny sense of timing. "There was a real indie ethic in the eighties that you weren't supposed to have hit records," Pavitt said in 1996, "but we admired labels like Motown and their hit factory mentality."[25] Seattle and Northwest bands that loosely fit into the prototypical grunge mode were quickly discovered by desperate record executives looking to cash in on Nirvana's breakthrough success, and for a few years in the early nineties, grunge eclipsed nearly every other form of music, spawning films, fawning features in glossy magazines, and even fashion in the form of designer Marc Jacobs's 1992 "grunge" collection. If the sight of Kate Moss mincing down a runway in the Seattle uniform of flannel shirt, torn jeans, and a knit hat wasn't strange enough, the spectacle of a bewigged Matt Dillon strumming a guitar and playing a grunge musician in Cameron Crowe's 1992 film *Singles* was enough to make an indie musician puke.

Nirvana's success—whether the band members honestly enjoyed it or not—drew a line in the sand for the independent culture of the early nineties. No longer exclusively the territory of the tuned-in and networked few, indie's exposure to the mainstream turned what had long been signifiers of difference into easily identifiable marketed objects. Fifty-thousand-dollar cars sported bumper stickers reading "GIRLS RULE!" and the Spice Girls sang a diluted message of riot grrrl's rage for teen audiences who had never heard of Kathleen Hanna. Pretorn jeans were available at the Gap, and Manic Panic hair dye (long the choice of blue-, pink-, and purple-haired punks) made its way out of the bondage-gear shop and into the corner drugstore. The scenario Operation Ivy's Jesse Michaels described of being on tour and walking around town looking for the other punk rock kid who might be able to provide a place to crash became less and less feasible as punk and indie style, reincarnated as grunge, became just another identity for people to try on and reject. A subsequent wave of cynicism swept through the independent community. You were more likely to run into a frat meathead at a Screaming Trees show than you were a fellow record-collecting geek, and that scared away many people who had grown accustomed to the notion of indie shows as a safe, insular space.

It would be too easy and too reductive, however, to argue that grunge killed indie. It didn't. If it had, indie would not exist today, and it would not have begun its transformation that occurred in the wake of the inevitable loss of cultural interest in grunge. Grunge may have had its appeal, and some of the albums produced by Sub Pop in that era are fantastic records, but its musical style was too inadequate to evolve over time, and Sub Pop was unable to sustain the hype. Pavitt left the label in 1996, and two years later a lack of funds forced the label to seriously downsize in staff and space. As the nineties unspooled amid a muggy mess of circumstances, including the repercussions of twelve straight years of Republican presidencies, an economic recession, Operation Desert Storm, Rodney King's beating and the subsequent urban rioting that followed the acquittal of his Los Angeles Police Department assaulters, the soundtrack of countercultural anger had to change. And it did: hip-hop's urgent, urban beats and furious lyrical assaults seemed much more relevant to the zeitgeist. But where did that leave punk, indie pop, grunge, postpunk, and the ever-multiplying musical subgenres that constituted indie? What about the zines, comics, and independent publishers that had proliferated throughout the eighties and nineties? Did they cease to matter? Of course not. But in the wake of its emergence into the mainstream, indie was forced to reinvent itself, and, for a period, that reinvention meant that it needed to stop looking outward and to start looking inward, where all ideas begin.

seven

Brighten the Corners: The Reinvention of Indie Rock

*I don't understand what they mean
and I could really give a fuck.*

Pavement, "Range Life"

In 1991—the same year of Olympia's IPU convention and *Nevermind*'s release—filmmaker Richard Linklater made a movie called *Slacker*, starring a number of nonactors from Linklater's hometown of Austin, Texas, including a few indie musicians as cast members. *Slacker* is essentially a film about nothing, but its nothingness also predicted the coming changes in indie rock. The characters wander around Austin discussing UFOs, the Kennedy assassination conspiracy theories, and Madonna's Pap smear. Like many twenty-somethings who were living through a prolonged recession and post–Cold War ennui, the characters in *Slacker* are dealing with being "the first generation that were not better off than their parents," according to the film's cinematographer Lee Daniel.[1] Cast member Kalman Spelletich recalled that "we'd just come out of eight years of Reagan, and we were really fucking bummed out. People felt disempowered, like they were standing at the edge, screaming, and we don't have a big enough bullhorn because we don't have the money to buy the thing."[2] With the release of Douglas Coupland's novel *Generation X: Tales for an Accelerated Culture*, Nirvana's *Nevermind*, and *Slacker* all in the same year, America was suddenly interested in understanding the boomer spawn who were making this art, and it seemed like they might not be as interested in reinventing society as their parents had been. However, many young indie artists—Linklater and his cast and crew included—found that life on the creative and financial margins of society suited them just fine. The film's production designer Deborah Pastor remembered that she and her Austin friends "were constantly having to explain why you were going outside the fold, and [why] it wasn't a bad place to be—it was the place to be, because these people were smarter and funnier and thinking farther."[3]

The indie rockers who emerged in the aftermath of grunge's hype came across as similarly low-key. They didn't take it for granted that they recorded for labels that allowed them creative freedom, but they didn't always make a big deal about it. When Seattle's scene flamed out, what indie bands wanted to do was play around, make music on their own terms, and reinvent indie music as something low-fi and DIY—to take it back to its punk roots but with a different kind of beat and a less strident lyrical flow. Yet even the most stalwartly indie bands of the latter half of the nineties faced complicated new ideas about how indie was being defined. Even if they were signed to an indie label, odds were that the label was partially owned by a major or distributed by one. If it wasn't, the crappy economy made it harder than ever for their backers to make ends meet. Nascent underground bands—the kind that had struggled for years for even a mention in the pages of a hard-to-find zine—were now being discovered by millions in the pages of *Spin* or the *Village Voice* just as their recording careers were getting started. As the information age began to take control of our cultural communication, nothing stayed underground for very long. The changes in sound, ethics, and ideals that shaped indie music around the turn of the twenty-first century had a profound impact on indie rock: the term that evolved to encompass independently made postpunk music in the nineties and today. Nowhere is that impact more prominent than in the story of Pavement, a band that inherited indie's freedom but chose not to make a big deal about it, preferring to engage in sonic experimentation and identity play, and the Silver Jews, whose charismatic and reclusive leader David Berman would become indie's poet laureate. Along with these bands, their labels, Drag City and Matador Records, would stand as polar opposite examples of how indie music could be disseminated to an audience. In the indie music community, it was high time for a change, but that change would prove to be complicated. In the midst of the changing landscape of indie music, punk's anger and frustration, which had been so radically reinvented in Olympia and Seattle, was being supplanted by sounds and lyrics that were low-fi, apolitical, and lackadaisical. Punk still existed, but it spun off into its own scene, with its own sounds and rules, and indie rock began to evolve.

Among the many people who were creating this new genre was songwriter and guitarist Stephen Malkmus, whose band Pavement was preparing to release its first full-length album, *Slanted and Enchanted*. Malkmus and his childhood friend Scott Kannberg had begun Pavement as a studio band in their hometown of Stockton, California, which Kannberg has described as "devoid of any cultural or musical significance."[4] Malkmus's description of his hometown supports that notion, sounding like something from a post–*American Graffiti* vision of the American West: "Stockton's got dirt-weed and noise coke and people cruising down the strip looking for fights," he said in 2004.[5] In the tradition of many other bands who came from similarly outlying places, Pavement's sound was the product of multiple influences that might not have collided if its core members had grown up in more sophisticated environments. Both Malkmus and Kannberg started off as fans of the bombastic arena rock band Kiss before they discovered punk. The LA punk scene of the eighties—including bands like Black Flag, the Minutemen, Flipper, and the

Germs—had a particularly powerful impact on them, along with the category-defying band Devo, which Kannberg said "changed the landscape for me," and the UK postpunk bands the Fall and Gang of Four.[6] Malkmus and Kannberg played in a couple of short-lived bands while they were still in high school, but Malkmus soon departed for the University of Virginia in Charlottesville, where the missing pieces of Pavement and the beginnings of the Silver Jews would fall into place.

Though UVA is best known to outsiders for its basketball teams and business school, it also has historically had a decent-sized music scene. Like Olympia, Washington, Athens, Georgia, and Chapel Hill, North Carolina, Charlottesville was one among a number of towns that were spawning what was beginning to be known as "college rock": indie rock made by brainy, curious people drawn to schools in smallish towns with good bookstores, coffeehouses, and clubs. To the advantage of Malkmus and countless other musicians, all of these college towns were also home to excellent college radio stations. Calvin Johnson of Beat Happening has described how much of an impact being a DJ for Evergreen State's KAOS had on his own musical development, and Malkmus had a similar experience at UVA's WTJU in the late eighties. By that time, college radio stations were finally moving away from playing the same stuff as mainstream radio and were becoming a viable outlet for indie bands. Mike Watt recalls that "the college radio stations were actually the first part [to change] when the campuses started to change" and became more indie friendly in the early nineties.[7]

Robert Nastanovich, station manager at WTJU, a self-described noisemaker who grew up in nearby Richmond, Virginia, was more interested in going to shows than attending classes. Another UVA student, David Berman, often turned up in the same places, "a ringleader and a party machine," Nastanovich recalled, "so smart that he did well in school with minimal effort."[8] Malkmus, Nastanovich, and Berman would meet and form a couple of short-lived bands before Malkmus returned to Stockton, where he reunited with Kannberg and met an off-kilter aging hippie named

Gary Young, who played the drums and owned a recording studio. Malkmus, Kannberg, and Young got together and recorded enough songs for an EP that they called *Slay Tracks*, which they self-released in 1989 under the Pavement moniker (copies of this rare EP now sell for hundreds of dollars). *Slay Tracks* found its way to a New York bass player named Mark Ibold, and via Ibold to the rising UK band the Wedding Present, who in turn recorded a version of Pavement's song "Box Elder," and performed it on John Peel's highly influential UK radio show. The Wedding Present never secured Pavement's permission to record the song; nonetheless, along with the positive reviews *Slay Tracks* was getting in zines, the cover brought Pavement a degree of attention they hadn't been expecting. With its illegible cover text and the band members identified only as "S.M." (Malkmus) and "Spiral Stairs" (Kannberg), *Slay Tracks* seemed to deliberately defy interpretation, a sign of things to come in Pavement's development as a band.

Pavement recorded another EP, *Demolition Plot J-7* in 1990, which attracted the attention of Drag City records, a fledgling indie label. Founded by Dan Koretzky and Dan Osborn in Chicago, Drag City used the profits from its first release by the band Royal Trux to fund Pavement's next EP, *Perfect Sound Forever*. Malkmus soon moved to New York (New Jersey, actually, but he worked as a security guard at Manhattan's Whitney Museum), where he reunited with Nastanovich and Berman. The three of them began recording tracks "on a Walkman-style tape recorder," and when Berman got to know Drag City's Koretzky, according to Nastanovich, "He convinced [Koretzky] that we were a palpable lo-fi act."[9] They called this new band the Silver Jews, slang for blond Jewish people, and played together in the evenings after work. As Pavement's reputation began to grow, the Silver Jews were often described as a Pavement side project, but it is Berman's distinctive songwriting, guitar playing, and singing that characterizes the band's music. Berman tried to play down the connection by listing his Pavement bandmates under pseudonyms, calling Malkmus "Hazel Figurine," continuing in the tradition of obfuscation and identity play that had begun on the early Pavement releases. The Silver Jews released two EPs on Drag City before Berman left New York to pursue a graduate degree in creative writing at the University of Massachusetts. By 1994, the Silver Jews would reunite and release their first LP, *Starlight Walker*, just as Pavement's fame crested.

Pavement's real leap forward came with the release of *Slanted and Enchanted* in 1992. Their Drag City recordings had gotten them good notices in fanzines and big magazines like *Spin* and *Rolling Stone*, but Pavement felt they were outgrowing their tiny record label and tried to arrange a deal with one of the bigger indie labels of the time, like SST or Sub Pop. In the end, they wound up on another small indie label but one that would soon eclipse its humble beginnings, thanks to the bands it represented and the canny sensibilities of its founders. Matador Records was founded in 1989 by Chris Lombardi, who was joined a year later by *Conflict* zine writer and former head of indie label Homestead Records, Gerard Cosloy. Cosloy possessed an uncanny ability to find bands that boasted both indie credibility and commercial appeal; a major label A&R executive called Cosloy "a rare visionary" who has been "right since he was 18 years old."[10] In the year before *Slanted and Enchanted*'s release, indie labels like Matador were facing a distribution crisis, because Rough Trade, the main distributor for many indie labels, had gone bankrupt. Major labels swooping in and cherry-picking hip bands also hurt indie labels. In 1991, Cosloy told the *New York Times* that major labels were "vultures" and that "they're eager to take the lead from the indies, and when major labels start taking bands away, there's nothing left to support the indie network."[11] SST founder and former Black Flag guitarist Greg Ginn was similarly bitter: "A lot of groups went chasing after that [major label] dream," including SST's own Sonic Youth, "and it produced worse music without reaching the goal of selling more records."[12]

In this unstable climate, a release by a critically acclaimed but still mostly anonymous band from Stockton/New Jersey/Charlottesville might not have seemed like a big deal, but *Slanted and Enchanted* had leaked to the media long before its official release.

Leaks are commonplace today because of file sharing, but back in the early nineties when everything was on tapes and vinyl (and the occasional CD), the album's early arrival gave critics a chance to start peeing their pants about it ahead of time. *Spin* reviewed the album in advance of its release and declared that "Pavement makes things happen where nothing happened before" and implied that the band's mix of cutting-edge sound and bicoastal group of semianonymous musicians was "too perfect" and had been "charted out in some indie rock boardroom."[13] By this time, Pavement had added a second drummer, Steve West, to supplement Young's sometimes erratic playing (Young eventually left the band), and bassist Mark Ibold was also a full-time member, so the band had a fuller and more rounded sound that was developing into a unique melding of classic rock, noise rock, and punk. Robert Christgau of the *Village Voice,* another advocate for the band's evolving style, described it as "noise [that] doesn't give up without a fight . . . and tune [that] digs where it's coming from."[14] Many critics commented on Pavement's image, trying to puzzle out what it all meant. The band members looked like frat guys, except for Malkmus, who had good cheekbones and sported a smart-guy smirk. The fact that nobody in the band looked like a rock star or acted like one onstage—even in the Calvin Johnson "I'm just goofing around" mode—further complicated critics' jobs of slotting Pavement into a category. Prior iterations of indie rock had been so much about image, style, and putting a point across to the audience about politics, identity, or independence itself that these college-educated guys in polo shirts presented a conundrum that was terribly hard to figure out.

For audiences who were discovering Pavement, the bottom line was that the music was good. It was also different from anything else under the indie rock flag at the time, and Malkmus's lyrics made up a big part of that difference. Malkmus has often been compared to the avant-garde poet John Ashbery because, like Ashbery's poems, his lyrics are anything but linear or preachy. They play with image, metaphor, abstraction, and language in a hyperliterate manner that hadn't been heard before outside of

Dylan and a handful of other songwriters. *Slanted and Enchanted* starts off with the song "Summer Babe," which in any other hands would be yet another anthem to a briefly glanced at cutie, but in Malkmus's words turns into a wistful paean to a girl who's "eating her fingers like they're just another meal" while she's mixing drinks on the "protein delta strip."[15] The liner notes to Pavement albums added to the layers of obfuscation in Malkmus's wordplay, because they were typically hand scrawled and almost illegible. Malkmus, however, was direct about this propensity for confounding his audience. In the song "In the Mouth a Desert," he sings, "Pretend the table is a trust knot we'll put our labels down," and "wait to hear my words, they're diamond sharp," a combination that invites the listener to take a moment and listen to Malkmus like a friend, like one of us, while at the same time the "diamond sharp" wordplay guarantees second-guessing. This back-and-forth combination of openness and mystery would become one of Pavement's hallmarks.

With the advance critical hype over *Slanted and Enchanted*, Matador had to scramble to ship enough copies to meet the demand. When thirty thousand records arrived at the label's New York office, so did the sheriff, prepared to evict the company for unpaid rent.[16] Matador met the bill, but it was a painful reminder of how tenuous the whole indie record business really was. As a result of fatigue from trying to make ends meet, in 1993, Matador brokered a deal with Atlantic Records. Under the terms, Atlantic would assume responsibility for distributing and marketing a select few Matador artists, including Pavement, Liz Phair, and the Fall. Phair's 1993 album *Exile in Guyville* had been a breakthrough indie album, selling two hundred thousand copies, a pittance in today's market but an impressive number for an indie label at the time. Phair's and Pavement's success gave Matador the leverage to pursue the success that Cosloy and Lombardi eventually admitted they had always wanted. "People think we're an elitist label that doesn't want to sell any records," Cosloy told the *Los Angeles Times*, and Lombardi chimed in, "We've always wanted to sell as many records as we possibly could."[17] Matador's decision to sign with Atlantic may have been a strategy for survival, but the move looked to some like a crass bid for cash, in the same vein as Sub Pop's tongue-in-cheek motto "World Domination" was an off-putting notion to indie stalwarts who were still hand selling their music on cassettes. Matador did its best to downplay the relationship with Atlantic even as it milked the major label for cash, and today its Web site says explicitly that the album had "no Atlantic logos ever on packaging." Robert Christgau made a prediction for Pavement's future in light of these behind-the-scenes maneuvers when he reviewed their *Watery, Domestic* EP in 1993 and wrote that "nobody this good stays in Indieland forever."[18]

Pavement's next release, *Crooked Rain, Crooked Rain*, in 1994, could be perceived as the band's biggest bid for mainstream success. Instead of sounding like UK indie favorites the Fall, an accusation Pavement had dealt with after *Slanted and Enchanted*, *Crooked Rain* sounded more like Led Zeppelin—arguably one of the least indie bands of all time. "I like the purity," Malkmus said of classic rock. "Rock and roll should be about cigarettes and alcohol and fun and shagging and making out and stuff like that."[19] More than any other Pavement album, *Crooked Rain, Crooked Rain* is top-down, pedal-to-the-metal, balls-out rock (a friend of mine once described it as a "great album for road trips"), and it reflects Malkmus's admittedly middle-class roots. "I mean," he reflected, "we are nice suburban boys in the end," and nice suburban boys of his generation venerated classic rock as much as they venerated punk.[20] This attitude stands in huge contrast to the punks of the eighties, who hated arena rock bands and constantly mocked and disparaged them. Pavement's bombastic rock and guitar solos, however, were yet another sign of how much indie had changed since then. Audiences accepted this shift in Pavement's sound as part of their evolution as opposed to seeing it as a betrayal of some set of values or ethics they had never really preached about in the first place. When Pavement talked shit about postgrunge poseur bands the Smashing Pumpkins and

Stone Temple Pilots in its song "Range Life" ("Stone Temple Pilots, they're elegant bastards"), the band had it both ways: it could put down crass sellouts of its own generation even as it recycled riffs from crass sellouts of the past.[21]

While Pavement were watching their video for the song "Cut Your Hair" go into rotation on MTV, the Silver Jews focused on simply managing to play and record. Berman, still the band's prime mover, wrote all the music and lyrics, performed the vocals, and played guitar. He recruited a rotating cast of supporting musicians (including Malkmus, Nastanovich, and new Pavement drummer, Steve West, all part-time members of Berman's crew) that was constantly shifting, lending the music a shambling, off-the-cuff feel that clearly reflected its indie roots. The band recorded its first two albums on a Walkman, the ultimate lo-fi recording technique, but when the time came to record the third album, *Starlight Walker,* in 1994, it had moved up to a recording studio. The following album, *The Natural Bridge,* which came out in 1996, further polished the Jews' country/rock sound. Unlike Pavement, which had been touring incessantly and even played nineties alt-rock megafest Lollapalooza in 1995, the Silver Jews never played live. Berman disliked performing, agreeing only to participate in the occasional poetry reading, and the ever-shifting band lineup would have made it impossible for him to assemble a touring band in any case. So the Silver Jews' reputation grew solely through its records, slowing the word of mouth about the band. It would remain mostly an act for indie connoisseurs.

Berman released another Jews album, *American Water,* in 1998, and his first book of poetry, *Actual Air,* arrived a year later. Both this album and Berman's book would bring his cerebral but visceral writing skills into focus for a number of readers and listeners who had never heard of him before. *American Water* once again features Malkmus, who can be heard singing and playing on most of the tracks. The first song, "Random Rules," opens the album with a brilliant couplet sung in Berman's world-weary drone: "In 1984," he sings in a sepulchral tone, "I was hospitalized for approaching perfection / Slowly screwing my way across Europe, they had to make a correction."[22] The band behind him is tight and melodic, countrified and raw edged. It sounds nothing like Pavement, yet Malkmus's playing and singing enhance Berman's in a manner that elevates the whole album. *Pitchfork* hailed the effort, saying that the band was now a "full-fledged contender for the American indie throne," a mantle that didn't sit entirely comfortably with Berman, who still had no interest in touring and was busy finishing up the poems that would appear in *Actual Air*.[23] The news that Berman, who had a graduate degree in creative writing by this point, was finally publishing a book of poetry made some fans of the band nervous, not out of doubts about Berman's writing but because previous books published by rock musicians had always been met with nasty reactions from the literati. Even Bob Dylan's *Tarantula*, a tossed-together assortment of poems and lyrics, was critically drubbed at the height of his sixties rebel fame. Berman's book, however, enjoyed a very different reaction.

Actual Air was released by Open City books, a small indie publisher, in 1999. Founded by the late novelist Rob Bingham, the press began as a literary magazine, and Berman recalls that "the literary journal had come out with three or four issues when I met Rob Bingham. We became great friends. His mother was the poetry editor at Grove [a publishing house in New York]. For a couple years, he tried to get me to work up a manuscript to show his mother, which I finally did, so she passed it on to the guy who really ran the show in poetry, but it languished in piles and stacks."[24] Bingham believed in Berman's work despite this setback, so he expanded the journal into a press to publish Berman's poetry. The gamble paid off. While *Actual Air*'s poems are sometimes willfully obscure, Berman balances that abstraction often enough with black humor and a weary worldview that appealed to a much larger audience than the Silver Jews had managed to attract at that point (though *American Water* was showing signs of being their breakthrough). The book earned accolades in some very mainstream venues: the *New Yorker*, *Entertainment Weekly*, and *GQ* all gave it enthusiastic reviews, and prominent poets Billy Collins and James Tate provided cover blurbs. The *New York Times* gushed that "Berman's is a funny, smart, on-again, off-again poetry of great promise."[25] In many ways, just as indie rock was nudging its way toward the mainstream, *Actual Air* helped to open the doors for independent publishing to do the same.

Berman is pensive about the differences between writing lyrics and writing poetry. To him, they don't necessarily require different processes; rather, they are actions with different outcomes. When we spoke in 2008, he was in the midst of finishing the latest Jews' recording, *Lookout Mountain, Lookout Sea*. Noting that he had read a number of poets as he wrote that album's songs, Berman says, "Reading Mallarmé and Emily Dickinson had a lot to give me. Phrases from Emerson and Whitman and Roger Miller are weaved in there." The Silver Jews' recurring themes of Americana gone wrong are closely reflected in this choice of poets, and Mallarmé's surrealism has also colored much of Berman's work. But Berman's work, like the best of the craft, pulls from these influences without copying them, and many nonpoetry readers, who found his poems accessible without being dumbed down, picked up copies of his book. With the success of *Actual Air* (which to date has sold an estimated twenty thousand copies—an impressive number for a small press poetry book), Berman says that expectations of his songwriting have changed. "The lyrics are now being held to a higher standard," he admits. "Up until the last year, I've always used a different standard for judging good lyric writing than I have for good poetry, but the activities are cousins, like mowing and raking. In both, I'm shooting for a nice-looking yard." For Berman, adjusting to these different identities of poet and songwriter is akin to a shift in behavior: "Poetry is like putting on a funny suit," he says. "And lyrics are like marching down Main Street in that funny suit."

After the release of *American Water* and *Actual Air*, things finally seemed to be falling into place for Berman. While his success didn't match the level enjoyed by his friends in Pavement, he was managing to survive. "Starting in 1997," he says, "I stopped having to work. *American Water* helped. Bingham gave me an advance for *Actual Air*." However, throughout this time Berman was struggling with drinking and drug use that escalated to an intentional overdose of Xanax. He spent time in a psychiatric ward and finally, with the encouragement of his new wife and bandmate, Cassie, eventually checked into rehab in 2004. Berman is frank about the difficulty of trying to stay sober in the "fuck the rules" world of indie rock: as he told the *Washington Post*, "I didn't have any models of artists getting sober and still doing well. I had models like Paul Westerberg," the famously drunk front man of the Replacements.[26] Berman's drug problem had another unfortunate side effect: "I fell into great amounts of debt in the early 2000s," he admits. At that point, the Jews very rarely played live gigs. Berman had begun traveling to do poetry readings after the release of his book, but he still showed little interest in playing music in front of an audience. The debt from his drug abuse changed that attitude. "One day I realized I could save myself," he says. "It was out of the blue. I could go on tour and make money and save myself." After the release of *Tanglewood Numbers* in 2005, the Silver Jews embarked on their first-ever tour and played to rapturously receptive audiences across the country and in Europe.

While Berman was struggling with the worst of his addiction in the late nineties, interband relations had soured for the members of Pavement. After *Crooked Rain, Crooked Rain,* the band turned its back on the classic rock sound and released an oddball album that tossed out verse-chorus-verse song structures and reached out into genres like country and punk for inspiration. *Wowee Zowee* was met with disappointment from critics and fans. The fact that the album was released only a year after *Crooked Rain, Crooked Rain* indicates Matador's enthusiasm to expedite a follow-up album to Pavement's best seller, but as a result, the record felt rushed and scattered. The 1997 release, *Brighten the Cor-*

ners, made further nods to Pavement's pop and classic rock influences, prompting one interviewer to ask Malkmus in 1997 what he thought of the accusations people were making about Pavement's selling out. "I think we sold out on *Slanted and Enchanted,*" he replied. "We made a bunch of singles before that; we were part of a real noisecore art underground. [*Slanted and Enchanted*] sounds so lo-fi now, but then I felt it was such a pop album."[27] Obvious rifts had developed between Kannberg's more melodic songwriting style, as evidenced on *Brighten the Corners,* and Malkmus's continued interest in abstraction and experimentation. Indie bands had historically navigated this kind of push and pull—even Mission of Burma featured two singer/songwriters with extremely different tastes and styles—but the tension is not always easily relieved, especially when a band finds itself in the wake of its biggest hit and under pressure from its ambitious label to produce a follow-up.

Matador continued to aggressively promote Pavement even as the band's album sales were steadily shrinking. The label even brought in a successful pop producer, Nigel Godrich, who had polished the sounds of formerly indie acts like REM and Beck, to whip Pavement's sound into radio-friendly shape. However, it was the wrong cultural moment to try and break the band through to the masses. Popular music tastes were moving away from rock sounds and toward pure, manufactured pop. In 1996, the best-selling album was Alanis Morissette's *Jagged Little Pill,* which was at least a tiny bit aligned with indie sounds in its guitar work and postfeminist girl-power lyrics. By 1999, the year of Pavement's final album, *Terror Twilight,* Billboard's best seller was the Backstreet Boys' *Millennium.* The contrast between the Backstreet Boys and Pavement couldn't be clearer: their sounds had nothing to do with one another, and the moment of indie's potential crossover into the mainstream seemed to be over. Britney Spears's *Baby One More Time* was also released in 1999, indicating a seismic shift from the record industry's fleeting interest in grunge bands and homegrown indie sounds in the early part of the decade. In the midst of these changes, Pavement's breakup in 1999 didn't come as a surprise to anyone who attended its final live show in England and saw a pair of handcuffs dangling from Malkmus's mike stand. Those handcuffs encapsulated what being in Pavement had begun to mean to him: it was a trap, he wanted out, and that was the end of the band, though Matador listed them as "on hiatus" for half a year. Communication between band members quickly deteriorated to the point that Steve West, the band's drummer, is rumored to have discovered on the Internet that Pavement broke up.

Matador continued to forge ahead after Pavement's split, promoting the other bands on the label and extricating itself from its contract with Atlantic when that company didn't work out. In 1996, Matador entered another contract with Capitol Records. When that company faced bankruptcy in 1999, Matador was able to buy back its shares and returned to being a truly indie label for some years afterward. It also moved on post-Pavement and began releasing albums by many of the most important indie bands of the time: Toledo's legendary and durable Guided By Voices; Scotland's touchy-feely Belle and Sebastian; the volatile, soulful singer-songwriter Chan Marshall, better known as Cat Power; the New Pornographers; Yo La Tengo; and Kannberg's post-Pavement band the Preston School of Industry. Stephen Malkmus's solo albums were also released by Matador, as were the new albums and back catalog reissues of the newly reunited Mission of Burma. In 2002, still able to sniff out an indie band that might end up selling a lot of records, Cosloy signed the New York–based band Interpol, whose album *Turn on the Bright Lights* became Matador's best-selling debut to date. The label, however, had some help in moving that many CDs; it had entered into a deal with Warner Music Group's Alternative Distribution Alliance, which maintains a guise of independence by not mentioning Warner on its Web site and promoting itself as "a one-stop shop for independent labels."[28] Matador's cofounder Chris Lombardi chalked the deal up to a survival strategy: "I still think the major labels will betray a band for a dollar," he admitted, "but today everything has changed. Matador needs the major labels. We'd never have a best-selling album if we didn't have this partnership." Changes in distribution pressured other indie labels to make similar deals. Chain music stores such as Best Buy, for example, required that CDs were "packaged according to certain guidelines and [had] to stock large amounts of inventory in case an album was a best seller."[29] These restrictions and the onus to produce enough inventory to meet Best Buy's bottom line were impossible for most indie labels to manage; thus, entering into deals with majors for distribution felt a bit less like dancing with the devil.

For major labels in the current decade, indie bands remain commodities to be bought and sold. A Universal Records executive was quoted by the *Los Angeles Times* as saying, "We rely on the indies to be the minor leagues for our major league teams. The indies find markets we didn't even know existed, and we can take the band and make them huge."[30] Lombardi scoffed at this attitude, but the fact remained that Matador had a knack for finding bands that made money, even if making that kind of money meant the bands eventually defected to major labels. Interpol, which broke through on Matador's label in 2004, released its most recent album on Capitol Records. Other indie bands from the nineties also made the move to major labels in the next decade: Modest Mouse left the tiny Seattle indie Up Records for Epic Records in 2000; Death Cab for Cutie defected from its long-time label Barsuk for Atlantic in 2004. Indie bands who stayed on indie labels did manage to have breakthrough records, such as Arcade Fire, who remained with Merge Records even after their debut album *Funeral* sold nearly a million copies, and their labelmates Spoon, who signed with Merge after a deal with major label Epic went very sour. But the bands that chose to stay indie viewed the decision as a practical one. Arcade Fire's Régine Chassagne admitted that the band flirted with major label executives, but she insisted that "right from the start, we made it clear we'd never sign with them. I mean, why would we?"[31] If Arcade Fire and Spoon were making a living on Merge, and they had the creative freedom to record what they wanted on those labels, then why make the move to a major? Pavement had the same attitude in the nineties. Increasingly, for bands that were offered major label deals, taking those deals or remaining on an indie label was indicative of a kind of flexibility bands hadn't had in the past. In the eighties, major label deals were the death knell for bands like Hüsker Dü and the Replacements, who found their sound polished and refined to the point that it became almost unrecognizable. Today, indie bands face the same problem when they move to a major, and on top of these concerns, they have to deal with being marketed in venues they might not have considered appropriate when they were still recording on indies— car commercials, fashion shows, soap operas, and so on. (Though as we will see, that commercialization can happen even if the band remains on an indie label.)

Some bands, however, remain stalwartly independent, and much of their ability to maintain that status is due to their labels. The Silver Jews' label, Drag City, remains free of corporate ties as of this writing and continues to foster close relationships with its artists. David Berman says that Drag City serves as his network, as the people who help him out when he needs it, much like labels like SST and Dischord helped build their artists' careers over time. Berman casually accepts his current position as one of indie rock's most important singer/songwriters; now that he's touring regularly, he's busier, and he admits, "I've got an intern recently." He moved to Nashville a few years ago and says with tongue-in-cheek awareness that "it's fun for me to try and out write Music Row. They're going to know my name." Berman may be half joking, but for many of his followers, the idea of a corn-fed country star like Kenny Chesney singing one of his songs elicits a sense of subversive glee.*

---

*Nonetheless, Berman was ultimately unable to overcome his longtime discomfort with touring and performing live. On January 22, 2009, he announced that the Silver Jews would be disbanding and that all future tour dates (with the exception of one farewell concert) were canceled.

When the best indie rock breaks through into the mainstream, as when fearless freaks the Flaming Lips somehow managed to make a hit album about pink robots or Pavement cheerfully skewered the Smashing Pumpkins on one of its songs even while it was playing beside them at a festival, it's both a surprise and a pleasure to see hardworking musicians getting paid for doing something they enjoy. Bands who remain truly independent won't get paid much, but for many earning a living is enough.

★

Poet/songwriters like Berman, along with superliterate musicians like Malkmus, changed the rules of indie songwriting at the outset of the twenty-first century. They made indie rock a safe place to be bookish and smart, and their compatriots in the indie press world—themselves gearing up for a sea change in the way books and magazines are made—welcomed that atmosphere.

eight

Scan, Kern, Layout, Print: Indie Publishing in the Twenty-first Century

The thirtieth of January 2008 is bitterly cold. Funnels of icy wind blast down the Avenue of the Americas in Manhattan, among the clutches of bundled-up New Yorkers hustling for the subway. Scattered handfuls of people race through the blustery weather, crossing the street toward the Hilton Hotel, where the Associated Writing Programs conference is about to start. Many of the eight thousand estimated attendants push boxes and overflowing bags of books through the revolving chrome door, greeting friends as they nudge through the packed lobby. Flyers and signs advertise readings featuring such big marquee names as Martin Amis, John Updike, and A. S. Byatt, but for many the main attraction of the AWP is the book fair, which spreads over three entire floors of the Hilton's conference center. The publishers of books and magazines, along with literary organizations and graduate programs, purchase booths and tables for the three-day duration of the conference, and to some extent, the three-story structure of the AWP book fair mirrors their status: well-funded presses and long-established organizations have elaborately designed booths on the bottom floor, which is packed wall to wall with people dressed up in suits and fancy conference wear, jostling each other to gawk at famous writers and lining up to get books signed. As you ascend the escalator to the second floor, the energy begins to shift. The press names represented are more obscure, the table layouts are funkier and more likely to feature handcrafted displays than giant glossy blowups of book covers, the printed matter on hand is more eclectic, and the people staffing the booths are comfortably dressed in jeans, boots, and sweaters, ready for long walks and subway rides back to friends' apartments where they can crash on the couch. By the time you arrive on the third floor, the displays are even funkier, including a booth covered in AstroTurf and another decorated with tinfoil sculptures, touting books and magazines that cover a dizzying variety of topics and forms. AWP estimates that more than four hundred presses and magazines participated in the 2008 book fair, the majority of them independently owned and operated.[1] It's likely that most of the writers attending the conference will eventually see some of their work appear in an independent magazine or in a book produced by an independent press. Even as zines fade from the cultural spotlight, a new generation of independent publishers has emerged to take up the mantle passed on from the prior generations of independent presses. And in spite of financial and distribution challenges, the number of these small press publishers is growing faster than ever before.

I spend most of my days at AWP manning the table for Pavement Saw Press, a one-man operation based out of Ohio that has been producing poetry books for more than ten years (including my work). This year the man himself, editor David Baratier, is unable to attend the conference, so my fellow Pavement Saw author Rachel M. Simon and I are doing what all small press authors eventually have to do: selling our own books. Since I worked in an independent bookstore for many years and subsequently founded and ran an independent magazine, selling printed matter is second nature to me, and the atmosphere at the book fair is amiable enough to make time pass quickly. Sometimes, I'll run out to attend one of the hundreds of panels and readings going on downstairs, but for the most part, I prefer to hang out at the book fair. We're surrounded on either side by independent literary magazines (one of which bills itself as "a journal for the terminally ill"), and across the aisle is the table for Austin, Texas–based Effing Press, which makes beautiful letter-pressed, hand-stitched chapbooks and broadsides. Scott Pierce, Effing's editor, shrugs off our seemingly remote location in the farthest corner of the third floor. "All the interesting people are up here," he says. AWP's conference, though officially designed for students and faculty of the many creative writing programs at colleges and universities across America, has also become a gathering place for hundreds of independent literary communities from across America, many of which have no academic affiliation. By the end of the first day, I've met dozens of people whose work I've come across at some point in time, some of whom I've published in one of the indie magazines I edited or who have published me, and I've swapped books with other small press authors who are here to network and share ideas. These people are not here to make money, if there is indeed any money to be made. By the end of the conference, we've recouped just enough to pay for the table, but that's about it. My giveaway AWP tote bag is so stuffed with free books, magazines, and conference swag that I have to pay a friend to ship it all back home to me in Oakland. That seems like a fair trade.

Nobody starts an independent press or magazine expecting to make a living, and most people who publish, edit, or write for independent media have one or more day jobs, which may or may not have anything to do with literature. The revival of small presses in the present decade is a reflection of our times. Just as indie experienced a resurgence and reinvigoration in the Reagan era and many writers of the time found a venue in zines, the Bush years also inspired writers to create a platform for expressing themselves. The increasingly conservative political climate that followed in the wake of 9/11 and the Iraq war coincided with huge increases of students entering MFA programs in creative writing and, after graduation, those writers were looking for places to publish their work. When they discovered that making it out of a major magazine's slush pile is about as likely as being struck by lightning while fiddling in a wheat field, many of those young writers decided to create their own magazines and book presses, where they could publish the work of their friends, associates, and like-minded strangers.

Laura Moriarty, the deputy director of Small Press Distribution, who has been involved in independent publishing for more than thirty years, argues that "the conglomeration of the media is actually resulting in people on the other end, our end, saying, 'Okay fine, we'll make our own party.' And it's kind of like people did in the sixties, but there's more of it."[2] Just as independent record labels were beginning to assert themselves as a viable alternative in the post-Nirvana landscape, in the late nineties, many independent presses and magazines began offering an alternate take on arts, culture, and news that became increasingly important in the wake of the "dumbing down" of many mass media outlets, and their community focus was crucial amid the shuttering of many local and alternative newspapers. Like many other forms of independent culture, independent publishing often begins with one individual reaching out to his or her networks and in those networks finding a way to create a plausible business model that can survive and even thrive without the kind of budget available to magazines that showcase more pages of advertising than they do content or books that appear to have been written for no purpose other than paying someone's mortgage. This contrast is not always purely black and white: subversive authors publish via mainstream outlets, and major magazines cover underground art, but these examples are often the exception. However, when we read the stories of the people who run independent presses, a common thread of commitment to the form becomes clear: it's a labor of love, it's a struggle, and it's something they're all passionate about. And the present decade has seen some of the greatest growth in independent publishing since the sixties, even if that growth is sometimes threatened by the constant struggle to break even and a struggle to succeed among the media conglomerates.

If indie culture and independent art always stand in opposition to something (independent record labels in opposition to major labels and manufactured musicians, crafting in opposition to generic products offered by chain stores like Ikea and Target, independent comics in opposition to shiny superheroes, and so on), independent publishing has historically existed in opposition to mainstream publishing. Major publishing is big business, and it plays by big business rules. The bottom lines for choosing which books to print often comes down to making money, which means that vapid books proliferate on the best-seller lists and receive the biggest advances and promotional budgets: chick lit, made-up memoirs, and *The Da Vinci Code* are just a few examples of cash-generating books of questionable literary value. For writers who venture outside of profitable genres, however, the struggle to find a publisher often means that they eventually turn to independent presses, which have historically been more willing to take risks on authors whose work might not generate a lot of money. Mimeo magazines and small presses in the fifties and sixties provided writers with a cheap and easy method to publish their work when academic and popular journals ignored their work, and the same thinking fueled the zine revolution of the eighties. In 2008, most major publishing houses and mainstream magazines (like major record labels) are owned by conglomerates. In 2001, America Online purchased Time Warner thanks to approval by the Federal Trade Commission and soon controlled multiple media outlets, including Comedy Central, CNN, Warner Music, WCW Wrestling, and the Time Warner publishing group, which housed nine different book imprints.[3] By 2007 this became an untenable business model due to the fact that the books were not making enough money to be worth Time Warner's while, and Warner Books was acquired by a different conglomerate: Hachette Livre, France's largest book publisher.[4] The conglomeration of book publishing often means that risk-taking authors get shunted in favor of profitable ones, and first-time authors whose books may be critically lauded but don't sell well are often dropped. It also means that fewer authors will make it into print, period. Just as fewer bands get deals when there are only four major record labels, the takeover of publishing by corporate interests means that writers have a smaller chance of landing a book deal. The magazine world is also controlled by large corporations. Condé Nast owns the *New Yorker*, *Vogue*, *Wired*, and multiple other titles; the Hearst Corporation not only holds controlling interest in more than thirty daily and weekly newspapers, but also publishes about twenty magazines; and *Rolling Stone*, which began publishing during the countercultural press revolution of the sixties in San Francisco, is currently part of founding editor Jann Wenner's Wenner Media, which also owns *Men's Journal* and *US Weekly* and publishes a nonfiction book imprint in partnership with Hyperion. In response to the corporatization of print media, more and more independent presses and magazines have begun to emerge.

Among the many book presses to emerge out of the underground in the last decade, Akashic Books epitomizes the fighting spirit of the early punk underground, but it also represents a successful, growing independent press that has been able to survive for more than a decade in spite of the odds brought on by the reorganization of mainstream publishing. Founded by Johnny Temple in 1997 and based in Brooklyn, Akashic (a Hindu term describing a universal library) began as an outlet for Temple's interest in one particular book, Arthur Nersesian's *The Fuck-Up*, which, as Temple recalls, "some friends and I had all read and loved. It was a little sort of cult classic within my social circle, and it was self-published."[5] Nersesian, who had been writing in underground journals for years, got an agent for *The Fuck-Up* in the late eighties. Nersesian titled the novel *The Fuck-Up* because "I needed something to grab people's attention."[6] However, *The Fuck-Up*—the story of an aspiring writer who winds up working at a porn theater—got rejected by every publisher Nersesian's agent queried. In 1991, Nersesian published the novel himself, and it slowly gained a cult following of curious readers, including Johnny Temple. Temple had begun thinking about starting an independent publishing company because he had a history of working as an independent musician and liked the idea that he might be able to apply the principles of an indie record label—the willingness to take on risky artists, to provide fair contracts to musicians, and to build a relationship with a community of listeners—to the business of book publishing. Temple and his partners contacted Nersesian about "letting us launch our book publishing company with his novel," and Akashic was born.

Before he became a publisher, Temple had for years been a touring musician in the band Girls Against Boys and had recorded for the indie labels Dischord and Touch and Go. When Girls Against Boys was offered a deal with Geffen Records in 1996, Temple, who praises his experiences working with indie labels, looked at this windfall in a pragmatic manner: he decided to take the cash and start his own indie label. However, his plans quickly took an unpredictable turn. "For the first time in my life," he says, "I had some disposable income, and so I decided to start this record label I had always wanted to do. However, I found by the time I actually started it, I was increasingly burnt out on the music business. I was playing in two bands at the time, and so I already had enough music in my life." Temple's musical burnout turned out to be a blessing in disguise. Nersesian's *The Fuck-Up* not only sold very well for Akashic, but it was soon picked up by an unlikely mainstream outlet: MTV Books bought the reprint rights in 1999. The book has since gone through twelve printings. The success of Nersesian's book indicated that independent publishing might actually be a viable venture, and publishing offered Temple an outlet that music didn't: "I realized that it was everything that I had wanted out of a record label, but since it was books and publishing, I had a little bit more critical distance because I'm not a fiction writer myself, so there was a certain amount of magic to the fiction which was really compelling to me."

Temple received help and business advice from several similarly minded independent publishing companies, including Henry Rollins's 2.13.61 and Incommunicado Press. "When Akashic started out in ninety-seven," Temple reflects, "there were a lot fewer indie publishers, and there were a lot fewer that had connections with independent culture." Rollins's history as a member of Black Flag—a band that had pioneered the early DIY touring circuit—helped him understand the value of networking for independent artists, a philosophy that Temple shared. Rollins and other publishers "helped us tremendously in our early days, with advice and contact information [with printers, distributors, and so on], and in turn I've tried to be helpful; now that Akashic is somewhat established, I've tried to reach out and help up and coming independent presses."

Akashic's slogan, "Reverse Gentrification of the Literary World," reflects this philosophy of reaching out not only to help other presses, but also to reach readers and audiences that might not otherwise be exposed to literature. "The idea is that publishing really is a gentrified world," according to Temple, and "almost everybody who works in the publishing business is middle class, or upper-middle class, or upper class. You don't see many people from working-class backgrounds or poor backgrounds in book publishing." Akashic's list of authors reflects this interest in breaking boundaries, featuring a number of authors from the African diaspora, Caribbean writers, gay and lesbian writers, and Latin American writers. The press began by publishing two or three books a year; currently, it publishes twenty-five titles annually, with only four people on staff responsible for all of the editing, publicity, accounting, and marketing. "We're just bombarded with submissions every single day," Temple admits, but the press still makes a concerted effort to maintain a diverse list. For Temple, this is simply part of Akashic's mission. "Our dream is to sell books beyond the sort of people that read literary publications and present literature in a way where it can be more deeply woven into the fabric of our society." He stresses the idea that his ideal audience would include "people who tend to be sort of ignored by the mainstream publishing business," and to that end, Akashic participates in a number of social justice projects and community activities, including the Brooklyn Book Festival, an international gathering with a "strong community bent," and "really famous and really obscure authors." The 2008 Brooklyn Book Festival, which took place on September 14, attracted thousands of attendees, more than sixty vendors including both independent and mainstream publishers, and authors ranging from highbrow novelists Russell Banks and Jonathan Franzen to the legendary Joan Didion to the up-and-coming independent writer Tao Lin and Brooklyn-born novelist Jonathan Lethem, in addition to nearly a hundred other authors both famous and obscure. Panels included a discussion of independent music and publishing with Fugazi's Ian MacKaye and Sonic Youth's Thurston Moore, book-making demonstrations, readings from every conceivable genre, and discussions of literature as social change.

For all of Akashic's success and growth, Temple is realistic about the difficulties of running a press today, given the nature of the publishing business and the current economic recession. "The economy of book publishing is really, really difficult," he admits. Reading as a recreational activity is declining nationally and has been for years, and even formerly successful big publishers are struggling to deal with shrinking audiences for books and steadily declining profits. For independent publishers whose readership is small to begin with, that decline hits hard. "I would love to always stay completely independent, the way we are now, and not have to take on any investors," Temple says, "but if a recession were to hit, that might make it very difficult to survive the way we are now." About a year before I spoke with Temple, Soft Skull Press, another well-respected New York–based indie publisher with a cutting-edge group of authors under its wing, found itself on the verge of collapse due to the bankruptcy of its distributor, Publishers Group West. Because bigger distributors like Ingram deal with distributing books in bulk, a small press often fails to meet the distributor's bottom line. Ingram is a wholesaler, which means that bookstores must order a certain number of copies of a book from Ingram in order to stock it at all—in the same manner that music vendors like Best Buy make it difficult for indie labels to sell through them because of the enormous number of CDs they require the label to send them for inventory. For an independent press, the reality is that rising printing costs make it impossible to afford to print enough copies to sell in bulk via Ingram. Indie presses will more often sell a couple of copies to a bookstore, a few copies online, a few more at a book fair, and several at an author's readings, so independent presses need distributors that are willing to work on a smaller scale. Publishers Group West, which represented a number of small, independent presses and helped to get their books into stores and with online vendors, had for years given small publishers a decent rate and had helped them survive, but the downturn in the book publishing economy had crippled PGW's operation, and its bankruptcy left all of its publishers in the lurch and deeply in debt because PGW had fallen so far behind on payments to its presses. Richard Nash, Soft Skull's editor, took what Temple calls "heroic" measures to keep the press independent and tried to fund-raise enough money to avoid being bought out by a bigger publisher, but that became unrealistic, and Soft Skull was acquired by Counterpoint, a bigger independent publisher, which less than a week later was itself bought by a mainstream publishing company. Nash described this turn of events by bluntly declaring that PGW's parent company, Advanced Marketing Services, did not do enough to support PGW when it purchased the company: according to Nash, "The independents got fucked by the Enron of publishing" when PGW went down on AMS' watch.[7] Temple is aware of how tenuous Akashic's survival is in the wake of these shake-ups; in spite of its successes, any independent business is vulnerable "whether the economy goes into a recession, or your distributor goes bankrupt . . . there's no padding for a company like Soft Skull or Akashic, so if something kind of traumatic happens, I could find myself in a situation where I have to take on investors or something." For independent publishers, taking on investors can mean the loss of some control over the business because the investors might demand to have input into the titles the press releases and the way the company is run, and for publishers used to answering only to themselves, their authors, and their audience, that kind of compromise can be difficult. Temple is optimistic that this scenario can be avoided for now but, like many other people involved in independent publishing today, he's also aware that securing outside support can simply be a necessity in tough times.

The 2007 bankruptcy of Publishers Group West caused a ripple effect throughout the independent publishing business. The bankruptcy resulted in the presses being owed money by a company that no longer existed, and in a world where every dollar counts, and even a successful press like Akashic "has never made a profit," according to Temple, going into serious debt can be terminal. When distributors don't pay presses, the presses in turn can't pay their bills. While some presses were able to scrape together the funds to survive the bankruptcy (McSweeney's Books, for example, recruited some of their famous contributors and held an eBay auction; on their Web site, they explained to readers that they had lost 30 percent of their revenues, including those owed for Dave Eggers's book about a Sudanese refugee, *What Is the What*, which were earmarked for charity), the blows kept coming.[8] Early in 2007, another distributor, the Independent Press Association, shut its doors due to fiscal mismanagement. During its lifetime, the IPA was a distributor for many independent magazines, and up until its bankruptcy there had been an upsurge in new titles and circulation. The IPA had begun with the mission of helping independent publications and for years had provided indie magazines with bargain-rate distribution. After the IPA collapse, many of those magazines lost the fight to survive. Among the losers was the publication I edited and wrote for, *Kitchen Sink Magazine*, a quarterly arts and culture journal, which I founded with a group of friends in 2001.

At that time, although newsstand sales and magazine subscriptions had been plummeting for decades, the idea of regularly being able to disseminate ideas via a portable print medium was irresistible to a number of people in the indie community. After all, zines, for all of their ability to sneak subversive, confessional, or just plain weird ideas out into the world, rarely find themselves on the magazine racks of any bookstore or newsstand, independently owned or not. Zines are often just too small to make a casual browser lean over and pick one up, and their limited distribution can make accruing new readers difficult. Though zine distributors do exist, they are strapped for cash and staff, and their range of distribution is limited by the fact that most zines have fairly minuscule print runs. Blow up a zine to magazine size, however, and you have something that might get people's attention. Likewise, color covers, perfect binding, and bigger page sizes allow writers and designers a lot more freedom in layout and content. There's more wiggle room in producing a magazine, and at a time when indie as a print medium was spreading its wings beyond its eighties incarnation, the idea of putting together one that might cover bands, artists, writers, and comics artists who might not otherwise receive media exposure seemed like a good idea.

Kitchen Sink, like so many indie projects, started as an idea in response to a void: Jeff Johnson, Jen Loy, and myself, all members of *Kitchen Sink*'s founding editorial and publishing staff, had previously worked together on *Fabula*, an independent magazine that had gone deeply into debt and ceased publication. So we figured we had learned our lessons and could make a better, more tenable business model for a new magazine. But like a lot of indie publishers, we were more than a little naive. We got together in 2001 with several friends who came from working on indie comics, zines, and alternative news weeklies and decided that an arts and culture magazine focused on essays and first-person experiences rather than the typical assortment of reviews and blurbs was sorely needed to serve the Bay Area's booming indie community, which was receiving little coverage from local media. A year later, after a lot of fund-raising and no less than ten meetings where we debated about what title to give the magazine (we decided on *Kitchen Sink* because we liked the "everything but" idea), we released our first issue, with the tagline "a magazine for people who think too much."

From the beginning, that mission statement attracted a high caliber of writers, many of whom felt restrained by the tiny word count limits and inherent strictures of writing for mainstream magazines, which were relying more on shorter and shorter articles, and our decision to design the magazine without photos and to instead use only illustrations primarily done by comics artists made the publication unique. We also received 501(c)(3) nonprofit status, which enabled us to apply for the very scarce grant money available to magazines. After the publication of just a few issues, we received the Utne Independent Press award for Best New Magazine, along with best magazine awards from all three of our local free weeklies. We had fun and cared deeply about what we were doing, but to be frank, publishing a magazine was a huge pain in the ass. All of us had full-time day jobs, several editors left to pursue grad school or have kids, interns showed up once to work and never came back, burnout and resentment were rife, and raising enough money to print each issue was a constant battle. Advertising money was scarce, and it was tough to get readers to commit to a subscription. We had to get creative, or the funds would soon run out. Jen Loy, who was our editor in chief for the first few years of publication, had recently bought a café in downtown Oakland, and through her decision to start featuring live music and art shows, she hooked into Oakland's rapidly growing art and music scene. Using Jen's connections, we started throwing benefit parties and art auctions to raise money for each issue. Every three months, the pattern repeated itself: solicit articles and answer queries, edit, copyedit, lay out, book a band, hang some art on the walls of a local art-friendly collective warehouse, invite a few hundred guests, have a party, clean up, count the money raised, pay bills, recover from hangovers, do some more editing and lay out, and send the issue to the printers. Even if this fund-raising plan rapidly increased our readership and reputation for being the spark for a thousand drunken hookups, it put a mighty strain on all of the staff.

When the Independent Press Association approached us about distributing *KS*, we jumped at the opportunity. We were increasingly exhausted by the fund-raising cycle, which having a bigger distributor would partially negate—or so we thought. Up to that point, we had distributed the magazine on our own, loading up cars with boxes and taking copies to local bookstores and magazine shops, selling copies at parties, and bribing friends and family to subscribe. The chance to go national and to increase our circulation fivefold was hard to turn down. Since our writers and illustrators were all working for free, the additional exposure seemed like a fair trade for their effort. Over its five years of publication, *KS* had come to rely on our network of friends who ran other independent magazines for advice and camaraderie, including *Punk Planet, Clamor, Bitch, Other, McSweeney's Quarterly, The Believer,* and Watchword Press. We staged a series of local readings called "Indie Mag All Stars," and reached out to one another when times got rough financially to help with fund-raising ideas, so we all came to feel like we were part of an unpaid, overworked gang. Many of these magazines also chose to sign with the IPA, mostly because there were few viable alternatives for distribution. So when the IPA sent out an announcement that it was shutting its doors and declaring bankruptcy just after New Year's in 2007, at which point they owed us close to ten thousand dollars, we and our friends at other indie magazines knew we were fucked. The IPA had fallen so far behind in payments that we had had to raise enough cash to print the magazine for several quarterly cycles, and this resulted in their owing us a growing amount of money. The IPA, like a number of nonprofits, had always tended to be somewhat dysfunctional in its operations, but for the last year that we worked with them, they were clearly struggling to make payments, always a dangerous sign. Jeremy Adam Smith, a former interim executive director of the organization, wrote on *Other* magazine's blog right after the bankruptcy that "the IPA story is one of bad management and bad faith; if not for that, it might still be around supporting indie titles, who as a group will survive this crisis and keep on innovating."[9] Jeremy, as it turned out, was only a little bit right. Along with *Kitchen Sink*, our friends at the venerable indie magazines *Punk Planet* and *Clamor* were out of luck; neither survived because the debts owed to them by the IPA could not be recouped. *Other*, which had been publishing on a smaller scale, survived the shift, as did McSweeney's and its lit crit magazine *The Believer*. *Bitch* magazine pulled through as well, because, as editor Andi Zeisler explains, "We had built up a really loyal group of donors that we were able to go to for emergency funding at the time."[10] After the PGW collapse and the IPA collapse, the landscape of independent publishing looked increasingly bleak.

But that was not the end of the story. Just as indie music had been forced to change in the wake of the grunge/riot grrrl implosions but had come back with even greater significance and strength in the new decade, indie publishing has historically experienced a similar cycle of surges and dips. Among the many people who've made a longtime commitment to working in indie publishing, Zeisler still carries the torch for independent magazines. *Bitch* was founded by Zeisler and her former publishing partner Lisa Jervis in 1996 (Jervis left the magazine in 2006). Jervis and Zeisler originally published *Bitch* as a traditional zine, "but each issue that came out was a step in the general direction of becoming a full-fledged magazine," Zeisler recalls. "Whenever we had extra money, for instance, we did something to make it more magazine-y, whether it was changing the size or adding a color to the cover or adding more pages." The zine community could have taken this shift the wrong way, since many zinesters at that time stuck to the idea that "having your zine distributed by certain distributors, or getting a bar code so that your zine could be sold in Barnes and Noble" could qualify as selling out. "Being a zine was definitely part of what *Bitch* was, content-wise," Zeisler asserts, "but it was also a somewhat temporary state of being until we could become a magazine." The shift to magazine format, according to Zeisler, was "more in line with how we saw *Bitch*'s mission and development."

That mission has always remained the same in the ten-plus years of *Bitch*'s existence. The magazine's tagline, "Feminist Response to Pop Culture" has always run below its provocative title as the magazine has expanded in distribution, print run, and size. "I actually think the idea that pop culture can be a locus of feminist activism has gained a lot more traction over the years," Zeisler says, "not necessarily because of *Bitch*, but because there's just so much *more* pop culture out there, many more people talking about it." In the twenty-first century, the growing number of information sources about celebrity and popular culture via blogs, Web sites, television, and podcasts have presented a challenge for *Bitch*. The magazine has had to deal with "increasingly blurred lines between what does and does not constitute popular culture" at the same time that it also stretches to include some of those media in its own mission in order to keep up with the attention-deficit nature of the times. Nonetheless, *Bitch*'s ability to maintain its original concept has earned it a loyal and diverse readership, one that it maintains today.

Even after *Bitch* survived the IPA debacle, Zeisler admits that "it's always, always been a struggle to stay afloat, because print publishing gets exponentially more expensive, but resources are shrinking." Zeisler is referring not only to the cost of printing itself, but also to the available number of readers who can fund those print runs. Part of the problem indie magazines have always faced is getting themselves onto newsstands. When your subscriber base is tiny, attracting new readers via newsstand sales is a crucial part of your survival—which is another reason why the IPA collapse had such a big impact in the indie magazine community, since it got many indie mags onto newsstands. According to Zeisler, the other side of *Bitch*'s financial struggle is simply about getting noticed. "From a broader societal perspective," she says, "there's just so much media out there now that it's very easy for independent publications to get lost or drowned out in a shuffle of bigger, flashier, louder offerings." Many publishers in the indie community echo this sentiment. Print media increasingly cater to a smaller and smaller audience, partially thanks to digital media and partially thanks to an overall cultural decline in reading as a recreational activity. In a shrinking market, independent magazines like *Bitch* are an increasingly rare commodity. For Zeisler, the biggest blow after the IPA collapse is "the loss of camaraderie and resource sharing that was one of the reasons that so many magazines joined the IPA to begin with—that's huge." Since the IPA had presented itself as an "organization that had started with the explicit goal of helping independent, mission-driven publications to thrive," its betrayal of those same publications continues to hurt even those that survived.

In spite of the reality of indie print media becoming endangered species, both Zeisler and Johnny Temple are cautiously optimistic about the future. Zeisler reminds me that *Bitch* "has lived through two iterations of a culture declaring that the end of print is nigh. And in neither time did the end of print actually come to pass, and really exciting independent magazines continued to launch." Temple acknowledges that in the world of book publishing, technology has actually made the venture more pragmatic. "With the passage of time, it becomes easier and easier to start a publishing company," he says, "because . . . in the past ten years technology, desktop publishing, and all sorts of things have continued to advance. And with these advances it makes publishing more affordable." What's impressive about the number of new presses and the still-surviving independents that brought their wares to the AWP book fair in New York in January is not only the sheer diversity and volume of exciting books and magazines they're producing, but the surge of interest in print media in the wake of digital media threatening to decimate it. Just as indie rock in the last decade has valued a return to "authenticity" in music production, emphasizing lo-fi sound and primitive recording methods and rediscovering genres like folk and country music, independent publishing has simultaneously returned to low-tech means of production—including letterpress printing, hand-stitched binding, and xeroxing—while at the same time using technology as a tool instead of crouching in a corner and hiding from it.

The arrival of Amazon.com in 1994, with its deep discounts on books and cheap shipping, posed an immediate threat to independent bookstores, which had long relied on community support to stay afloat, a premise that passed on to independent publishers. The relationship between independent bookstores and indie print media has always been symbiotic. An indie bookstore is typically more willing to commit to selling small press items on consignment or to host events for independent publications that might not bring in a ton of money, and because their staffs are usually highly literate and attuned to news about new books and magazines that might otherwise stay off the radar, independent booksellers are crucial to the survival of small presses and magazines. When they began to vanish from the landscape of many cities (Cody's Books of Berkeley, California, one of the most venerable independent bookstores in America, closed its doors in June 2008, while I was in the midst of writing this chapter), indie publishers had to take stock of the new publishing and selling landscape and quickly shift their survival strategies. For many of them, the Internet actually turned out to be a useful tool for networking and sharing resources, the same strategies that had enabled indie to assert itself as a viable subculture in the first place. Online, that interaction came in the form of blogs.

Ron Silliman, a member of the earlier generation of independent publishers and writers who had begun the mimeo magazine movement in the sixties, was one of the first creative writers to embrace blogging as a means for disseminating his ideas about poetics, independent publishing, and community. Silliman's Blog, which he began in 1999, regularly receives upwards of fourteen hundred hits a day—a surprisingly large number for a blog that appeals to a niche audience of poets and poetry publishers. "I think at the very beginning, the people who were reading [the blog] were people who tended to have aesthetics very close to mine, and gradually that expanded out," he says. "I was starting to get readers who have aesthetics who are quite at odds with what I do. Sometimes because they like the negative energy, or at least the cognitive dissonance." Silliman's vocal stance against what he calls the "school of quietude"—poetry that hews closely to the academically established lines of confession, lyric, and New England in autumn types of settings—quickly attracted an audience of similarly minded avant-garde adherents. But Silliman's Blog has also been highly attractive to readers who seemingly visit only to get into flame wars in the comments box. The fact that a blog about *poetry*, and specifically about avant-garde poetry and poetics, is attracting an audience of that size is startling, but it also reveals a need writers have for a venue where they can hash out ideas. "What's really happening," Silliman says, "is that the definition of the relationship between the poet and an audience is undergoing really significant changes." Those changes are fueled by the Internet's expanding role in what were previously scattered communities of readers and writers. The networking opportunities provided by blogs, social networking sites, and e-mail has actually been a very empowering thing for small presses and magazines in spite of the doom and gloom message that the age of print media is over. If you're an independent publisher, via a blog, you can network with readers, run excerpts from books, and build a community that's not limited by your own zip code.

Small Press Distribution's Laura Moriarty notes that even in the wake of the PGW and IPA collapses, the number of new indie presses continues to grow. "We usually take on about thirty [new presses] a year," she says, "and I think we took on fifty last year [2006] so there are more, and a lot of good ones." Moriarty sees this resurgence of interest as a product of the energy and networking ability of the new generation of publishers. "These people were raised by boomers," she argues. "All incredibly individuated and creative, and they've got their parents to help them, and they're really following in the footsteps of the people from the sixties," the originators of the small press revolution, who are revered in this new community. And the fact that there *is* a community of small presses, for both books and magazines, is what Moriarty sees as the glimmer of hope for independent publishing's future. The new publishers SPD picks up are "incredibly networked. And they're good at things, so they're making books that are objects that people want to buy," reflecting the larger cultural shift back to craft and design being part and parcel of any object's value, whether it's a book, magazine, or CD. Most crucially, though, Moriarty observes that the new generation of publishers is aware of its audience: "They want to read their version of their generation," she says, "so those books are necessary to those people; there's a community, and they're wanting them."

That sense of community is arguably the greatest contribution independent publishers provide for readers and writers. Just as the early independent presses and mimeo magazines of the sixties found an audience hungry for new ideas that were not being expressed in mass media, indie publishers—in spite of financial setbacks and great odds against them—continue to cater to a similarly minded audience today. I can speak from experience that working on an indie magazine feels like wearing a badge of honor, a sense of "Yeah, I made this, and you're reading it, and now we can talk about it, and maybe I can help you make a magazine too." And the aesthetics of indie magazines and presses and their increasing interest in low-tech but very cool-looking methods of printing and binding make them visually arresting and immediately differentiate them from other offerings. Those same aesthetics also came to color much of what we can today identify as "indie style": a return to the value of handmade objects, an interest in things made with care, and a collective desire to forge a relationship between maker and consumer. As the twenty-first century began to evolve, so did the aesthetics of indie, in all of its various forms.

nine

Hands On: The Crafting and Indie Design Movement

San Francisco's Fort Mason was originally built in the 1860s for defense during the Civil War. Its long, barnlike buildings hover over the bay on rickety-looking piers, but the fort has withstood several reincarnations. After its closure as a military base in the mid-1960s, its buildings were converted into a center for arts organizations and nonprofits, including several museums and theaters, a music school, and environmental organizations. Today, even while its cultural heart has shifted, it still looks like a military base. As crowds of tourists wind their way up the hill toward the fort from nearby Fisherman's Wharf, they pass by thick stone walls, cannon mounts, and the officers' headquarters, now converted into a youth hostel, all of which offer wide, sparkling vistas of the bay and its two bridges. On a bright, gusty July morning, among the crowds of fanny-packed and souvenir-fleece-jacket-clad out-of-towners who flood San

Francisco year-round are a number of younger people with messy-looking hair, many of whom have the glazed look in their eyes that indicates they recently rolled out of bed. They're dressed in clothes that often look—and mostly are—handmade: elaborately knitted scarves, repurposed thrift-store dresses decorated with felt patches and dime-store lace, screen-printed T-shirts, sweatshirts, jackets, tote bags, and hats. The members of this part of the crowd peel off from the tourists and make their way down a very long and steep staircase carved into a hillside, at the bottom of which the fort's Festival Pavilion, a long, slim rectangle of a building, is playing host to San Francisco's first annual Renegade Craft Fair.

Founded in Chicago in 2003, the Renegade Craft Fair in 2008 has spread to three cities—Brooklyn, Chicago, and San Francisco—and is probably the largest craft fair in America today. Sue Daly, Renegade's organizer, is herself a crafter who pinpointed a need in her growing community for a gathering where crafters and shoppers could come together. Today, Renegade has about two hundred vendors per venue and gets applications from twice that many. The fair is juried, which means, according to the Renegade Web site, that vendors are judged according to "how your items fit in with our vision of 'Renegade,' meaning crafts that are DIY and contemporary, [and] the quality and uniqueness of your wares."[1] On first glance, the range of vendors in San Francisco is overwhelming. Tables lined up in three aisles stretch all the way to the back of the pavilion, a cavernous building with a high, echoey roof that reverberates with music played by the DJ tucked in the back. The ATM machine, brought in for the event and placed near the entrance, is flashing "OUT OF ORDER," so someone has helpfully tacked a handwritten sign onto it informing fairgoers that there's a working ATM in one of the nearby buildings. The sign is written in curvy red script and decorated with small hearts, hinting at the emphasis on ornamenting the most pedestrian kinds of objects that await inside.

It's just after 11 a.m. on a Sunday, and the fair isn't too crowded: there are one or two people browsing each table. The first table I pass is covered in lamps made from recycled teacups; next to this are several tables sporting clothing items with antler- and owl-themed designs. A group called Thread Banger offers a sewing machine at its table so customers can alter any garments they purchase right on the spot. A guy with a Snidely Whiplash mustache wearing a fitted vintage suit and fedora sketches a woman in front of his booth, which advertises "unflattering por- traits while you wait." The displayed portraits, emphasizing every pimple, wrinkle, and nose hair, bear out this promise. Fur- ther on, the emphasis on recycled and repurposed goods remains prominent: there is a table of "new jewelry from forgotten arti- facts," more jewelry made from vintage typewriter keys, and Velcro-adjusted skirts put together from what look like fifties and sixties fabrics that will fit "almost everyone." In other cases, craf- ters are trying something different; a vendor called Brookadel- phia sells Lucite and gold-plated necklaces that mimic the nineties trend for nameplate necklaces, replacing first names with the phrases "Post-Modern" or "Post-post-modern," or the words "Obama" or "Veggie." There are a lot of T-shirts for sale, but some stand out for their unique designs, including one with the words "Joan Didion" printed across the front in large block letters, and the city-themed shirts from Campfire, a group of artists from Akron, Ohio, that showcase striking fonts and illustrations for a seemingly endless collection of cities and towns: "City of Bicycles: Davis," "City of Stumps: Portland," "City of Charm: Baltimore," and "City of the Sunny Side: Oakland."

There are more than 150 vendors at Renegade this year, a large percentage of them young and female, and aside from those selling crafts, there are also representatives from craft-friendly magazines *Venus* and *ReadyMade* and the craft-vending Web site Etsy.com. The magazines and Web site are all part of the crafting community; however, their growth in circulation and popularity is indicative of the gradual shift of crafting's position from an underground DIY movement to becoming much more visible in mainstream culture. As I'm standing taking notes near a table selling knit neck warmers, a young female vendor interrupts me to ask what I'm doing. She says she's concerned that I might be from a corporation and that I might be stealing ideas from crafters. I reply that I'm a writer doing research, and she explains that idea theft is a real problem for crafters; as DIY design and crafting get greater exposure, original designs, most of which aren't copyrighted, are easily appropriated by businesses that can manufacture cheaply made copies. The growth of crafting in the years since 9/11 has been phenomenal: one estimate places the amount of dollars spent on crafting supplies at twenty-nine billion dollars in 2002, a number that has likely grown exponentially higher in the years since.[2] Etsy.com reported in November 2007 that sales for that month alone totaled $2,966,160.[3] As crafting gets bigger and bigger, the danger of its DIY, recycling, community-oriented message being diluted and changed—much in the same way that indie rock, comics, and magazines were appropriated by mainstream culture—is real. Yet on the whole, crafting today retains most of the original spirit of community, reinvention, and transformation of everyday objects that have been the hallmarks of the trade from the beginning. Crafting's emphasis on recycling is especially prescient; long before Al Gore warned the world about global warming, crafters were reusing everyday goods and turning them into useful and unique items, like garden planters made from old tires and glass bottles repurposed as hanging lights. The idea of taking a commonplace object or everyday piece of clothing and making it unique not only builds on folk art traditions, it also mimics the punk and indie culture's longtime emphasis on celebrating difference and making do with what you already have at hand. Many crafters have designed zines or flyers for bands; others are influenced by riot grrrl's message of female empowerment, since the majority of crafters are women who operate their own businesses. Yet some crafts at Renegade resist both reproduction and a simplistic definition, and in doing so reinvent and help reinvigorate the idea of what crafting can be. The most prominent example at the San Francisco fair is right up front.

From the outside, the Postcard Machine looks like a large

white box—nothing that would stop a passerby in her tracks, except for the sounds that are emanating from it. As a pair of women walk by, a robotic voice suddenly bursts out of the box, saying, "Welcome to the Postcard Machine possibly from the future." The women stop and look around before they realize that the voice is coming from the box in front of them, which, upon closer inspection, turns out to have a Postcard Machine logo on the front, along with a spinning dial labeled with themes, a screened-over window, and a few open slits. The women take a few steps closer to the machine, which tells them in the same robotic voice that they have a choice of postcards but will need to spin the dial to pick a theme. "What colors do you prefer," the machine queries, and once it gets their answer (orange), it asks them to flatten their bills. In between quips and queries, it makes a series of blips, boops, and beeps that elicit a storm of giggles from the women and passersby. The sounds are almost impossible to reproduce in typeface, but suffice to say that it sounds like a wiseass, funny, possibly tipsy robot. Within a minute or so, two dollars have gone into the machine through a slit (to the sound of a long "booooooop") and two handmade postcards have emerged.

I move around to the side of the machine and it unzips to reveal a grinning young blonde woman in black eyeglasses. Michelle Ott not only invented the Postcard Machine, which is making its fourth appearance at a Renegade Craft Fair, but she also makes the postcards and sits in the machine (which is really a modified tent), interacting with people all day. When I ask how it's going, she says the only problem is that people keep mistaking her for the ATM since the real ATM is broken. As is the case with many crafters, Ott invented the Postcard Machine as a method to encourage creativity and interaction. In her case, that kind of interaction was important because she was stuck near the South Pole when the idea came to her. The Postcard Machine began when Ott was working as a janitor at the McMurdo Station in Antarctica, where employees have "a little tiny craft fair on the holidays, just tables where you can sell your wares."[4] Ott has a long personal history doing mail art projects, beginning when she was young and her grandmother lived far away, and she realized that "the huge pleasure of getting mail means you have to send mail." Over the years, Ott began to see her postcards "as a little sketchbook" and a way of keeping in touch with friends during her travels. At one point, she tried a mail art project, in which "[I] would do a set of a hundred postcards, stamp them and then address them to myself, and leave them all over the place traveling, and then see what I'd get back." Many of them did come back to her, and the range of responses ran from a woman working in a glassblowing studio in Portland, to a man who listed the exact location along with the date and time when he found the blank postcard, to an anonymous response detailing the writer's "five fallacies about life."

The success of that craft project inspired Michelle to do something that would engage people in more direct interaction. "In Minneapolis," where she previously lived, "I had helped another person with a Valentine's making machine that was very different but a similar idea," she recalls. In Antarctica, the long months of extreme isolation inspire McMurdo employees to come up with creative attempts at entertainment, and "in that kind of really small community you kind of know everyone," she says, so initially she made the postcards for each individual on the spot. The idea worked, and people loved interacting with her inside of the machine, which at that time consisted of a large cardboard box. When she returned to the United States, Ott began thinking about ways to take it on the road to craft fairs. "A friend of mine said, 'You know, you can get those tents that you go hunting in,'" she remembers, "and I was like, 'What the heck is that?'" It turned out her friend was talking about the one-person rectangular tents that act as a hunter's camouflage, so she "started trying to design and make it, but I don't have a sewing machine that works like that, and I don't know those tools and materials." Eventually, she found a company that manufactures outhouse tents, and the Postcard Machine was born in its current collapsible and portable form.

Ott's first venture in the new Postcard Machine was at the

Oakland Art Murmur, where she ironed out some logistical problems, learning that the machine "can't take wind, and I can't really be on a hill" because it will tip or fall over. Eventually, she took her creation to the Renegade Craft Fair in Chicago, where the challenge of being inside the machine for eight hours a day, two days in a row in hot weather was negated by the fact that she "sold three hundred postcards that weekend, which means I talked to every single person [who approached me] about a postcard, which is so cool." Since then, she's traveled to the Renegade Craft Fair in Brooklyn and is now working at the San Francisco incarnation as well. When I ask her why interaction with people is so important to the Postcard Machine project, she says that she "hope[s] to inspire people to send other people mail. I hope people buy them and think they're really great postcards, but my bigger goal is that people get them and go wow, I'm gonna send postcards to people." Ott does put a lot of thought and time into designing the cards, which are made from recycled and salvaged materials and hand stitched around their borders, and she designs a special postcard for the location of each craft fair she visits. The biggest draw of the project is the chance for interaction and the sense of surprise. "The cool thing is that the people who like the Postcard Machine really just like it," she says. "It's fun and it just feels good to interact with them." Some people have a prickly reaction, as I witnessed at Renegade; they glance over and keep walking, or they visibly recoil. Ott can see everyone who approaches from inside, and she's "gotten some dirty looks and people who were like it's not that cool or something, which is fine, totally fine." For the most part, however, "the people who like it just laugh a lot," she says, "and that's the best part. A huge element for me is that it's a surprise, that they're gonna put two dollars in, and they don't really know what they're gonna get out of it."

Ott admits that traveling to craft fairs like Renegade is more about breaking even and getting a chance to meet people and see friends than it is about making money. "I stay with friends and I usually make enough to make back the entry fee," she says.

"Those big fairs are expensive," but now that the cost of manufacturing the machine has been recouped, she's hoping to take it to some music festivals and other events and start to "put it in the plus." Like a lot of crafters, Ott is both thrifty and resourceful; she recycles all the paper scraps from manufacturing the postcards into more postcards, gets lots of materials from the East Bay Depot for Creative Reuse, a recycling center for education, arts, and crafts, and makes her own screen prints at home. In the past few years, she's been spending time with a number of busking street musicians, and she hopes to take the Postcard Machine out and start "using it like I first intended it, going out renegade, out on the street, going to where there's people in parks and seeing what happens." The success of this machine has also inspired her to do another crafting project, this time for herself. "For my birthday I'm gonna do a cake and balls machine," she says with a laugh. "You just stick your hand in, and you either get a cupcake or a meatball in your hand. Extra icing or extra sauce."

*

Standing behind a table decorated with intricate doilies reading "HANDMADE NATION," a longtime crafter and craft organizer named Faythe Levine is chatting with passersby about her own project, a long-gestating, soon-to-be-released documentary film about "the rise of DIY art, craft and design."[5] With her elaborate tattoos and vintage skirt, Levine's look fits right in with many of the crafters and shoppers around her. Her open, friendly expression invites people wandering by to stop and hear more about the film and its accompanying book, which she and her creative partner, Courtney Heimerl, began working on in 2006. Levine attended the first Renegade Craft Fair in Chicago back in 2003, and "even at that first show, I talked about how this would be a great thing to document, because it was really really obvious that something big was going on." She says that the early version of Renegade was "super, super DIY," in contrast to the more elaborate displays surrounding us in San Francisco, and "people had blankets on the grass selling their stuff." The rootsy, hands-on vibe of that first Renegade fired Levine up enough to start a craft fair in her adopted home of Milwaukee, to eventually open a craft shop of her own, and to begin exploring the idea of making a documentary film about the growing craft movement. Eighty hours of footage, nineteen thousand miles of travel, and twenty-four filmed profiles of crafters later, the film is finally near completion, and Levine will leave the San Francisco Renegade and head almost immediately to Los Angeles, where she is helping stage a large art auction to raise funds for the film's completion and release. Levine is humble about her knowledge of the crafting community she's been part of for many years, and her efforts to document that community in a film have been made as a pure labor of love.

When I reach her on the phone at Paper Boat Boutique, her Milwaukee-based craft store, Levine admits that she's pretty tired from all the traveling, but she's used to splitting her time between filmmaking, running her shop, playing the musical saw in her band Wooden Robot, and making her own crafts. "I think that it's really common for anyone that has creative drive to be involved in multiple mediums," she says, shrugging off her own ability to juggle so many creative endeavors as no big deal. Originally from the Pacific Northwest, Levine discovered the punk and zine communities as a teenager, which would eventually help her make connections with like-minded DIY artists in the crafting community. "I still am in touch with some of the people I met when I was fourteen that I was pen pals with," she says. "Those sort of connections sustain through your life." Of her teen years and introduction to punk, she says, "I lived in the suburbs of Seattle, and there was this great all ages venue, so I got introduced to hardcore and riot grrrl at the same time." She asserts that riot grrrl "made an incredible impact on me because I was a teenager and saw all these strong women just deciding to do whatever they wanted." Riot grrrl's emphasis on feminist notions of DIY, along with the "whole underground music community," helped lead Levine to zine making, which was "my gateway drug to realizing that I would do whatever I wanted, and by myself." Both riot grrrl and music zines in the nineties were known for utilizing cheap and creative methods for design and printing, and "as soon as I realized that people were just making zines about whatever," Levine says, "and kind of hand assembling and printing, silk screening, and spray painting stencils, I was totally hooked."

Levine first tapped into the growing network of crafters in "2002 or 2003, which was around the time that I finally started going online." Prior to discovering the growing number of Web sites, listservs, and message boards for DIY crafters, Levine admits she was "more like a handwritten letter, hardcore non-e-mailer." Levine's own crafting projects bear out this love of old-fashioned communication methods. One of her own best-known crafts was the Messenger Owl, a stuffed felt owl with a pocket in the back for handwritten messages, which was featured on the HGTV show *That's Clever* in 2004. The owls were so popular that Levine had to hire a friend to help manufacture them, giving her an early glimpse into the growing popularity of crafting. Once she heard about the Renegade Craft Fair through *Venus* magazine—one of the earliest magazine proponents of crafting—she applied online, a process that eventually led her to communication with other crafters. Once online, Levine "started being involved in message boards and wanted to organize a fair in Milwaukee to bring them out here, and so then I started Art vs. Craft [a Milwaukee-based craft fair] soon after that."

Within a few years of her nascent involvement in crafting networks, Levine began to seriously consider the possibility of filming a documentary about the subculture. Since crafting is a visual medium, a film seemed like a logical way to represent it as a subculture—Levine could not only travel and interview crafters; she could show them at work, thus passing on the idealism of DIY to the film's audience. With some commercial production experience under her belt, Levine knew her way around a camera, but she really wanted the film to be from an insider's point of view. "I realized there's all these television shows about craft," she says, referring to a growing number of TV networks and shows with hyperperky hosts who are usually former models rather than true crafters, "and I thought it would be a good idea to make a documentary about this movement before someone came along and did some sort of exposé." Levine approached her friend Courtney Heimerl about collaborating on the film project, knowing that she wanted "to work with someone I was comfortable traveling with," since Levine was already planning on covering a lot of ground. Heimerl agreed, and the two women set off on a cross-country, year-long trip to make their documentary in true DIY fashion: one camera, one person doing sound, and a lot of driving. Levine found the people she profiles via the same networks of crafters she'd been working with at fairs and through her shop. "A lot of the people [I filmed] were people I already had relationships with," she says. "It made the logistics of approaching people a little easier from the production side." Along the way, she did end up filming "a handful of people I met through word of mouth," but the biggest challenge by far was trying to capture the very diverse, individualistic world of crafting in a single film. "I could still be interviewing people," she admits. "There are so many amazing people doing incredible things that it was difficult to decide to stop."

When I ask her whether or not any of the people she talked to make a living from crafting, she says it's really on a case-by-case basis. "The one thing about the DIY art and craft community is that there's not one type of person, so people's comfort levels and what they're trying to do are very different," she explains. "There definitely are people who are making a living off what they make. Sometimes someone had a supportive spouse who has insurance and that kind of security. Oftentimes people are doing a day job, and then crafter by night." Even as crafting grows, the economics of attempting to make a living from art remain challenging in the American economy, which is reliant on cheaply made goods. So some of Levine's compatriots who have tried to make a living from crafting have found it too difficult, "and

[they] just did it part-time so they don't lose their inspiration and excitement about why they are making things." Levine herself bartends in Milwaukee a few nights a week to help with the bills, and she acknowledges that her film was made on credit cards and the generosity of others. Many of the vendors I spoke with at Renegade bore out the notion that they weren't necessarily there to make a big profit—many of them hoped only to recoup travel expenses, get a chance to see San Francisco, and meet friends.

*

Most of the vendors at Renegade are young women who are operating small businesses, a phenomenon that is still unique in the larger indie culture. Crafting as a subculture may be inherently female in some ways; after all, sewing, knitting, and making jewelry and soaps are all tasks that women have been doing unpaid for thousands of years. Some observers have treated the number of women drawn to crafting as trivial: an article about the Brooklyn Renegade in the summer of 2007 joked that "the fair's status as cute-girl central ('crafts babes,' one man panted) add[s] to [its] appeal."[6] Other writers and cultural observers have been more astute in their analysis of crafting's potential as empowering for the women who participate. Rob Walker has argued that instead of simply a time-killing occupation for bored cuties, "the D.I.Y. craft movement offers a new way to resolve an old tension between traditional domestic skills and participation in the (economic and creative) marketplace: by combining them."[7] Levine falls squarely on Walker's side of the argument. "The important thing is that it's a powerful creative movement that's mostly women, and I don't know if that's ever existed before," she says. The inherent sense of camaraderie with other women attracted Levine to the community in the first place, but she's also aware of the potential misperception of crafting as a silly pursuit. "Especially now," she says, "there's a little bit of a backlash of a lot of women who are involved in the community trying to prove that this isn't just cute girls making cute stuff. This is a valid movement of women being creative, not just owls and mushrooms. It's a real thing." Unlike the indie music, publishing, and comics communities, where women still play a smaller role, crafting doesn't require women to fight against any inherently sexist stereotypes. Rather than seeing crafting as exclusionary of men, Levine says, "It's really empowering to identify with other women who are living a similar lifestyle and who you can rely on and call or e-mail for advice." In documenting this subculture, Levine hopes to spread that message. Being a part of a real community of female artists, she says, "is a really powerful thing."

Levine's documentary and the growing scale of craft fairs like Renegade indicate a major shift in crafting's position from small-time hobby to big-time cultural force, and *ReadyMade* magazine provides the how-to manual for aspiring and accomplished crafters alike. Launched in December 2001, *ReadyMade*, which today is one of the biggest and most influential DIY and crafting magazines in America, with half a million readers, was founded by Shoshana Berger, who serves as editor in chief, and Grace Hawthorne, the magazine's publisher. Berger and Hawthorne came together to start *ReadyMade in* 2002 just as the Bay Area was reeling from the dot-com bust, which had left a number of young creative types who had gone to work doing design and writing for Internet start-ups newly unemployed and looking for other outlets for their creative impulses. These newly idle twenty- and thirty-somethings often found that their DIY hobbies of knitting, carpentry, and sundry other crafting projects moved at a much slower pace than their work in the Internet world, and many of them welcomed the downshift. In the years since, *Ready-Made* has grown rapidly in both circulation and staff, reflecting crafting's growing popularity. The magazine's office is located on a side street in the mixed-industrial area of Berkeley known as the artisan district because of its population of potters, small presses, and live/work spaces. Walking into the office, the immediate sound of hammering and sawing, along with the acrid scent of glue, clearly demonstrate that *ReadyMade* is a hands-on operation. The magazine does almost all of its manufacturing on-site, so the craft or design projects that the magazine walks its readers through have been tested out before it begins to circulate, thus lessening the chances of bodily injury or crafting disaster for those trying things at home.

Shoshana Berger's office is a bit quieter than the front of the office, where the designers are putting together what looks like a massive piece of bedroom furniture. On one wall of Berger's office, a series of interlocking wooden boxes houses a variety of found objects, and, typical of any editor's office, books and magazines are scattered on every other surface. Berger, who is in her thirties, is a Berkeley native and admits that growing up in that city's climate of experimentation, environmentalism, and eclecticism had a huge influence on her own interest in crafting and design. "It's kind of a rite of passage to be interested in salvage," she says of her upbringing.[8] Berkeley is not only home to the East Bay Depot for Creative Reuse, but it is also home to Urban Ore, a salvage and scrap yard that stretches over several city blocks. Berger jokes that salvage "and therapy are the two pinnacles of being a Berkeley native, and my father was a professor of engineering at UC Berkeley so he always had a shop in our basement and always had my sister and I tinkering with things." Berger's father's background helped her to begin to see the potential of renewability in things that might have otherwise seemed like they couldn't be reused. "He was a child of the Depression," she says of her father, "and there was always this kind of inherited sense that resources should not be looked upon as eternally renewable."

With her interest in salvage and crafting firmly inculcated, after college Berger moved into a West Oakland collective artist's warehouse called The Compound, where "everyone who lived there was an enormously innovative reuse designer in that they would just really make something out of nothing all of the time." Among her fourteen housemates, "one of them was making Adirondack chairs out of redwood fencing, the other one was salvaging old barn doors and hardware and building these elaborate storage things in his loft and reusing old vacuum cleaners and turning them into lamps." Every issue of *ReadyMade* echoes that ethic, the DIY nature of the work using materials others might have perceived as garbage. "The ingenuity in that space among this group of maybe fourteen artists was just so inspiring to me," Berger emphasizes. Culturally, these artists and crafters were doing something radical in a very consumer-driven moment in American culture, one that was particularly prominent in the Bay Area. The dot-com boom had attracted many young businesspeople to the area, including artists, designers, and writers. All of a sudden, your friend who for years had brewed coffee in the mornings and done illustrations all night in her studio just for the pleasure of it was making a ton of money designing Web sites, and this new climate polarized the difference between indie artists and artisans and their counterparts who were suddenly very interested in profitable enterprise. "A lot of wealth was being generated in the dot-com boom, and a lot of people were being very flagrant about how they spent money," Berger recalls, and "The whole [climate] of young twenty-something culture shifted a little bit, and I think in reaction to that, we just wanted to be scrappy."

In 2002, at the apex of the boom, Berger was working as a journalist and editor for several different magazines, so the idea of starting a magazine about craft and DIY design—topics she was intimately familiar with—seemed like a natural course of action. Prior to launching *ReadyMade*, she "had never experienced the business and the violent economics of magazine publishing, so that was a real crash course." When the dot-com boom swiftly became the dot bomb a couple of years later, one of the greatest ironies for the indie subculture was that independent magazines, record labels, and businesses in the area suddenly had a better chance of succeeding. The playing field had been blown flat with the demise of so many Internet magazines and start-ups. With almost nothing in the way of competition from other magazines or venture-capital-funded Web sites, *ReadyMade* quickly went from being a quirky indie magazine with a "very indie, very campy, and very kind of nudge-nudge, wink-wink you're in on the joke" editorial stance to a bimonthly publication with broad audience appeal and a significant circulation. When I ask if the original

ReadyMade conception was to be a small-scale indie magazine or a large-scale glossy, Berger thinks for a moment and says, "I think we always thought we wanted to be inclusive rather than exclusive. We wanted it to feel like a cooperative because the whole idea is that design should be open source and that ideas should be open source and . . . there was a lot of interest in open-source technology at that time where people were starting to break through the idea of intellectual property." She compares this moment to the growth of free music on the Internet, arguing that *ReadyMade*'s growth, and the growth of crafting along with it, both followed in the footsteps of the rapid and self-empowering ability to disseminate ideas and products, along with the chance to discover previously unknown pockets of community that the Internet opened up.

ReadyMade's content, which is 60 percent reader generated, according to Berger, reflects the eclecticism of the multifaceted crafting community. The most recent issue has features on everything from how to make your own yogurt to making cork-wrapped lamp bases, photo-print dresses, and pom-pom socks for kids. There are many features dedicated to DIY artists and designers, and a lavish spread showcasing the self-designed live/work loft of a young couple that designs "gift-worthy objects d'art."[9] There are also book reviews, music reviews, and featurettes on wallpaper, clothes-drying racks, and reuseable grocery bags—all reflective of the wide range of crafting pursuits. In the last few years, *ReadyMade*'s staff has expanded from seven people to nearly twenty. The growth spurt the magazine is experiencing was partially enabled by "a larger conglomerate who is helping publish the magazine," Berger says. "We have more resources; before it was a very hand-to-mouth enterprise." Working with a corporate partner has not resulted in editorial changes ("They haven't meddled in that," according to Berger), but there have been some shifts in the magazine's content—the music reviews are a new feature—that might appeal to a wider audience outside of the craft community. Berger says that taking on a partner was something *ReadyMade* had been planning to do for years in hopes of increasing its circulation, and thus far the experience has been fine. The magazine's circulation and distribution have grown, and the staff has grown along with them. She does admit that "there is definitely a step-up in the pressure we feel in terms of delivering on numbers and making sure we meet their expectations financially . . . they didn't just invest for free."

The growth also means that *ReadyMade* cannot produce every project in house. "We try to make most of them," Berger admits, but "some of them we'll have the contributors send them in and trust that they are being honest and not leading us down a garden path." She points out that at a bigger magazine, say, *Martha Stewart Living*, "they have a section of the building just for building props," whereas *ReadyMade* has only a small amount of space for manufacturing. "So we kind of do it by hook or by crook," Berger laughs. "We have friends of the magazine who do props for us in their shops, 'cause we don't really have a proper warehouse or a proper garage." In its leaner days, *ReadyMade* was more heavily reliant on interns, the unpaid, unsung heroes of any indie venture. "The magazine was basically founded by interns," Berger admits. "We used to have like ten interns coming through, half of our manpower." And *ReadyMade* interns, who glommed onto the magazine as an incubator of cool ideas, stuck around: "In the first three or four years," she says. "We couldn't kick them out. It became their slacker job. They would just stay for a year or two years, and it was unbelievable." Today, *ReadyMade* only has two or three interns at a time, and they "really stay for three or four months, and that's it." With its recent shifts toward a bigger audience, its growing numbers of paid staff, and slick covers featuring models posing while in the midst of a crafting project, it could be argued that *ReadyMade* is selling out. Berger explains, however, the advantage to these changes is that the magazine is taking the idea of DIY to a wider audience than ever before.

Berger views the mainstream interest in DIY design as part of a larger cycle of consumerism. "As with every great grassroots idea," she says, "it gets co-opted by the mainstream and gets kind of chewed up by the great maw of consumer culture and spit out as DIY: the Ersatz version, DIY: the Urban Outfitters version, DIY: the Scion version, and that's just how consumer culture works." She goes on to argue that "it's a totally healthy pattern because what that causes is a chain reaction in the community that built it in the first place to find alternative paths and to skirt that way and find something new." Faythe Levine goes further, stating that the growing interest in crafting is a kind of backlash against the accelerated nature of consumer culture in the twenty-first century. "Doing things by hand," she says, "whether it's sewing or handwriting a letter or playing music or whatever that may be, is something that does slow people down, and I think that's a big part of the attraction." Walking around the Renegade Craft Fair, Berger's and Levine's arguments begin to make sense. Even if the crafts and designs on display could easily be replicated by a chain store like Urban Outfitters or Target, those mass-produced designs would not have the intrinsic value of a handmade object. For the maker, the process of looking the buyer in the face, of talking to them, and of sensing their interest in the value of that same object—even if it's only a postcard—adds a layer of personal investment into the transaction that would be impossible to re-create on a mass-market level. Even on Etsy.com, the crafters who sell their wares tell little stories about themselves, about the crafts, and often interact directly with customers. While the idea of getting to know your customer isn't new, it is inherently and inarguably indie. Bands that play small clubs often sit onstage, sweaty and maybe a little drunk after a gig, and sell copies of their own records and tapes. Indie magazine editors always carry a copy of their magazine around with them, just in case they meet someone who might be interested in it. Comics artists trade sketches for more comics with other artists in their network. Even if crafting can be mistaken for a frivolous pursuit, the fact is that it represents both a viable creative subculture and a business alternative at a time when corporate conglomerates are making it more and more difficult for artists to remain truly independent in most other mediums. As popular culture speeds up, and takes indie with it, crafting, as Faythe Levine says, is a good reminder that we can still slow down and do things on our own.

ten

Branded: The Big Indie Crossover

On a rainy October morning in 2007, I'm sitting at the head of a scuffed wooden table in a fluorescent-lit third-floor classroom on the UC Berkeley campus, teaching a writing class focused on underground music. It's the last day of our discussions of punk and indie, and my students are showing signs of weariness about the topic. They've read Michael Azerrad's book *Our Band Could Be Your Life*, a chronicle of punk and indie bands in the eighties, they've watched *We Jam Econo*, a documentary about the Minutemen, and they've been subjected to daily blasts of music by Fugazi, Sonic Youth, Dinosaur Jr., and other indie bands of the eighties and nineties, resulting in sensory overload for those unfamiliar with the genre. My students are an ethnically mixed group from wildly varied backgrounds, ranging from newly arrived immigrants to upper-class Southern California valley girls to engineering savants to young hippies from rural Oregon. As members of the highly desirable eighteen-to-twenty-two-year-old demographic of college students, they are a marketer's wet dream. But at a time when indie rock and indie style are spreading over mainstream culture like a rash, the majority of my students don't identify as indie fans, much less as members of any indie subculture like the ones they've been studying. When I ask if they listen to indie rock, a few nod, but only two actually support indie music by going to shows or buying CDs from the local independently owned record store, Amoeba Music. The rest rely on BitTorrent or swapping music with friends, and their taste is eclectic: many prefer hip-hop; some like classic rock; others just listen to "whatever." When I ask how they would define indie in 2007 after doing research on punk ethics, corporate record companies, and the history of DIY, a few respond by blurting out band names: Mates of State, Tegan and Sara, Modest Mouse, Death Cab for Cutie. After a few minutes, one student who's been quietly thinking makes a puckery face and says sardonically, "Indie's really just hipsters in skinny jeans. That's all it is anymore."

Many of my students agreed with that assessment, and given the tenacity of the vogue for skinny pants, it's likely that you could make the same argument today and be at least partially correct. In 2008, the term "indie" is more difficult to define than in decades past. The signifiers of indie in popular culture are multifarious and often puzzling due to their blatantly corporate ties: iPods are indie (since indie artists like Feist sing in iPod commercials); American Apparel, the trendy retailer of thirty-dollar T-shirts and leggings, is indie (since it advocates for fair wages for its garment workers and because its advertisements, with their images of skinny, young, nearly naked hipster girls, look like porn for indie fans); Toyota Scions are indie (because Toyota has marketed them with a DIY crowd in mind by making them easily customizable); bands who used to be on indie labels but are now on majors are indie (because they have some sort of sound or look that helps them sustain indie cred even while they're playing stadium tours); Chuck Taylor sneakers are indie; tattoos are indie; shock-fiction writer Chuck Palahniuk is indie; shag hair-cuts are indie; male facial hair is indie; eyeglasses are indie (especially if they're thick framed); and, yes, skinny jeans, for reasons probably known only to the first band member to sport them in a video to the delight of some fashion designer, are also indie. The list goes on. Indie, like punk and many other subcultures before it, has been branded by corporate culture and repackaged as an aesthetic.

Nowhere is the evidence of indie's gradual transition from off-the-radar subculture to fashion and lifestyle trend clearer than in the success of a retail chain that has exploited indie music and blatantly borrowed from crafting and DIY styles. Urban Outfitters, the Philadelphia-based chain of clothing and home furnishings stores, was founded in 1970 as a single boutique called the Free People's Store. Its owner, Richard Hayne, was at that junction in tune with the hippie counterculture and its taste for handcrafting. Hayne's boutique was "a general store for students, offering affordable yet fashionable clothes and assorted bohemian bric-a-brac."[1] The store paid homage to the San Francisco Digger's Free Store and other alterna-boutiques of the era by showcasing a free box for customers who were too broke to afford the wares on sale, but behind the store's bohemian aura, Hayne was a savvy businessman who redyed bulk-purchased T-shirts, painted salvaged crates for shelving, and marketed the hippie lifestyle even while he personally distanced himself from the counterculture. "I would never and did not ever characterize myself as a hippie," he told a reporter in 2003. "But," he said of his nascent retail empire's affinity with alternative culture, "it is fair to say we were influenced by the fashion of the times."[2]

With his prescient sense of upcoming trends, Hayne began building a chain of retail outlets and clothing brands, including the wholesale line Free People, Anthropologie, which attracts a thirty-to-forty-five-year-old female clientele, and Urban Outfitters, which went public in 1993. Targeting the eighteen-to-thirty-year-old demographic coveted by marketers, Urban Outfitters' combination of trendy clothes with kitschy home decor items and bric-a-brac made it an ideal store for any city with a large population of college and postcollege young people with large disposable incomes. The chain grew rapidly, and currently there are more than 140 Urban Outfitters stores in the continental United States alone, with more in Europe and Canada. In 2008, the chain's sales grew even as the U.S. economy sagged: its Web site estimates fiscal sales for 2008 to be $157.7 million.[3] Today, the store's style leans heavily on indie as a guiding light. On an August afternoon in 2008, just before the fall semester is about to begin, the Berkeley store is crammed with credit-card wielding parents and their teenage kids. Most are shopping for housewares, but it's doubtful that many of these parents are interested in some of the store's edgier offerings, like the "ghetto pint glass set" (emblazoned with the words "pimp" and "ho"), the strap-on tequila bandolier, the "Rock Star Rehab" board game, or the fifties-style faux-Bakelite ashtrays. They also pass on a DIY screen-printing kit, along with a number of crafty items that bear some resemblance to wares at the Renegade Craft Fair. The main draw for the store's usual clientele, and Urban Outfitters' greatest homage to indie, is in the clothes.

For years, broke punks and DIY crafters have revamped thrift-store clothes into something different and individualistic; at Urban, you can purchase an "Urban Renewal" cowboy shirt that's been fitted with an empire-style elastic waistband and an interior tag reading "made in India" for fifty dollars. Shoppers can buy skinny jeans for boys and girls in every color and denim wash imaginable, whereas punks in the eighties and nineties had to "peg" their own jeans with safety pins or find a friend with a sewing machine to do it for them. There are Chuck Taylors, long the sneaker of choice for Nike-hating indie rockers and their fans (ironically, Nike acquired the Chuck Taylor brand in 2003). There are leather biker jackets, temporary tattoos, Mexican tooled leather purses, baggy house dresses, biker boots, and, of course, T-shirts emblazoned with every crafty-looking owl design (currently the emblem in vogue), eighties hair-band logo, and sarcastic/ironic/self-loathing word and phrase you can imagine. All of these items at one point in time meant something if you were a part of the indie subculture: they were signifiers of difference and rebellion, most often purchased at yard sales and thrift stores or borrowed from friends, or, even more meaningfully, homemade. Today, these items are made in factories in China, Sri Lanka, India, and Turkey, where conditions for workers are notoriously close to slave labor at best. And these items are being offered to customers by a CEO who, in opposition to the store's countercultural image, contributed thirteen thousand dollars to the notoriously homophobic senator Rick Santorum and his political action committee and is known to have ties to multiple right-wing causes.[4]

Knowing these facts, Urban Outfitters doesn't sound like an indie-friendly business, and yet, based on its marketing, consumers might easily be tricked into believing that it is. The store plays a constant soundtrack of indie rock, with the CDs of featured artists on display right up front. In 2007 and 2008, Urban Outfitters joined with Toyota to sponsor the Free Yr Radio tour, a series of in-store performances by trendy indie bands, including Tapes 'n Tapes, the Klaxons, and nineties freak-out heroes Dinosaur Jr. The tour was ostensibly put on to benefit a few of the dwindling number of America's independent radio stations, but its aggressive promotion of the Toyota Yaris made the idea a little suspect. "There is a big risk of offending people and looking like you are trying too hard when you do things like this," admitted Toyota spokesman Chad Harp, but like Urban Outfitters, Toyota has a history of attempting to appeal to a DIY-friendly (or at least DIY-associated) crowd.[5] In discussing the marketing of the Toyota Scion, *New York Times* columnist Rob Walker says, "Scion has been shrewd in noting the intense passion around the DIY community and wants to associate itself with that."[6] Urban Outfitters has been equally shrewd in aligning itself with Toyota; through that relationship, it's able to capture another group of consumers. However, Urban Outfitters' version of "trying too hard" occasionally crosses over from promoting DIY-friendly Toyotas to rumored copying from DIY culture. The store's alleged copies of a number of indie designers are chronicled on blogs and crafting message boards, including the Web site urbancounterfeiters.com, which offers full-color evidence of some creepily similar items. The interior of the stores—which resemble the kind of artsy loft many people imagine that indie kids inhabit in meccas like Williamsburg, a trendy neighborhood in Brooklyn, with casually placed piles of Chuck Palahniuk novels, discarded indie rock CDs, and crafty-looking gimcracks—is strategically designed at the Philadelphia headquarters. Employees—all of whom look like people you'd run into at the Pitchfork Music Festival, sporting shag haircuts, slouch boots, and tattoos—run around the store clutching clipboards outlining lifestyle displays passed on from company HQ. For anybody who wants to know what it feels like to be indie, Urban Outfitters is a one-stop shopping emporium for trying on that identity.

The popularity of indie as a brand is due in a great part to the unprecedented rapid acceleration of trends in popular culture. Whereas it took years for indie bands to gain a following in the eighties and nineties due to lo-fi and low-tech methods of print and music distribution, today, the dissemination of music and art moves at a faster pace than ever before. MySpace made it possible for bands to post MP3s of their own tracks to their own pages, negating the necessity for a manager or any other kind of middleman who might have previously shopped their music around to venues and record executives on their behalf. BitTorrent and many other MP3 file-sharing sites are natural places for indie music to thrive. Since most indie artists still face the reality of not making a living from their music, giving it away for free seems like a fair trade for building an audience through word of mouth, a tradition that goes back to the punk era. Bands back then usually didn't mind if people traded taped copies of their albums as long as those same people turned up for their shows, and the same is true today for many indie bands. The ability to network and communicate as well as promote and sell your work on the Internet has made a huge difference for independent artists today.

For those artists that work to build their own audiences and

communities, technology also helps enable them to stay connected outside of their immediate geographic area. Matt Hart, the
editor of *Forklift, Ohio*, "A Journal of Poetry, Cooking and Light
Industrial Safety," lives in Cleveland, Ohio, which is not a city that
immediately comes to mind when one talks about indie ("We're
taking over the city one weirdo at a time," he says of his group of
creative local friends).[7] Yet Hart has been able to build a readership
for his journal, an audience for his band Travel, and a network of
writers and musicians all over the country because, according to
Hart, "Nowadays, especially for writers, I don't think it really matters all that much where one lives. By my lights, the Internet and
e-mail have blown the world so wide open in terms of access to
journals, other writers, setting up readings, et cetera. One can have
a pretty significant community just by corresponding with people
electronically." Hart is currently writing a collaborative book with
a writer from Minneapolis; the two set up a Blogspot page that
only they have access to, where they write and share poems. In the
spirit of his commitment to making do with what's available, *Forklift*'s print style and aesthetic are pure DIY: "One issue was bound
with sandpaper with a bolt through the center," Hart recalls. "One
was a bag of chili mix with all the beans and spices; the recipe for
the chili was a jigsaw puzzle printed on the back sides of the poems." Yet *Forklift* is not available in most bookstores; instead, Hart
and his publisher, Eric Appleby, handle their own distribution and
sell copies through the journal's Web site, thus taking their very
handmade product to the world via a digital medium. Hart also be-
lieves in giving away his band's music instead of selling it and uses
file sharing for that purpose. "For [the band]," he says, "the main
thing is just to make the music and to make it easily available,
which is why all of our CDs can be downloaded for free at our Web
site." Hart's attitude about using technology to promote DIY creativity is pragmatic at its bottom line. "I've found that I enjoy making my own hoops and jumping through them at my leisure," he
says, and the Internet helps Hart and many other artists to make as
many of those hoops as they want.

As the Internet has grown, its corporate-controlled content

has grown along with it, but for the most part, it is still essentially a free-for-all, a place where pundits can expound on political blogs, collectors can go crazy on eBay, crafters can network on message boards, and writers can post their newest ideas and observations, all without a central controlling authority. In many ways, the Internet is still anarchic, and much of its anarchy is about speaking truth to power in the historical tradition of the best independent art. Interestingly, the accelerated speed of technology and information comes at a time when many low-tech forms of creativity are also making a comeback. "I'm a big believer in high/low dichotomies," says *ReadyMade*'s Shoshana Berger. "I think they create a productive tension, and that applies to art. It applies to what you're speaking of in terms of having the technology that enables you to do things in a much more efficient way, but still . . . wanting to feel some kind of organic connection to stuff that surrounds you."[8] The success of Etsy .com, the Web site started by a couple of twenty-something guys looking for a way for crafters to vend their wares easily online, is testament to this dichotomy, as is the recent surge of small press publishers who are bringing back antiquated printing methods, hand-binding books, pressing their own broadsides, and then offering up these texts for sale on blogs and social-networking sites and in e-mail blasts. If it's ironic that you can record antique-sounding tunes on a banjo and a harmonica into your laptop, post those songs on a MySpace page, and thus merge low-tech with the high, well, welcome to the new irony.

The end result of this ease of distribution and rapid flow of information has been a series of mixed blessings for the indie community. On the one hand, artists are more in control of how their work gets distributed and promoted than they've ever been before, with the proliferation of cheap and easy technologies for doing so. On the other hand, the Urban Outfitters conundrum rears its ugly head. The more overexposed indie music, comics, publications, and design get, the more those art forms can be co-opted by the mainstream and its masters. By the midpoint of the current decade, you didn't have to look far to find examples of fictional characters in movies and on television that were crazy about indie rock, quipping about comic books, and walking around in American Apparel hoodies and Urban Outfitters T-shirts. The 2004 movie *Garden State* wore its indie heart on its sleeve. Every character seemed to sport Chuck Taylors and a hoodie, and the soundtrack was littered with indie bands from Iron and Wine to the Shins, about whom Natalie Portman's character gushes, "The Shins will change your life," a quote that catapulted the previously semiobscure band into the pop culture spotlight. "I think people are sick of fakeness," Shins singer James Mercer said of the band's newfound popularity, and whether or not listeners felt like the Shins were in some way "realer" than Coldplay—a very slick, major label band also featured on the film's soundtrack—the band was suddenly exposed to a whole new world of fame.[9] The Shins' label Sub Pop, sensing the potential for another album that might prove to be as popular as Nirvana or the Postal Service, its best-selling bands up to that point, poured a lot of money into making the band worthy of Portman's quirky character's loving hype, and four years after the film's release the Shins are still one of indie's most popular bands. Similar exposure occurred for bands that appeared on the television show *The O.C.*, on which the character of Seth Cohen, a quirky kid growing up in the Los Angeles suburbs, regularly expounded about comic books, underground films, and his favorite band, Death Cab for Cutie, whose music played constantly on the show's soundtrack. Soon enough, the band left its tiny indie label Barsuk Records for a major deal with Atlantic and a lifestyle of stadium tours and guest appearances on *The O.C*, where it played a set at the show's fictional club the Bait Shop for an affluent audience of very blond, very tan, very skinny girls—probably not the typical audience or venue that indie bands imagined for themselves in the past.

This new audience, which discovered indie not through word of mouth or any kind of network of indie artists, plays a big part in the changing image of indie culture today, and it's not just Urban Outfitters and Toyota that have tapped into it. "There is an intense hunger out there for 'the custom,' the 'personal,' the 'individual,'" says Rob Walker, who writes about marketing and has chronicled the journey of many artists and designers from the underground to the mainstream. "If any brand can associate itself with those ideas successfully," he continues, "it probably helps them in the marketplace." While iPods, for example, may not necessarily be inherently indie, "Apple in general might still have some of that [indie appeal] because it was the underdog for so long." Likewise, the iPod carries a cultural cachet because "that group [of indie fans] puts a high value on design and aesthetics and style as somehow inherently virtuous." The success of American Apparel, another brand aligned with indie culture, stems from the fact that its T-shirts and hoodies are also customizable to the individual. "Its T-shirts serve as the blanks used by lots of independent creators and designers," Walker observes, and the store's "particular vision of youthful sexiness" in its advertising helps to further broaden its appeal. The increasing use of indie rock in advertising furthers the message that indie is something anyone with a dollar can buy. Whereas bands licensing songs to advertisers may have previously been perceived as selling out and betraying the community (something Kurt Cobain was acutely aware of), today having your song in a car commercial is just status quo. "By and large," says Walker, "there's no penalty for licensing a song for commercial use anymore, and that's partly because there's more of an emphasis on 'indie' as a business idea than a cultural idea."

Whether or not the exposure of independent culture is a good or bad thing for the artists behind it (or for popular culture), the fact remains that with its opening up to anyone and everyone, the idea of what indie means is up for grabs. In nearly every large city in America—and in many smaller cities too—it's not difficult to find an indie-friendly music venue, a crafting collective, and a comic book shop selling racks of Fantagraphics titles. But in most large cities, it's also easy to find hordes of the skinny-pants-wearing hipsters my student was referring to when she argued that indie has lost its meaning today. But what *are* hipsters? They're young people who proliferate in major cities, crowding galleries, clubs, and bars, drinking Pabst Blue Ribbon and smoking Parliaments, appropriating indie style and aligning themselves with independent artists but not necessarily making art of their own. Are hipsters indie? Many hipsters share an interest in indie music and style, and the original Beat Generation–era idea of the hipster certainly fits with the idea of what indie originally meant. John Leland writes in his book on the history of hip that "when America had a center, hip was outside of it," and today, "hip is exactly what it has always been: an undercurrent of enlightenment, organized around contradictions and anxieties."[10] In that light, being a fan of indie culture, if not a participant in it, makes hipsters indie. The term "hipster" today carries such a pejorative connotation, however, that nobody with a grain of self-awareness wants to be identified as a hipster, yet they continue to proliferate, much to the chagrin of many independent musicians, artists, and writers.

The cover text of the August 2008 culture-jamming independent magazine *Adbusters* screams "Hipster: The Dead End of Western Civilization" over a photo of a disaffected-looking young guy with a beard. When the writer Douglas Haddow goes to a club and sees a girl wearing "an American Apparel V-neck tee, nonprescription eyeglasses and an inappropriately warm wool coat" and asks her whether or not she's a hipster, she screams, "Fuck no!"[11] Haddow goes on to argue that the primary problem with hipsters is that they cull so many signifiers from working-class culture and attach themselves to viable creative communities but contribute nothing to culture or society in return. "With nothing to defend, uphold or even embrace," Haddow argues, "the idea of 'hipsterdom' is left wide open for attack. And yet, it is this ironic lack of authenticity that has allowed hipsterdom to grow into a global phenomenon," primarily because, unlike the artists who created the indie community and strive to keep it solvent today, hipsters don't seem to make or do anything.[12] Hipsters can logically be compared to marketers: they take whatever they can from creative communities, but instead of being inspired to do creative work of their own, they simply turn other people's original ideas into trends and passively follow along with whatever's in style. In a 2003 article about the rise of hipster style bible *Vice* magazine, Vanessa Grigoriadis argued that "by definition, hip taste is embraced by hipsters because the masses don't get it—and can't buy it," yet even at that early date, *Vice*'s editors were aggressively pursuing movie deals, a television show, and promoting the Vice clothing line, pushing their own version of a hipster subculture into the mainstream.[13] If hipsters have borrowed from indie, they've also helped to exploit it.

Kathleen Hanna, who as a member of the influential bands Bikini Kill and Le Tigre, has seen indie go through more than one occasion of "selling out," is thoughtful about the state of the independent community today. After Nirvana's success, Hanna saw "people in the indie scene who never thought about careers or anything [going], 'Oh, Nirvana totally knocked Guns N' Roses off the face of the earth.' And ever since then," she says, "it was like what is the mainstream gonna farm from the indie scene next." Nearly twenty years after *Nevermind*'s release, Hanna feels like popular culture is still waiting for the Next Big Indie Thing in spite of indie's current trendiness. "It's weird because it almost seems like this superlong drawn-out horrifying transitional point," she says of the intervening years. "It's almost like this pregnancy where the baby never gets born. I feel like it's been as if, 'The baby's coming! The baby's coming!' and it's five years later. And the woman weighs three hundred pounds . . . and is not having the kid." Hanna argues that the technology available today might eventually "displace the major labels," but that it also poses problems for people who come from the pre-Internet version of the indie community. "For me there's a nostalgia for pre-Internet society," she admits, "and that's the thing people aren't getting today. We wrote letters to people and got responses back—we traded a whole culture through the mail." Hanna, who is currently taking a hiatus from music to pursue a graduate degree, notes that the pressure the Internet puts on indie bands today is in complete opposition to the tapes-and-mail culture she and her friends helped create. "Because of MySpace," she sighs, "you better have a hundred thousand hits on your Web site, or on your MySpace, before you can think to go on tour."

When a friend of mine was attempting to book shows for his band in San Francisco, club managers told him that giving them a CD (which the band had painstakingly created covers for) was pointless; they just wanted to be referred to a MySpace page. Yet the proliferation of bands on MySpace leads to problems in terms of building an audience. On the one hand, it's easy for anyone with time on their hands to click a button thousands of times until one has enough "friends" to guarantee a few people turning up if one goes on tour. On the other hand, as indie music multiplies and changes, niche audiences abound, many of which are too small to make much of an impact. If you want to make music by throwing a mouse against a wall, sampling its squeak, and manipulating that sample, there are enough people on the Internet that you could conceivably build up a microaudience of fans of mouse-tossing tunes. There are thousands of bands in this position, and their number grows every day thanks to cheap recording software that is readily available. If you want to make mash-up albums consisting entirely of illegal samples of other artists like the musician Girl Talk (aka Gregg Gillis), build up a fan base via YouTube clips of your frenetic live shows, and give away your music on a pay-what-you-can basis, you can do that too. Girl Talk, according to the *New York Times,* is doing well enough that Gillis has been able to quit his day job at a biomedical engineering company and pursue music full-time, a pretty good measure of one's success as an independent musician.[14] And if you're Radiohead, one of today's most successful rock bands, you can extricate yourself from your contract with a major label, record an album, sell it on a pay-what-you-can basis, and still make millions of dollars. When Radiohead decided to pursue this route to release their most recent album, *In Rainbows,* the move was lauded by both indie and mainstream press as a revolutionary act. Fans could choose their price and download the album for a limited time, and hardcore fans with cash could purchase an eighty-dollar box set with a limited-edition book included. Nine Inch Nails tested a similar maneuver, allowing fans to download an album for free but also offering an "ultra deluxe" version of the album signed by the band's front man, Trent Reznor. In both cases, the bands must have been aware that these giveaways would earn them enough kudos from fans to put butts in seats on their upcoming tours, but it also looked like a move toward independence and extricating themselves from stifling major label contracts.

As much as these moves toward giving away music are welcomed by fans who are tired of paying almost twenty dollars for a CD, and may indicate the end-time for major labels—something that indie artists have predicted for years—the result is that online you can be confronted by way too many options for listening. Before I changed my MySpace profile to private, every single friend request I received was from an indie band, and I received dozens a week. There was no way that I had time to listen to all of that music, and no way I was going to cover any of those bands in my magazine, which didn't even run music reviews. Likewise, the sheer numbers of writers who are marketing themselves online makes it impossible to know which blogs are worth reading, which online journals post quality work and not dreck, which writers are aggressively promoting themselves in pursuit of book deals, and which ones are simply writing for writing's sake. Crafting is experiencing a similar flood of goods. Etsy.com is a fantastic resource for crafters and consumers alike, and many crafters have been able to use Etsy in order to turn crafting into a viable business. But if you go to Etsy and type in "wallet," you get more than six hundred wallets; if you type "journal," you get eight hundred journals; and if you type "tote bag," you will get nearly two thousand totes. Some people are patient enough to click through two thousand images of totes until they find the perfect one, but in an accelerated culture where time is a precious commodity, most people aren't, and this produces the kind of nostalgia for pre-Internet indie culture that Kathleen Hanna was talking about. The crafting community's message of slowing down and taking the time to make something on your own can become lost in a sea of tote bags, even if every one of them is special and unique.

Thus we arrive at the point where indie is simultaneously reaching a stage of oversaturation and corporatization, and it's debatable whether we should just stop using the term "indie" altogether. Just as the idea of "alternative" music and culture began to seem dated and clichéd after marketers seized it in the nineties, the term "indie" today has been stripped of much of its original meaning. In a post on the MP3 blog Moistworks, writer Alex Abramovich asked several of his writer and musician friends to provide their own definitions for the term "indie" in 2008. Writer Douglas Wolk mentioned that today there are four major labels, and if a band is affiliated in any way with them, it is now technically dependent instead of independent and thus cannot be called indie. "To claim that a band can be 'indie' without being financially independent of the major labels is to pretend that industrial capitalism does not exist," Wolk argued. Carl Wilson pointed out that in its broadening and co-option, the term has been stripped of meaning: " 'Indie' now connotes such a hodgepodge of economic, social and aesthetic associations that it is irrelevant," he wrote.[15] Abramovich's post netted nearly sixty responses ranging from tirades against the writers who argued for indie's demise to those that pointed out the healthy and thriving indie community that still exists in spite of commercialization. But most of the blog's arguments about the term's inexorable slide into meaninglessness ring true. Etymologically, since the term "indie" connotes independence, when it's applied to rock bands recording for major labels, cars manufactured in factories, iPods, or six-hundred-dollar purses, as seen in a recent Bloomingdale's catalog, it really has lost its meaning.

Does this loss imply that people aren't making independent art anymore? The answer to that question is emphatically no. The opening up of independent creativity to so many individuals logically means that at least some of those people will be inspired to make art on their own. And the broader audience for indie today also means that its music, art, and writing will diversify beyond its traditional white, upper-middle-class/middle-class makeup. Much as the expanding audience for hip-hop has allowed that culture to evolve and change, the same may happen for indie. Reinvention should not be a perceived as a sacrifice for the independent community either: it's something indie has repetitively dealt with in the past. Each time indie culture has gone through a change, it has reemerged as something new, and each reemergence has ushered in a new cadre of artists. For some participants, however, the sheer scale of indie's current popularity has become too much to deal with on a daily basis. A few months after I wrote the introduction to this book, Jen Loy and her partner Nicole Neditch sold Mama Buzz café, one of the places where the Oakland Art Murmur began. They were increasingly frustrated by the growing crowds of hipsters attracted to the party scene of Art Murmur without making any kind of creative contribution to it. Vandalism, violence, and burglaries were becoming an increasing problem on Art Murmur nights. Today, both Jen and Nicole are still involved in creative pursuits, but they've distanced themselves from the Oakland art scene. After *Kitchen Sink Magazine* folded, many of the people who'd been involved decided to focus on their own projects instead of making the sacrifices of time and money inherent to starting another independent publishing venture. But both Jen and Nicole and the former *Kitchen Sink* staff are all consulting with new indie ventures, offering advice, doing some volunteer writing, and helping with fund-raising. For many of us, indie has proven to be a lifelong commitment even if our participation in it waxes and wanes.

On the other hand, the majority of the people, publications, and groups profiled in this book are doing just fine more than a year after I wrote the introduction. Unnamable Books is still hanging on in Brooklyn and now regularly hosts events by local and visiting authors; the Pitchfork Music Festival had another successful year in 2008, and one of its headlining acts was the reunited Mission of Burma, who played a full cover set of its landmark album *Vs.* that was webcast to fans all over the globe. Mike Watt still plays and tours with a dizzying number of acts and regularly keeps in contact with his fans via the blog on his Web site, and Berkeley's 924 Gilman Street still hosts shows every weekend. Faythe Levine's documentary about crafting, *Handmade Nation,* is on the cusp of its release; Daniel Clowes's newest graphic novel, *Mister Wonderful,* has just come out in print. *Bitch* magazine and Akashic Press continue to print challenging, cutting-edge literature, and Small Press Distribution works with more presses than ever before. More and more people are also starting their own labels, magazines, presses, and art and craft collectives. The difficult task of choosing who and what to profile for this book required narrowing down to a handful of examples from the thousands of individuals and groups I encountered and read about. Entire genres and subgroups had to be left out for the sake of brevity, and they continue to multiply every day. Clearly, the flame of independent culture has not gone out for the many people who remain committed to it.

The word "indie" may have lost much of its luster, but as America struggles through a painful time economically, culturally, and socially, the idea of creative independence remains crucial. As popular culture turns again and again to mass production and passive acceptance of the status quo, art that evolves outside of corporate America can and does make a difference in the way people think. That is what indie was once all about and what it will be about in the future, even if we cease to call it "indie." To make something on your own, regardless of its potential to bring in money, lends the end product an inherent sense of value that would be absent if it were a copy of a copy of a copy. Writing at a time when creative independence was perceived as a radical act, Frank O'Hara explained that writing was simply an act of will, not something done according to any established pattern. "You just go on your nerve," he wrote, and the same sentiment holds true today. Independence means rebellion, risk, tenacity, innovation, and resistance to convention. It is rooted in the past and recycles and reimagines the past, but it is always ahead of its time. It will always value collaboration and networking, the sharing of resources, no matter how scarce, and the one-of-a-kind contribution of each individual. Even if it is reduced to a cliché, somebody watching that cliché will already be thinking about and planning ways in which that cliché can be reimagined. That is what it means to be indie.

Notes

Introduction

1. http://newpages.com/bookstores/newyork_bookstores.htm.
2. Stats retrieved on July 16, 2008, from Alexa, http://www.alexa.com/data/details/traffic_details/pitchforkmedia.com?q=.
3. Readbuzz.com.
4. Stereogum.com, Pitchfork Music Festival review, http://stereogum.com/archives/concert/pitchfork-music-festival-2007-sunday-715-rating-62_005865.html.
5. interviewsarchive.com.
6. From an interview with the author, August 3, 2007.

One: Constantly Risking Absurdity

1. Constance Lewallen, *Joe Brainard: A Retrospective* (Granary Books/University of California, Berkeley Art Museum, 2001).
2. Marjorie G. Perloff, " 'Transparent Selves': The Poetry of John Ashbery and Frank O'Hara," *Yearbook of English Studies* 8 (1978): 177.

3. Donald Allen, ed., *The Collected Poems of Frank O'Hara* (New York: Knopf, 1971).
4. Terence Diggory, "Questions of Identity in 'Oranges' by Frank O'Hara and Grace Hartigan," *Art Journal* 52, no. 4 (Winter 1993): 42.
5. Diggory, "Questions of Identity," 50.
6. Frank O'Hara, *Meditations in an Emergency* (New York: Grove, 1996).
7. Brad Gooch, *City Poet: The Life and Times of Frank O'Hara* (New York: Harper Perennial, 1994), 280.
8. Ibid., 3.
9. Steve Silberman, "Allen Ginsberg's Celestial Homework," http://www.levity.com/digaland/celestial/.
10. Barbara Ehrenreich, *The Hearts of Men: American Dreams and the Flight from Commitment* (New York: Anchor Books, 1987).
11. Alan Lomax, quoted in R. Serge Denisoff and Jens Lund, "The Folk Music Revival and the Counterculture: Contributions and Contradictions," *The Journal of American Folklore* 84, no. 334 (October–December 1971).
12. Ibid., 397.
13. Peter Coyote, *Sleeping Where I Fall* (Washington, D.C.: Counterpoint, 1998).
14. All quotes from Peter Berg are from an interview with the author, January 16, 2008.
15. All quotes from Hal Reynolds are from an interview with the author, October 19, 2007.

Two: Get in the Van

1. Minutemen, "This Ain't No Picnic," *Double Nickels on the Dime*, SST Records, 1984.
2. *We Jam Econo: The Story of the Minutemen,* director Tim Irwin, Plexifilm, 2005.
3. Mike Watt, "Paranoid Chant," *Paranoid Time*, SST Records, 1980.
4. *We Jam Econo.*
5. Sonic Youth, "Providence," *Daydream Nation*, Enigma Records, 1988.
6. All Mike Watt quotes are from an interview with the author, November 21, 2007.
7. *American Hardcore,* director Paul Rachtman, Sony Pictures Classics, 2006.
8. Minutemen, *Project: Mersh,* SST Records, 1985.
9. Michael Azerrad, *Our Band Could Be Your Life: Scenes from the American Indie Underground, 1981–1991* (Boston: Little, Brown, 2001).

10. All quotes from Clint Conley are from an interview with the author, October 22, 2007.
11. All quotes from Roger Miller are from an e-mail interview with the author, October 18, 2007.
12. Azerrad, *Our Band*, 107.

Three: Homegrown

1. Aaron Cometbus, *Despite Everything: A Cometbus Omnibus* (San Francisco: Last Gasp, 2002).
2. All quotes from Jesse Michaels taken from an e-mail interview with the author, December 2007.
3. *Slingshot #62,* Autumn 1988.
4. Gavin McNett, "The Day Punk Died," Salon.com, April 2, 1988.
5. Brian Edge, ed., *924 Gilman: The Story So Far* (San Francisco: Maximumrocknroll, 2004), 38.
6. Ibid., 8.
7. All Lawrence Livermore quotes are from an e-mail interview with the author, January 18, 2008.
8. Edge, *924 Gilman,* 10.
9. Ibid., 153.
10. Ibid.
11. Cometbus, *Cometbus Omnibus.*
12. Operation Ivy, "Here We Go Again," *Hectic* EP, Lookout Records, 1988.
13. Operation Ivy, "The Crowd," *Energy* LP, Lookout Records, 1989.
14. Cometbus, *Cometbus Omnibus.*
15. Flipside, 1988. Retrieved from http://www.operationphoenixrecords.com/flipsideoperationivy.html.
16. http://www.greenday.net/hitlistinterviewbj.html.
17. James Sullivan, "Growing Up Without Growing Old: Lookout Records Celebrates 10 Years of Promoting Punk Bands," *San Francisco Chronicle*, January 4, 1998.
18. Rob Harvilla, "Kerplunk: The Rise and Fall of the Lookout Records Empire," *East Bay Express*, September 14, 2005.
19. Edge, *924 Gilman,* 104.

Four: Xerox, Staple, Repeat

1. Steve Clay and Rodney Phillips, *A Secret Location on the Lower East Side: Adventures in Writing, 1960–1980* (New York: Granary Books, 1998).
2. Ibid., 29.

3. Jerry Gafio Watts, *Amiri Baraka: The Politics and Art of a Black Intellectual* (New York: New York University Press, 2001), 46.
4. Ibid.
5. Clay and Phillips, *A Secret Location*, 257.
6. All quotes from Laura Moriarty are from an interview with the author, January 8, 2008.
7. Daniel Kane, *All Poets Welcome: The Lower East Side Poetry Scene in the 1960s* (Berkeley: University of California Press, 2003), 31.
8. All quotes from Ron Silliman are from an interview with the author, November 8, 2007.
9. Bruce Southard, "The Language of Science Fiction Fan Magazines," *American Speech* 57, no. 1 (Spring 1982): 19.
10. Ibid.
11. Stephen Duncombe, *Notes from Underground: Zines and the Politics of Alternative Culture* (New York: Verso, 1997), 7.
12. Ibid., 158.
13. Mike Gunderloy and Cari Goldberg Janice, *The World of Zines: A Guide to the Independent Magazine Revolution* (New York: Penguin, 1992), 4.
14. Duncombe, *Notes from Underground*, 159.
15. http://www.larkfarm.com/factsheet_five.htm. Gunderloy turned down an interview request for this book.
16. Cometbus, *Cometbus Omnibus*.
17. *Punk Planet*, issue 51, 2002.
18. Cometbus, *Cometbus Omnibus*, 2.
19. *Maximumrocknroll*, issue 200, January 2000.
20. Ibid.

Five: Like a Velvet Glove Cast in Iron

1. Fredric Wertham, *Seduction of the Innocent,* quoted at http://www.dreadfuldays.net/soti/soti_chapt01/soti_chapt01.html.
2. Senate Committee on the Judiciary, *Comic Books and Juvenile Delinquency, Interim Report,* 1955 (Washington, D.C.: United States Government Printing Office, 1955).
3. Patrick Rosenkranz, *Rebel Visions: The Underground Comix Revolution, 1963–1975* (Seattle: Fantagraphics Books, 2002), 4.
4. Ibid., 15.
5. Ibid., 52.
6. Ibid., 68.

7. Ibid., 69.
8. Ibid., 86.
9. Ibid., 71.
10. Ibid.
11. All Douglas Wolk quotes are from an interview with the author, May 28, 2008.
12. Ted Rall, "The King of Comix," *Village Voice,* June 27, 1999.
13. Ibid.
14. Ibid.
15. Mike Wyma, "Drawing on Life: Agoura Publisher Sees Redeeming Value in 'Alternative Comics,'" *Los Angeles Times*, June 25, 1987.
16. Ibid.
17. Brian Hood, Nick Mercer, Q&A with Jaime Hernandez, *Anthem Magazine,* March 12, 2008.
18. Ibid.
19. Dez Skinn, *Comics: The Underground Revolution* (New York: Thunder's Mouth Press, 2004), 252.
20. All quotes from Daniel Clowes are from an interview with the author, June 9, 2008.

Six: We're Gonna Have to Be the Band

1. All quotes from Calvin Johnson are from an interview with the author, April 14, 2008.
2. Azerrad interviewed in *The Shield Around the K: The Story of K Records,* director Heather Rose Dominic, Northstar Films, 1999.
3. Ibid.
4. Ibid.
5. Ibid.
6. Beat Happening, "Indian Summer," *Jamboree,* K Records, 1988.
7. http://www.krecs.com/html/info/.
8. All quotes from Kathleen Hanna are from an interview with the author, October 26, 2007.
9. "What Is the International Pop Underground?" K records Web site.
10. *Shield Around the K.*
11. Ibid.
12. Nitsuh Abebe, "Twee as Fuck: The Story of Indie Pop," *Pitchfork,* October 24, 2005.
13. Chris Nelson, "The Day the Music Didn't Die," *Seattle Weekly,* August 8, 2001.

14. *Don't Need You: A Herstory of Riot Grrrl*, director Kerry Koch, Urban Cowgirl Productions, 2003.
15. Ibid.
16. "Kathleen's Herstory," Le Tigre Web site, http://www.letigreworld.com/sweepstakes/html_site/fact/khfacts.html.
17. Kill Rock Stars time line, http://www.killrockstars.com/about/timeline.php.
18. http://www.feastofhateandfear.com/archives/hanna.html.
19. Farai Chideya, "Revolution, Girl Style," *Newsweek*, November 23, 1992, 84–86.
20. Charles Aaron, "A Riot of the Mind," *Village Voice*, February 2, 1993.
21. Bikini Kill, "Double Dare Ya," *Bikini Kill* EP, Kill Rock Stars, 1991.
22. Aaron, "Riot of the Mind."
23. All Carla Costa quotes are from an interview with the author, June 8, 2008.
24. Stacy Trash, "The Kitty Collar: The Riot Grrrl Movement," 411 Mania .com, July 18, 2006, http://www.411mania.com/music/columns/42995/The-Kitty-Collar-07.18.06:-The-Riot-Grrrl-Movement.htm.
25. *Hype*, director Doug Pray, Lion's Gate Films, 1996.

Seven: Brighten the Corners

1. Brian Raftery, " '*Slacker*,' 15 years later," Salon.com, July 5, 2006.
2. Ibid.
3. Ibid.
4. Rob Jovanovic, *Perfect Sound Forever: The Story of Pavement* (Boston: Justin Charles Books, 2004), 30.
5. Ibid.
6. Ibid., 34.
7. From an interview with the author, November 21, 2007.
8. Jovanovic, *Story of Pavement*, 50.
9. Ibid., 84.
10. Eric Boehlert, "Matador is a hip but unprofitable label best known for launching Liz Phair. And for this Capitol is paying . . . how many millions of dollars?" *Rolling Stone*, June 27, 1996.
11. David Browne, "The Independents See Vultures Circling Overhead," *New York Times*, October 27, 1991.
12. Ibid.
13. Erik Davis, *Spin* magazine, quoted in Jovanovic, *Story of Pavement*, 96.

14. Robert Christgau, "Consumer Guide—Slanted and Enchanted," *Village Voice,* June 2, 1992.
15. Pavement, "Summer Babe," *Slanted and Enchanted,* Matador Records, 1992.
16. Boehlert, "Matador is a hip . . ."
17. Ibid.
18. Robert Christgau, "*Watery, Domestic* EP review," *Village Voice,* August 3, 1993.
19. Donna Gaines, "Stephen Malkmus of Pavement," *Rolling Stone,* March 20, 1997, 38.
20. Ibid.
21. Pavement, "Range Life," *Crooked Rain, Crooked Rain,* Matador Records, 1994.
22. Silver Jews, "Random Rules," *American Water,* Drag City/Domino, 1998.
23. Zach Hammerman, Pitchforkmedia.com, December 31, 1999.
24. All David Berman quotes are from an e-mail interview with the author, February 14, 2008.
25. David Kirby, "Books in Brief: Fiction & Poetry: *Actual Air,* poems by David Berman," *New York Times,* August 22, 1999.
26. David Malitz/*Washington Post,* Post-Rock podcast, June 27, 2008, http://blog.washingtonpost.com/postrock/2008/06/post_rock_podcast _david_berman_2.html.
27. Gaines, "Stephen Malkmus of Pavement."
28. Charles Duhigg, "Indie, Major Labels Tune into New Act," *Los Angeles Times,* August 14, 2005.
29. Ibid.
30. Ibid.
31. Darcy Frey, "One Very, Very Indie Band," *New York Times,* March 4, 2007.

Eight: Scan, Kern, Layout, Print

1. Associated Writing Programs 2008 Conference Web site, http://www .awpwriter.org/conference/2008ConfArchive/2008exhibitorslist.php.
2. From an interview with the author, January 8, 2008.
3. Federal Trade Commission Web site, http://ftc.gov/opa/2000/12/aol .shtm.
4. Hachette Livre company Web site, http://www.hachettebookgroupusa .com/about_company-history.aspx.

5. All quotes from Johnny Temple are from an interview with the author, June 4, 2008.

6. Daniel Robert Epstein, Arthur Nersesian interview, SuicideGirls .com, November 26, 2003, http://suicidegirls.com/interviews/Arthur +Nersesian/.

7. Priya Jain, "The Struggle for Independents," *Salon*.com, June 21, 2007.

8. http://mcsweeneys.net/books/bankruptcy.html.

9. Jeremy Adam Smith, "The Independent Press Association Is Dead," *Other* magazine blog, January 2, 2007, http://othermag.org/blog/?p =205.

10. All quotes from Andi Zeisler are from an e-mail interview with the author, June 17, 2008.

Nine: Hands On

1. Http://www.renegadecraft.com/sanfran/apply.html, accessed October 2008.

2. Pamela Danzinger, *Why People Buy Things They Don't Need* (Ithaca, New York: Paramount Books, 2004).

3. Etsy Storquecast, November 1, 2007, http://www.etsy.com /storque/section/etsy-news/article/etsy-statistics-weather-report-from -the-storque-newscast/541/.

4. All Michelle Ott quotes are from an interview with the author, July 10, 2008.

5. All Faythe Levine quotes are from a phone interview with the author, July 24, 2008.

6. Melena Ryzik, "Where the Crafts Babes and DIY Dudes Are," *New York Times*, June 24, 2007.

7. Rob Walker, "Craft Work: My Paper Crane," *New York Times*, July 2, 2006.

8. All Shoshana Berger quotes are from an interview with the author, November 12, 2007.

9. Melissa Kaseman, "Room and Board," *ReadyMade*, August/September 2008.

Ten: Branded

1. Jonathan Valania, "Clothes Make the Man," *Philadelphia Weekly*, June 11, 2003.

2. Ibid.

3. Urban Outfitters Financial Overview, http://www.urbanoutfittersinc
   .com/financial/index.jsp.
4. Valania, "Clothes Make the Man."
5. Courtney Harding, "The Indies: Tunes They Can Use," *Billboard*, June
   7, 2008.
6. All Rob Walker quotes are from an e-mail interview with the author,
   August 16, 2008.
7. All Matt Hart quotes are from an e-mail interview with the author,
   June 29, 2008.
8. From an interview with the author, October 26, 2007.
9. Jenny Eliscu, "Bruised Shins," *Rolling Stone*, February 8, 2007.
10. John Leland, *Hip: The History* (New York: HarperCollins, 2004), 14–15.
11. Douglas Haddow, "Hipster: The Dead End of Western Civilization,"
    Adbusters, issue 79, July 2008.
12. Ibid.
13. Vanessa Grigoriadis, "The Edge of Hip: Vice, the Brand," *New York
    Times*, September 28, 2003.
14. Rob Walker, "Mash-Up Model," *New York Times*, July 20, 2008.
15. All quotes in this paragraph are from the Moistworks blog post "In-
    dependent TM" by Alex Abramovich, April 30, 2008.

Acknowledgments

I interviewed so many people whose creativity, drive, and innovation were inspiring and humbling, all of whom helped me understand how crucial independent creativity really is. This book would not exist without your stories.

Thanks are due to my agent, Michelle Brower, who not only had the good taste to pick up an issue of *Kitchen Sink* but was the first person to take this project seriously and has been a joy to work with throughout the process.

My editor, Supurna Banerjee, has handled my mangled grammar and verbal diarrhea with good cheer and patience throughout. I owe her tons and tons of gratitude for her detailed, insightful editorial eye. Thanks to everyone at Holt for believing in this book.

Thanks also to Sarah Hays from Drag City, Nils Bernstein from Matador, Erika Clowes and Howard Wuelfing of Howlin' Wuelf Media for helping me arrange interviews.

The support of my colleagues in UC Berkeley's College Writing Programs has been invaluable. Heaps of gratitude are owed to Jane Stanley, who has been beyond accommodating and helpful at a time when I really needed help. Thank you to all of the faculty and staff.

The Mellon Faculty Institute not only helped me become a better teacher, but sparked my interest in doing research and provided invaluable support and guidance with working with Berkeley's phenomenal libraries and librarians.

All of my students have contributed to this book in their own ways and remind me daily of how absurdly lucky I am to have a job where I get to babble about writing and music and popular culture and engage in conversation with so many diverse, interesting, curious minds.

Lisa Fleming and Will Ulrich provided diligent and creative help with research. Derek Oye and Wilson Zheng slogged through hours of recordings and did a great job with transcription. Thank you all.

Jeff T. Johnson, Stefanie Kalem, Carla Costa, and Mike Larkin were all kind enough to provide feedback on the manuscript as it evolved. I couldn't have managed without your encouragement and brilliant ideas. Special additional thanks to Stefanie for suggesting the book's title.

Thank you, Sam Hurwitt, for your friendship, which means the world.

Thank you to my friends, colleagues, teachers, and those who encouraged, cajoled, gave advice, and helped keep me going: Mosi Reeves, Elka Karl, Jen Loy, Nicole Néditch, John Levine, Steve Tollefson, Gail Offen-Brown, Patricia Maughan, Andrew Demcak, Brenda Hillman, Robert Hass, Jen Tynes, Clay Banes, Erin Johansen, Lisa Drostova, Alex Green, Dylan Chivian, Michael Westerman, Jeremy Goody, Cole Coffee, David Baratier, Rachel M. Simon, and Debbie Hamati.

Thank you to everyone who wrote for *Kitchen Sink*, illustrated *Kitchen Sink*, read *Kitchen Sink*, wrote about *Kitchen Sink*, donated money to *Kitchen Sink*, and came to our readings and parties. You showed me that true community is possible, and I'm eternally grateful.

I am terribly lucky to have been born and raised in the Bay Area. The resources I needed to write this book are what make this place unique, and they're all independent: Moe's Books, Pegasus Books, Adobe Books, Green Apple Books, City Lights Books, Rock Paper Scissors Collective, Needles and Pens, Amoeba Records, Aquarius Records, Intersection for the Arts, Issues, Comic Relief, Doctor Comics and Mister Games, the Oakland Art Murmur . . . thank you for books, comics, records, anecdotes, art, magazines, all the stuff of life.

Thank you, Sage.

Thank you to my family: Lois Oakes, Betsy Oakes, Christine Gipson, Robert Oakes, Victoria Remler, Ava and Lior Remler, Melanie and Jennifer Shippen-Oakes, Robert Thompson, Duane and Adele Leonard. Dad, Grandpa, and Grandma, I miss you all.

Index

About the Author

KAYA OAKES is the cofounder of *Kitchen Sink Magazine*, which received the Utne Independent Press Award for Best New Magazine in 2003. Currently a writing instructor at the University of California, Berkeley, she has written music journalism, film and book reviews, and wrote a column on comics for Viz Comics' *Manga Vizion*. Her collection of poetry, *Telegraph*, received the Transcontinental Poetry Prize from Pavement Saw Press, and her poems have appeared in more than thirty journals and magazines. She has received writing awards from the Academy of American Poets and teaching fellowships from the Bay Area Writing Project and the Mellon Faculty Institute. Her Web site is http://www.oakestown.org.